Sarah Bernhardt in *Théodora*—1884

MAIN CURRENTS OF
MODERN FRENCH DRAMA

BY
HUGH ALLISON SMITH
PROFESSOR OF ROMANCE LANGUAGES IN THE
UNIVERSITY OF WISCONSIN

NEW YORK
HENRY HOLT AND COMPANY

To

THE MANY STUDENTS IN MY COURSE ON
THE MODERN FRENCH DRAMA
WHOSE FRESH INTEREST AND FRANK VIEWS
HAVE CONTRIBUTED MUCH TO THE PLEASURE
OF THIS STUDY

PREFACE

We have, nationally, a decided interest in the theatre. It is perhaps the one form of art — or near art — for which our passion approaches the universal and promises most for the future. The moving picture itself, detrimental as it seems to the legitimate stage, may be looked upon as a symptom of this passion. But more genuine evidence is abundant. While only large cities can have well established theatres and road troupes are expensive over great distances, small stock companies are frequent and usually supported in the style to which the members are accustomed, drama leagues and amateur performances are numerous, and, strange to say, plays are almost as widely read as novels, a use for which they were not primarily intended. Even to the college student, barbarian that he is supposed to be, this is the one genre of literature — assuming it is literature — of most general appeal. He goes in crowds into the drama courses, pays good money to see his fellow-students act and competes eagerly for a place in the cast, and finally, extremity of devotion, is occasionally induced a second time to listen to the reading of a Greek play.

However, the American public, intellectual or merely normal, is much less certain in its criterions for the drama than it is in its affection for it. This is only natural in a country so short of literary traditions and so new and varied in its culture and civilization. But it must be said also that the present diverse forms and conflicting cross-currents of the theatre might well puzzle a better grounded public. With the com-

mercial manager seeking to make the drama big and coarse
and the Little Theatre enthusiast wishing it small and fine, with
the actor-playwright endeavoring to hitch it to a theatrical star
and the social reformer trying to tie it to a propaganda stump,
its real course is naturally hard to discern.

The rôle of the public in this development is, it is true,
primarily static, although none the less important. It can not
create but it can record approval or disapproval, and it will
be, in the end, this yielding or this resistance which will determine the course of the stream. Audiences may become
surfeited by the prestidigital cleverness and artificial excitement of the Mystery Play but are not likely to seek long
cures in the realistic piece that is merely simple-minded. Reformers may wax eloquent over the Useful Play but the public
will hardly pay two dollars each for moral uplift, especially
after dinner on a busy day, and Static Drama is not very
moving. The general public is, after all, too big for the fixed
forms of the theatre. It can be carried along only by a drama
flowing in a broad stream fed by all the currents of life and
art, and not in the narrow channel of a system artificially constructed.

In this youthful abundance of our dramatic activity, promising no doubt, but also disconcerting, it is obvious that lovers
of good drama can save time, and even intelligent critics can
avoid much splashing up back-channels, through the study of
one of the oldest established theatres of another people, and
particularly one that has made many of the experiments we
are now trying, and has been, moreover, a powerful influence
in the development of our own drama, as it has of modern
drama the world over.

No other apology is needed, then, for offering another book
on the modern French drama. The subject is a fruitful one
both for the college student and for all of the general public

who are able, either through reading or seeing French plays, to profit by its study. In any case, the purpose of this book is to furnish the necessary orientation for such study and to inspire, if possible, its further prosecution. It is not meant to be either technically scholarly or complete. Stress has been laid on main currents to the point of obscuring minor movements or shades of difference, and on the most significant authors to the neglect of other good dramatists less important in the development of the modern French theatre. Above all has been the desire to make the subject clear and comprehensible to the student of French literature in his initiatory study of the modern drama. The strict adherence to this purpose of treating the landmarks of the modern French theatre will, it is hoped, sufficiently explain the omission of certain features usually found in other books, such as frequent résumés of plays and the mention of numerous playwrights, and also offer some apology for other *lacunae;* the author is aware of many of these at present and will doubtless learn of more later.

The author wishes to express his thanks to his colleague, Professor W. F. Giese, for numerous valuable suggestions concerning his manuscript, and to acknowledge the courtesy of the Oxford University Press, D. C. Heath and Company, the Century Company, and Henry Holt and Company in allowing him to reprint considerable portions of the introductions to plays of Dumas fils, Brieux, Curel and Maeterlinck which he had recently edited with these publishers.

H. A. S.

MADISON, October 1924

CONTENTS

INTRODUCTION

THE study of a literary genre so completely national as the French drama obviously offers a striking lesson for other peoples, and certainly for none more than for the Anglo-Saxon, whose point of view and dramatic qualities are markedly different from the French. In this lies one of the chief values of such study. Through contrast we see more clearly the dramatic virtues in which we may be deficient, and, further, we appreciate the worth of distinctive qualities of our own theatre by noting their absence in a foreign drama. In any case, it is well not to forget that our study is bound to be from an external point of view. However much we may be interested in the French drama, may become imbued with it and admire it, our standards of judgment and appreciation will always be largely determined by our social heritage as Anglo-Saxons and by the traditions of English and American literature. Our racial qualities, formed by centuries of development, can not be abdicated. Whether we are conscious of it or not, the final result of our efforts will be to see French drama through American eyes; hence it is but the part of wisdom to take all the advantage there is in distance and perspective in order to study it objectively, in its broad outlines and national characteristics.

No other product of their thought reflects better and more constantly the national genius of the French than the theatre. The drama is their oldest literary genre with a continuous history, and is, besides, a form for which they are peculiarly fitted by dominant racial characteristics; it has been an important, if not a preëminent branch of their literature at every epoch in their history.

The racial qualities which explain French drama in its distinctively national aspects are quite naturally the basic traits of the French people, those that may be considered largely as a heritage of the race, strengthened and developed by centuries of French history and civilization. Of these none is more an ultimate source than the strong feeling of social consciousness, the social instinct of the French. In its intensity, at least, it is unique, differentiating France from all other countries, and it is undoubtedly either a main or a contributing cause for most of the qualities that determine the character of French thought and literature.

Of the racial characteristics that have come down into modern literature the French seem to have inherited the greater number from the Romans and Gauls. The Franks may have furnished much of the sap and strength, the nutriment, to the French plant, but this is apparently of Gallo-Roman stock as seen in its fruits and flowers. The order and clarity of the French are undoubtedly due mainly to their Latin inheritance, as may be also, in part, their realism and positivism, their devotion to fact and to the useful rather than to imagination and the purely beautiful. Likewise, the particular flavor of much of their wit and satire is justly called the *esprit gaulois*. But these qualities and others besides, quite as important as factors in their literature, have certainly been strengthened or developed by this social instinct mentioned above.

The Frenchman is above all a social being, to an extent that is astonishing to Anglo-Saxons — provided they do not find it incomprehensible. Even conscience, the inviolate castle of Anglo-Saxon individuality, is in the French largely communistic. With the Frenchman this conscience is *devoir*, which we call *duty*, and which is substantially the force of public opinion. This is the Frenchman's supreme guide to life. In important matters he feels that he must live and act according to the standards set by his fellow-men. To have a clear conscience is to have their approval.

This social conscience is found in the earliest monuments of French literature, and persists with undiminished intensity in the latest. In their oldest national epic, Roland, in command of the rear guard, refuses to blow his horn and recall the main army lest any one may say that he feared the Saracens — " no evil song shall ever be sung of him " — and to the force of this sentiment he sacrifices twenty thousand of the flower of France. Likewise, Cyrano de Bergerac, in Rostand's drama, declares that his rule of life is to be *" en tout et partout admirable,"* a philosophy which makes him a popular hero of drama comparable to the epic Roland.

It is this desire for the approval and admiration of his fellow-men that has created for the Frenchman the *point d'honneur,* the focus of all his idealism in both life and literature; it may even overpower his national good sense and make of the most realistic and rationalistic nation the most chivalric and quixotic.

But the social instinct or social conscience is not only the Frenchman's cult in supreme moments; it is a religion which he practices daily, and which is an important source of his most common virtues, as well as occasionally the cause of a few of his failings. He not only lives according to the standards of his fellow-men but he lives with his fellow-men, and his qualities are developed to a striking degree by this fact. It is by this largely that he has brought conversation to the level of a fine art and the amenities and courtesies of life to perfection. This constant social contact and the importance given it have sharpened superlatively his wit, have developed his logic and clarity, as well as induced in him his measure and restraint. His chief business seems to be the exchange of ideas; he appears more concerned with thoughts than with the material facts of existence. He rarely gets excited over the latter, while he is continually in a state of greater or lesser excitation over the former.

But if the Frenchman's life is strikingly intellectual — and it is, as his literature constantly shows — he is primarily a public thinker, skilled in logic and trained in discussion. He is little given to purely speculative thinking and to meditation; even his imagination is usually under rein, and all undue profusion is rigidly pruned. Constant rubbing against one's fellow-men promotes realism and good sense but is fatal to extreme individualism and idiosyncrasy. There should be little place in French literature for fancy, mysticism, and even symbolism.

The Frenchman's conception of beauty likewise is created chiefly by his intellect and reason, with fancy and imagination subordinate and working under strict supervision. This beauty is above all that of form and harmony; in painting, line and drawing; in discourse, order and rhetoric; in literature, style and construction.

The distinctively French qualities, then, which we should expect to find dominant in drama are realism, rationalism, logic, order and clarity, seasoned with wit and satire; we should expect a drama concerned more with fact and truth than with the purely beautiful and poetic, interested and especially skilled in expressing mass psychology rather than individualism. We should not expect to find it richly imaginative or fantastic, and still less should it be speculative and mystical.

Add to this a condition in which the French theatre is probably unique. All French drama is, and has been in modern times, concentrated at Paris. It has practically all been written either by native Parisians or by Parisians through adoption, and, in either case, it is written for Parisian audiences. The result is that all French dramatists belong to one school, that of Paris; all are familiar personally with the plays of their predecessors and contemporaries. An important consequence of this unique situation is that continuity and tradition, which are perhaps inherently more important in the drama than in any other branch of literature, are particularly strong in the French theatre. Standardization, therefore, and perfection of technique through experiment and imitation are possible in the French theatre, and perhaps inevitable, to an extent hardly to be found elsewhere, and are unusually interesting subjects of study both as faults and merits. Certainly in no other theatre can it be more clearly seen that the evolution of the drama is dependent on the coöperation of three primary factors: the dramatist, the actor or organized stage, and the theatre-going public.

MAIN CURRENTS OF MODERN
FRENCH DRAMA

CHAPTER I

RÉSUMÉ OF FRENCH DRAMA BEFORE 1830

FRENCH drama is a thousand years old. Originating in the church in the tenth century, its development has been continuous and markedly in accord with French national character. It has had its periods of full bloom and brilliancy and its seasons of decline and fallen leaves, but it has never entirely disappeared nor lost identity; where one branch has withered, two have sprung from the same stock, and however much the species may have been improved or modified, the *genus franciscum* has remained recognizable.

The earliest known drama in France was in the Catholic mass, in which certain cardinal events of Christian religion were acted to make them more vivid to the people. The first two church dramatizations, made in Latin, were of Christ's birth and resurrection and were given at the Christmas and Easter services. From these two centers grew the Nativity and Resurrection plays of the early Liturgical drama, and by evolution and accretion, to be explained through the French passion for the theatre and love of completeness, these beginnings of the tenth century were expanded in the succeeding centuries, until they culminated in the fifteenth and sixteenth in the great Mystery plays, in which were incorporated practically

3

the entire Scriptures, along with much that was less orthodox.

In its inception then French drama was wholly pious and didactic, but, with the passion of the French for the dramatic *per se,* and for realism, and perhaps on account of a certain lack of reverence due to their keen sense of the ridiculous, it did not long remain so. Our chief interest in this early <u>history is to note the rapid growth of the dramatic impulse,</u> until it comes to use the original pious and didactic purpose largely as a moral pretext — a practice still in honor — and also to see the first appearance of racial traits that have remained distinguishing characteristics of modern French drama.

Early examples emphasizing the purely dramatic impulse are numerous. In a Latin Nativity play the episode of Rachel weeping over her children, slaughtered by Herod, has had a development that can only be explained by a desire to exploit the theatrical possibilities of a pathetic scene, one which in no way emphasizes a cardinal fact of Christianity. In the first really important religious drama wholly in French, the *Représentation d'Adam* of the twelfth century, we find that this dramatic interest, as compared with the purely pious one, has become the dominant preoccupation of the author, if it is not his primary purpose. He is concerned about style and composition for the sake of dramatic and artistic effect, he instructs his characters how to stand, speak and act in order to attain best these aims, and his emphasis is obviously determined by the dramatic possibilities rather than by the pious lessons to be taught. Moreover, not only is this play an excellent example of

French logic and clarity in its composition, and characteristic of French love of rhetoric in its speeches, but there
are a realism and attention to detail which are notable
in an early work of this character.   Cain is to strike
Abel furiously but without danger, since the latter is
instructed to place a sauce-pan beneath his garments;
and when the demons are taking the two brothers to
purgatory, they are told to treat Abel more gently than
Cain.   The play is written by a dramatist and not by a
priest, whatever may have been his calling.

Finally, in this play there is clear evidence that the
devils were already half-comic characters, since they are
specifically told to run about among the audience, partly
for the sake of exciting terror and partly for amusement.
The invasion of the comic has already begun.

Another early example of lack of complete reverence
in these sacred representations is, perhaps, to be seen in
a Latin form of the Saint Nicolas play.   A Jew has
placed his goods in the care of the Saint, and when his
wealth is stolen by thieves and returned by the Saint,
he is converted to Christianity.   In the scene where he
first finds that his money is gone, the Jew berates most
vigorously the image of the Saint for his negligence, and
ends by lashing it.   It hardly seems possible that this
lashing scene was carried out in a wholly serious manner,
and it is still less possible that it would be witnessed with
entire reverence by a French audience; in any case, it
would not be the only instance where the French have
jested a little with their saints.

This familiarity or levity, if such it be here, certainly
developed apace a little later, as did realism and farce.

In the *Jeu de Saint Nicolas* of Jean Bodel, in the thirteenth century, of which much is elevated in tone and purpose, there are whole scenes of drinking and gaming among thieves and roisterers, written with a realistic tone and in a language that makes the *mot propre* of Hugo and the Romanticists seem pale and that even equals at times the *mot malpropre* of Zola and the Naturalists. In fact it was this realism and coarseness, this over-development of the farce in sacred drama, that were the causes, officially, of the death of the religious theatre. In 1548 the Parliament at Paris forbade further representation of religious plays by the Brotherhood of the Passion because such performances resulted in holding sacred things up to ridicule. This drama, then, beginning in the Church with a wholly pious purpose, had not only been evicted long before from sacred places, but in the end was forbidden representation even in lay theatres, as being offensive to the religion by which it was created. However this may be explained, it is clear that other than purely moral and didactic purposes control the evolution of the drama, and this lesson might well be noted by the exponents of the Useful Play to-day, who would make the drama subservient to reform, a moral agency similar to the church or school.

The influence of the purely religious play on its successor, Classic drama, was slight, but its effect on French life in other ways was considerable; a drama that developed pieces sixty thousand lines long, requiring a week to be played and bankrupting, as they sometimes did, the city which staged them, could hardly have failed to leave important traces, in addition to such anachronistic survivals as the Passion Play of Oberammergau. Some of these effects are not always recognized. Perhaps not many stop to think that the " alligator " who swallows Punch in the marionette shows which delighted our youth, and which may amuse us still in many suburbs of Paris, is only the jaws of Hell through which the demons of medieval drama dragged the actors who had ended their rôle and who " got the hook." We may not have thought, either, why the French speak so familiarly the name of the Deity in exclamations and use the world *diable* with such incongruous adjectives (*bon diable, pauvre diable*) or in so many strange idioms (*faire le diable à quatre, etc.*). These usages are due to the fact that for centuries the Deity, angels and devils were actors on the French stage, appearing along with human beings, and with very similar attributes of character; popular conception and speech have been widely influenced in this way.

The origins of French lay drama, outside of the farce that was early introduced into the religious theatre, are less easily determined. The famous *Jeu de la Feuillée* of Adam de la Halle, in the thirteenth century, in which he satirizes most effectively his fellow-townsmen, a play that might have graced the first meeting of the Gridiron Club, does not seem to have had any immediate successors. It is not much before the fifteenth century that examples of the morality, *sottie,* and farce can be found. However, these lay forms prophesy much more clearly and, in some cases, influence the Classic drama of the seventeenth century.

The morality play in its regular practice of personifying abstract qualities obviously foreshadows later character comedy and shows the French interest in the universal and typical. Harpagon of Molière is only personified avarice, done, it is true, by a master hand, which could give individual life to an abstraction.

The *sottie*, of which the chief distinction from other forms is that it was performed by a society of *Sots*, or " fools," shows a tendency to biting satire, often on contemporary events and persons, and is thoroughly typical of a modern French practice.

But it is the farce especially that survives most noticeably in later drama. In its *esprit gaulois*, its effective and pointed brevity and its irresistible ridicule, it explains a whole side of Molière's comedy, and one which is not the least potent in maintaining the popularity of this great comic writer. In fact *Maître Pathelin*, the masterpiece of the farce, would be a masterpiece of genuine comedy also if it were not deficient in the higher artistry of style and the greater dignity of aim and conception. These qualities only the Renaissance could give, and until it came and raised the level of French literature, even a Molière could perhaps have risen no higher in the comic field than *Pathelin*.

The drama that grew from the Renaissance, the great Classic school headed by Molière, Corneille and Racine, is usually thought of as representing a complete break with medieval drama. The connection, it is true, is much slighter than it usually is between the different schools or movements in the evolution of a literary genre, but connection there is, none the less. The use of the comic forms of the medieval theatre in Molière was mentioned above, and, after all, Molière is immensely more real and a more important model for the modern theatre than are the tragic writers; his realism and democracy explain this sufficiently in present-day society, where the aristocratic spirit and cultured class have been submerged, and from which pure tragedy, born in the atmosphere of the seventeenth century, has almost disappeared.

However, Corneille, the creator of Classic drama in France in the seventeenth century, is explained almost as much by Alexandre Hardy, who is in spirit a writer of medieval drama, as he is by Jodelle, the first author of pure Classic tragedy; the action created by Hardy is the breath of life in Corneille's plays.

Excluding minor factors, we may say that three great dramatic principles were established by Corneille in the *Cid* and later plays, which justify his position as the creator of French Classic drama, and which have become the laws of worthy drama ever since his time. These major foundations of modern French drama are: interior or motivated action, free will or self-determination, and moral or mental drama rather than purely physical action or tragedy.

Through the first of these principles the play ceased to be merely a romance or a piece of action invented and controlled by the author; it is not simply a spectacle or a story, but furnishes food for thought, has a meaning and may illustrate a philosophy of life. With the second principle, by endowing his characters with free will and making them masters of their own fate, Corneille has given models that are real human beings, or at least are what real human beings think themselves to be; and we are able to enter completely into the lives of such characters, to sympathize fully and to rejoice and tremble with them. By his third innovation he has demonstrated that what is truly moving, poignant or tragic is not the physical fact, ruin, disaster, death, but the mental or moral distress or emotion of a dramatic crisis; the drama of the *Cid* is not Rodrigue's killing of Chimène's father, it is the Cid's struggle between love and honor, it is Chimène's distress, torn between love and duty.

In so far as innovations go, Racine did nothing beyond perfecting these principles, shortening and heightening the crisis, making it better motivated, more psychological, more human and emotional.

In the field of comedy Molière accomplished a very similar work, for he not only made comedy realistic and national and gave it social satire as its particular province — these are characteristics of good comedy everywhere — but, in his great character comedies, he also offers a dramatic crisis that is mental or moral and that is developed by the principle of interior action. The aim of the dramatist in either field is essentially the same, to seize a character at the psychological moment, and under the spot-light of the dramatist's keen vision to lay bare the secrets of the heart and soul. It is the drama of concentration and single purpose; there is no scattering, no distraction, no episodes; every action comes from some master motive in the character and is given to throw light upon this motive.

There can be no question that this conception of drama has much in it that is universally valid and that it has consequently served as a model for modern drama in all countries, and will doubtless continue to do so in the future. The plays of Racine, in *aim and composition,* are much nearer to recent drama than those of Shakespeare, despite the transcendent genius of the latter author, and this is true even of the present-day English theatre. But it should be especially noted how admirably this conception is adapted to the racial and national qualities that dominate French literature. With the law of interior action controlling, and the need to motivate every act in the psychology of the characters, is to be found the triumph of French logic and clarity. Tragedy is a mental and moral crisis which satisfies supremely the Frenchman's interest in ideas. His rhetoric is poured out in argumentative, intellectual suasion rather than in imaginative or poetic flights. Drama is will in action which accords with his positivism and good sense.

In comedy is found full scope for his realism and his moralistic trend; and particularly is its social satire pricked in by his keen wit, or splashed over the objects of his ridicule in the sallies of his *esprit gaulois.* Finally, the concentration of this drama and the brevity of a dramatic crisis satisfy the Frenchman's chief conception of beauty, which is that of simplicity, order and harmony.

It is obviously a mistake, then, to think of Classic drama as a system artificial for the French, imposed upon them by a study and imitation of the ancients and hampering their native genius. It only checked a profusion and richness which they have regularly pruned for the sake of clarity and symmetry, and held in rein a fancy and imagination which they most frequently keep under control as distracting to the concentration demanded by the actable play, which must present a complete demonstration in the narrow limits of two or three hours. If Corneille was seriously restricted by the rules of Classic tragedy, it was precisely in the qualities in which he was the least typically French.

The excellence of the Classic genre, at least for the French, could be abundantly proven by *a priori* reasoning, but this is hardly necessary since it has been so completely justified by experience. Not only was it the form for an unparalleled number of great plays in the seventeenth century, but its strength and solidity were so great that it continued in use until it had long outlasted its time. No pattern can remain in style for two hundred years and continue to fit its wearer. That the French should go on wearing the cloak of Classic drama long after they had discarded the wigs and laces with which it was matched, that they should write in the *style noble* and only of kings and lords long after kings and lords of the type of Louis Fourteenth or Louis Sixteenth had become anathema to the majority of the people, is striking evidence, first of the strength and glory of the Classic model, and second of the undoubted routine of the French, and particularly of the influence of theatrical tradition in Paris. The wonder is the greater since this mantle, worn by the giants of drama in the seventeenth century, had, on the pygmy shoulders of the eighteenth and early nineteenth century playwrights, shrunk to the dimensions of a strait-jacket. By servile imitation, without inspiration or growth, the rules and conventions of drama had crystallized into hard and lifeless formality.

The unities which restricted the action of a Classic drama to a single place and to twenty-four hours of time were observed in form without thought of the concentration and intensity of which they were more a product than a cause. Artificially elegant characters were staged, and spoke a language used by the highly cultured only, when a whole new class of French bourgeois had invaded the theatres and were hungry for plays which would touch their own life. Universal types were still paraded after Molière and his successors had rung on them all the changes possible, and writers seemed unaware that the study of humanity on the stage must correspond with the methods of study of the day, must turn from the deductive philosophy of the seventeenth century to the inductive methods of modern philosophy and of experimental science. Finally, most astonishing of all, during the first thirty years of the nineteenth century, the established theatres of Paris seemed to ignore that a great revolution had swept over France, over Europe in fact, and had overturned all the old foundations, State, Church, all the institutions of society, and even, for the time being, had shaken the traditional rationalism of the French from its throne and left them in a highly nervous state, a prey to hallucination and emotion, groping among the ruins in search of their lost guide to life. The theatre of this period was an anachronism, impossible to explain if it had really been alive. It is a mild phrase, then, to say that French drama in the beginning of the nineteenth century was ripe for a change; in truth it was more than ripe, it had already passed into the succeeding stage.

CHAPTER II

HUGO AND THE ROMANTIC DRAMA

THE period of modern French drama of which the chief developments are considered here comprises approximately the last one hundred years. Beginning with the Romantic school, formally inaugurated by Hugo's *Hernani* in 1830, we shall note the reaction against it in 1843, marked by the so called School of Good Sense, and shall trace briefly the minor stream of modified Romantic verse drama, which continues down to the present day, including that of Rostand. We shall then return to the main current, the Realistic prose drama, which developed about the middle of the nineteenth century from the double source of Romanticism and the *pièce bien faite* (well-made play) of Scribe, and shall follow its course through the evolution of its principal forms, the Social drama, the Thesis Play, and the Useful Play. In the recent theatre there will be noted particularly the attempt of the Théâtre Libre about 1890 to draw the drama into Naturalism and furnish it with a new technique, and a large place will be given to the playwrights of the last thirty or forty years.

Since the period in question is an important one in the history of the French theatre and particularly rich in its large number of authors and plays of at least respectable rank, this study must needs be strictly selective, devoted only to significant dramatists, and, above all, to those who may be of special interest to students of the theatre in other countries, in which the influence of French models during this time has been widespread.

Romanticism, which is European in extent, owes its growth to causes too diverse, and is too multifarious in its products, to permit of easy definition. Whether it be looked upon as an uprising of feeling and imagination against the dominance of rationalism; or an expression of the subjective, individual, and concrete rather than of the objective, universal, and abstract; or simply as a revolution against Classicism, seeking freedom from all restraint, depends upon the point of view from which it is studied. It was all of these and more. For our purposes, it will be simplest to consider only the rôle of Romanticism in the French drama, and to note the results when it is reacted on by the national genius of France, where, for obvious reasons, its duration and success have been more restricted than in some other countries.

While the general movement of Romanticism in Europe is closely bound up with social and political revolution and liberty, it owes its particular doctrine to the famous eighteenth century French author, Jean-Jacques Rousseau. Rousseau's philosophy was a call to return to nature. For him, all in nature was good, society and civilization were largely corrupting influences, and the rules and restrictions they had imposed should be thrown off. However, the influence of this philosophy can hardly be appreciated separate from the eloquence of sentimental appeal with which Rousseau endowed it in his various writings. In congratulating Rousseau on his treatise calling for a return to nature, Voltaire has pointed out the weakness of this philosophy and testified to the power of the plea in a single line: " You give me a desire to go on all fours again."

In France, the prestige of Classicism was such that Rousseau's doctrine made little immediate headway, and his influence was at first much more pronounced in England and Germany. When it did make itself more fully felt in France, it was greatly aided by the examples of foreign literatures. The early French Romanticists of the nineteenth century, besides taking Shakespeare as the model of all modern drama — a model whom they never really understood — were much inspired by Scott and Byron in their creation of Romantic historic literature and the proud, pessimistic hero. Also they were influenced by the writings of Lessing and Goethe, to whom attention had been attracted particularly by Madame de Staël's *De l'Allemagne*. It was, in fact, one of the comparatively rare periods in French literary history in which there was anything approaching a fairly general interest among French authors in the literature of other countries. A number of translations from foreign literatures were published about this time, and a few French authors learned sufficiently other modern languages to read foreign works in the originals. Finally, in 1827, a troupe of notable English actors came to Paris and gave successful performances of Shakespeare's plays, which stimulated powerfully some of the leaders of the Romantic school.

Among the early followers of Rousseau in France was Chateaubriand, who popularized the Romantic spirit in a general way; more specifically he turned attention to Nature, seen in her romantic and sentimental-moods, and, in such works as *René* and *Atala*, he greatly stimulated the vogue of the melancholy hero whose weeping sickness was so contagious during the following decades. Although not a dramatist, his influence on Hugo and other creators of French Romantic drama was very great.

Romanticism had already triumphed in other fields of literature, notably in lyric poetry, before it attempted to capture the theatre. It was on the stage that it had to fight its hardest battle and it was there that it attracted the most attention. The theatre by nature of its organization is usually conservative, and in France it is triply so, through the strength of French routine and because of its concentration at Paris. Quite naturally then, this was the last and most stubbornly defended stronghold of the Classic school.

The leader in this battle was Victor Hugo, and the chief manifesto of the school is his *Preface to Cromwell*, a long statement of principles written as an introduction to his first important play, *Cromwell*, which was published in 1827. This statement, with slight additions, covers the chief innovations proposed for the theatre.

There is much in the *Preface* that is of doubtful value or superfluous — first of all, at least three-fourths of the words. One can see that it is written by a very young man, although this alone does not account for all of its verbosity. The *Preface* is fairly consistent throughout in maintaining the doctrine furnished by Rousseau, that art should hold the mirror up to nature and that there should be no rules except those of nature, truth and life; but this doctrine, which had so often given the battlecry of reform, is hardly made clearer in Hugo's theory than it was later by his practice.

In the long pseudo-philosophic introduction of this *Preface*, Hugo makes much of the influence of Christianity in exalting God and humbling man, thus bringing to light and introducing into literature the earthly, the common, and the base, and he insists on the importance of this element, under the name of the grotesque, as a distinguishing characteristic of Romantic literature. " Christianity," he says, " brings poetry to truth. Like Christianity, the modern muse will see things with a higher and broader view. She will recognize that all in creation is not humanly beautiful, that the ugly exists along with the beautiful, the misshapen beside the graceful, the grotesque opposite the sublime, the evil with the good, the shadow with the light. . . . She will begin to do then as nature does: mingle, in her creations, without, however, confusing them, the shadow with the light, the grotesque with the sublime; in other words, the body with the soul, the animal with the spiritual."

Whatever may be the value of Hugo's philosophical explanation of it, the large rôle that the grotesque plays in Romantic literature is well known. Naturally this element appears in the theatre in the form of comedy, and this means practically the breaking down of the distinctions between comedy and tragedy, and the mingling of the two in the same play. While this was extensively practiced by the Romanticists — as it has been largely ever since — owing to the character of their drama and a frequent deficiency in humor on their part, this

principle did not attain its ultimate importance until later.
In the extension of the term in the passage above to include the earthly, the ugly, the evil, the physical and
animal, we find the chief field of the succeeding phases
of Romanticism; namely, Realism and Naturalism. Of
the last school particularly, one might say that its almost
exclusive presentation of the unlovely side of human
nature is a distinguishing characteristic.

As others had done before, Hugo attacked the Classic
unities of time and place, which demand that the action
of a drama should not exceed twenty-four hours and
that the place should remain unchanged. Although these
unities accord in general with the French native genius
for concentration and simplicity, and the choice of a
mental or moral crisis as the natural subject of drama,
their maintenance as hard and fast rules for all plays
could not be justified. Hugo's arguments are here conclu-
sive and have generally been accepted. He does not attack the unity of action, but in admitting secondary actions, and thus impairing simplicity of plot, he does
weaken it, and, deprived of the support of the other two
unities, it is, in the practice of the Romanticists, very
greatly compromised.

Classicism had devoted itself largely to an expression
of the universal in man, to the personification of abstract
qualities or at least to the presentation of typical characters. The Romanticists would turn to the concrete,
the individual, and often, in fact, to the exceptional. But
their really vital principle, in its ultimate development,
was to treat man as explained and modified by his environment. This environment appears in literature and the

drama in the form of " local color," and, as a rule, in the Romantic theatre it hardly serves beyond heightening the picturesque and striking, or giving atmosphere to a scene or play. Later, however, with the Realistic school this principle becomes the corner stone of their literature; man is treated as a product of his environment, and this doctrine, which is at the basis of Comte's positivism and Taine's determinism, becomes the dominant philosophy, replacing the deductive rationalism of Descartes.

According to the *Preface,* the drama should turn from the exclusive representation of antiquity to all history, but especially to the French, the announced ambition of the Romanticists being to create a great national, historic drama. For subjects it should no longer choose exclusively the nobility, and with this change, really a significant one in signalizing the rising tide of democracy in literature, would come, as a necessary corollary, the breaking down of the *style noble* and the substitution of the *mot propre;* the author should call a spade a spade.

Hugo makes a strong plea for lyricism as a proper element in drama, and naturally turns to Shakespeare for his model. It is interesting to note that this element, practically banished by the rationalism of the Classicists, but quite in accord with the emotional character of Romanticism, becomes in practice the chief merit of Hugo's dramas. Naturally he is a strong advocate of the use of verse as the proper language of drama, and his well-known changes in the Classic Alexandrine, breaking it up by double cesuras, relieving its monotony, and giving it much greater variety and pliability, thus enabling it to express colloquial speech and rapid dialogue, are most important reforms in the style of modern French verse drama.⌉

This theory of the new drama, destructive or simply reformatory as much of it was, does not, taken alone, give any very exact idea of the Romantic theatre. The proof of this is that most of the specific innovations proposed have been accepted since and incorporated in genres strikingly different from the Romantic one. The real character of the Romantic theatre, then, can be determined only by a study of its practice, and obviously the plays and dramatic career of Hugo offer the best examples for this purpose.

Victor-Marie Hugo (1802–1885) was only twenty-five years old when he wrote the *Preface to Cromwell* and only twenty-eight when *Hernani* was produced. We should remember that the Romantic movement was one of very young men. This not only explains many of its characteristics, of which some are laudable doubtless and others are lacking in wisdom, but further suggests a reason for the brief vogue of a great deal of the most highly colored Romanticism. A number of the Romanticists did not mature as such; they grew into something else, or at least their Romanticism changed hue. However, this is not the case with Hugo, who never grew up — perhaps because he was well satisfied with himself from the beginning.

Hugo was the son of an army officer prominent under Napoleon, and in his early youth traveled much, particularly in Spain, which doubtless explains some of his interest in that country, the scene of more than one of his plays. His mother was of a romantic temperament, addicted to novels which she is said to have tried out first on her sons; in any case, Victor Hugo was in his youth a great reader of such literature.

His education was in part in the well-known Lycée Louis-le-Grand at Paris. He had literary ambitions from the earliest age, and was a professed admirer of Chateaubriand. He received a prize for poetry at fifteen, and at seventeen was, with his brother, the founder and most voluminous writer of a short-lived literary magazine. His first published book, a volume of lyric poetry, appeared in 1822.

He had been converted to an ardent republicanism and entered political controversy, becoming a violent opponent to Napoleon III. This opposition led to his banishment from France in 1852 — an exile from which he refused to return until the fall of the Empire in 1870. Most of this exile was passed on the Island of Guernsey, where he wrote many of his notable works; the violent satire on Napoleon and the marked influence of the sea in much of his writing belong to this period. Returning to France in 1870, he took a prominent part in political and literary life up to his death. In 1875 he was elected senator. He had become a sort of literary idol in France, a rôle which he was remarkably fitted to cultivate and enjoy.

Hugo stands supreme as France's greatest lyric poet, and especially as an epic-lyric and satiric poet. As a novelist also, author of *Les Misérables, Notre-Dame de Paris* and many other romances, his fame is world-wide.

His writings as a dramatist, great as was his influence on the Romantic theatre, are of less value than those of the poet and novelist. His dramatic work was practically prescribed by his position as leader of the Romantic school and was not inherent in his genius, however much it may have been in his ambition, which was all inclusive. He lacked the specific ability of the dramatist, without which one may, it is true, write good literature cast in dramatic mold, but can hardly write a good play. It has been a frequent mistake to speak of him as a born or skillful playwright simply because his habitual turn of mind and language were theatrical; nothing could be farther from the truth since he was notably deficient in the really important qualities that are most necessary for writing a good play.

If one omits Hugo's youthful attempt, *Inez de Castro,* his first drama was *Cromwell,* finished in 1827. It is claimed that he had intended this for the great French actor Talma; but during its composition, owing possibly to Talma's death and also to Hugo's natural inclinations, the play entirely outgrew in length and complexity the limits of the theatre, and the idea of staging it was abandoned. It is vivid and interesting in spots, but on the whole is not a noteworthy contribution even to the somewhat doubtful category of the closet drama. The most important result of this attempt was the *Preface,* which has been considered above.

In 1829 Hugo wrote, in a very short time, *Marion Delorme,* in some respects one of the most characteristic of Romantic plays. This is particularly true in that it gives us, in Didier, the conventional Romantic hero, proud, mysterious, moody, fatalistic; and in Marion, the usual Romantic heroine who is redeemed through love. We find here, in the least complicated form, one of the best examples of Romantic philosophy, dealing with its characteristic theme, the apotheosis of a love, by preference irregular or immoral. For the Romanticists love was a god that could do no wrong. This philosophy, in its sincere unconsciousness, is perhaps not immoral, but it is at least unmoral, and what is worse, often absurdly untrue in its sentimental evangelism. *Marion Delorme* was forbidden by the censor and was not played until 1831.

Hugo then took up the subject of *Hernani*, which he wrote in a fever of composition, and which appeared at the national theatre, the *Comédie-Française*, in 1830, the first regular Romantic verse drama to be performed there, and marking by its advent the formal inauguration of the Romantic theatre. This was an event comparable with the appearance of the *Cid* in 1636,[1] by which the Classic theatre was established. The performance of this play, called the Battle of Hernani, was the final and decisive clash between the Classicists and the Romanticists. During its run, which was a considerable one, every line of the play was alternately hissed and applauded. The result was, on the whole, the triumph of Romanticism. Absurd as the play appeared from the Classic standpoint, and as much of it is from any reasonable point of view, its beauties are undeniable, and coming with the force and freshness of youth into the midst of barren artificiality, it won enthusiastic admiration.

[1] I have hesitated to change this sacred date — the only one my drama students seem to know — although it appears established that the *Cid* was not performed until January 1637.

In *Hernani* Hugo has probably displayed the greatest number of his merits and faults, which, considering the quality of the former and the quantity of the latter, is a remarkable feat for so short a play. Placed in colorful Spain, with its romantic bandit hero, Hernani, its famous Carlos V, and its absurdly jealous young-old nobleman, Don Ruy Gomez, all rivals for the hand of Doña Sol, it offered abundant opportunity for the mixture of mystery, history, and sophistry so frequent in Romantic historic drama, and above all for the antithesis which is the basis of Hugo's dramatic conception. Its secondary title, *Castilian Honor*, suggested by the cruel vengeance in the dénouement, resulting from the unreasoning jealousy and offended honor of Ruy Gomez, is, of course, only the famous *point d'honneur* of the French, the regular motive of their heroic literature, but it is here so enlarged and distorted through the usual magnifying powers of Hugo's vision, that he himself has failed to recognize its origin and has given it a foreign name. It is interesting to note that Corneille, in his most romantic moods, was subject to a similar hallucination.

As a dramatic composition *Hernani* is ridiculous, its plot being based on antithesis, with the principle of motivated, interior action violated so strikingly and so constantly that it seems intentional. Its dramatic figures all do exactly what they should not, according to all the laws of character and good sense, or rather each does in the end exactly what the other would be expected to do. For example, Hernani, the man of blood and steel, who thrills us for a whole act by his magnificent oaths of vengeance on the King, does nothing more daring than break a good sword on the pavement, and finally kneels at the feet of his father's slayer to receive the Order of the Golden Fleece and other blessings; the vindictive Don Carlos, so carefully groomed as villain for three acts, when the opportunity comes, ends by pardoning everybody; and the sixty year old Don Ruy Gomez, the generous and hospitable nobleman, is alone left to carry the tragedy to the end, which he does by wreaking a cruel vengeance on his rival and the woman he loves, and by killing himself like a sixteen year old Romeo.

But with all this, the play is filled with beautiful poetry by one of the master lyricists of the world, and abounds in pathetic and moving situations, in which the wonderful rhetoric and verse of the poet sweep us off our feet with passion and harmony, and disarm our criticism. Under the spell, we are unaware that the figures giving forth these divine voices are hollow, unlifelike creations, moved by the hand of the author in improbable, operatic action; charmed by the voice of the violin in the hands of a master, we care little that it is only inanimate wood patched together with glue. Even the most highly colored lines of melodrama are so draped with the mantle of poetry that they usually pass unnoticed. As a model for drama it is not to be imitated, but it contains many beautiful passages and scenes, and today, after almost a hundred years of life, with several hundred representations on the stage where it first appeared, it still continues to please and charm.

With the success of *Hernani*, the doors of the French theatre were thrown open to Romantic drama. In the next dozen years Hugo himself composed a half-dozen such plays, in the midst of a more voluminous output in the fields of lyric poetry and of the novel. His next piece was *Le Roi s'amuse*, in 1832. It is a striking drama, with some passages more dramatically powerful than any in *Hernani*, but it has also more exaggerated faults, is much less agreeable, and poetically is less beautiful. It was forbidden by the censor for its satire of Francis I, after only one representation, and although it has been played since, it is doubtless known to a wider public under the title of *Rigoletto* in Verdi's opera. It is interesting to see in this play the rising tide of Hugo's democratic sentiments and anti-monarchial tendencies.

From 1833 to 1835, Hugo, probably induced by the example of Alexandre Dumas, whose prose plays were having greater dramatic success than Hugo's verse theatre, wrote three dramas in prose, *Lucrèce Borgia*, *Marie Tudor*, and *Angelo*. The revelation afforded by these plays is complete, — and disastrous for Hugo's reputation as a dramatist. Stripped of the ornament of verse, and consequently of the beauty of poetry, his work stands out as lurid melodrama with few redeeming features. Take for example *Marie Tudor:* its history is often distorted or false, its characters stained by crime without measure or reason, and its action and dramatic effect dependent on chance and surprise to the point of the ludicrous. We never know when a cloak is pulled off or a cell door opened who will be revealed, but we may be sure that it will not be the person expected.

In 1838 Hugo returned to verse and wrote *Ruy Blas*, perhaps his best constructed drama, and next to *Hernani* his most successful. Here the leading characters seem more consistent and the plot and dénouement better prepared. However, this is only relative and this play also contains striking improbabilities of action and unwarranted conceptions of character. For example, the decisive action is hinged on the chance return of Don César on the very day of the dénouement, and on his accidental tumbling down the one chimney, of all the chimneys in Madrid, where his presence is significant, and where he alone, of all the persons in Madrid, could play the required rôle. Also one finds again Hugo's love of antithesis carried in his conception of character to the point of absurdity. Ruy Blas is a lackey, hence he has the talents of a prime minister and falls in love with the Queen. Don Salluste is a great lord with responsible charges, therefore he has the petty soul to carry out a mean plot against the Queen. Finally, in Don César, the debauched nobleman, companion of thugs and prostitutes, one finds quite naturally a delicate sense of honor and chivalry that scorns to take vengeance on a woman.

This way of conceiving life and character, so abundantly exemplified in popular literature everywhere, seems always sure of a sympathetic response from the unthinking multitude, and even from many who should know better. Whether this be due merely to a perverse chord in human nature or to a deeply ingrained fear of believing things are what they 'seem and ought to be, it makes a specious plea to a popular audience. In any case, this attitude appears closely akin to another universal prejudice which is inclined to accept satire and denigration of character as truth and realism, while the

praise of good qualities is likely to be called idealism or
exaggeration. This popular conception of life is one of
a number of factors, appearing in the drama about this
time, which tend to bring it down from the high literary
and cultural level where it had long been maintained to
the lower strata, intellectually and artistically, of a growing democracy, which was making itself felt in all phases
of life, social, political, and literary. Literature was being
brought more within popular conception.

One quality of *Ruy Blas* is worth particular notice.
The humor of this play, especially in the character of
Don César, is superior to that of any other piece of
Hugo and has done much to popularize it on the stage.
That this drama has not quite equalled *Hernani* in
public favor is owing undoubtedly to the superiority
of the first play in sheer lyric beauty, and is clear proof
that this poetry is the predominant merit of Hugo's
theatre.

Hugo's next and last play, *Les Burgraves,* in 1843,
marks an important date, that of the reaction against,
or failure of, the extreme Romantic drama. This play,
filled with epic and majestic poetry, lacks interest and
was coldly received. Hugo definitely gave up the stage
and turned to other work.

Most of the faults of Hugo as a dramatist, as well as
his merits as a poet, have been touched upon in the
examples of his drama treated; additional ones, perhaps
less original than copied on his part, will be treated in
connection with other Romantic dramatists, particularly
with Dumas. Those that are most natural or inherent
with him may then be summarized here, with further

brief explanations, where necessary, of their underlying causes.

One of the most notable qualities of Hugo is his intensity of vision and the bright light in which he sees all things. With him objects are regularly larger than life-size, and magnified in a light by which they are also distorted. This exaggeration is increased by a powerful imagination. He is, then, a painter of the most vivid pictures, for the creation and coloring of which he was endowed with an unrivalled mastery of words and verse. This panoramic visualization, which may be likened today to the moving picture, is Hugo's constant method. It takes the place of description, analysis, and even of the most serious historic deduction. Take as a striking example the philosophic-historic monologue of Don Carlos, in *Hernani,* before the tomb of Charlemagne. It is nothing but a magnificent series of elaborate pictures or visions. One can almost say that this is Hugo's sole method of serious thought — if it can be a method of serious thought.

With the qualities mentioned, Hugo is naturally exceedingly picturesque, although his work often lacks measure and may be marred by bad taste. This, as we have seen, is especially due to his love for antithesis and for violent contrast. By temperament, then, Hugo is primarily a writer of melodrama. His worst plays, those in prose, are melodramas, and what saves his verse dramas from a similar charge is that they are the work of a great lyric poet. Some of the outright and exterior melodrama of his prose plays may be due to the example of Dumas, in whom its genealogy is clearer and can best be treated, but it is important to note also that Hugo's basic conception of life and drama is really that of melodrama.

What this conception is, as seen in his plots and characters, has already been described; it seeks for the striking, the unusual and surprising, which are the regular province and resource of melodrama, and it abandons the principle of logical, interior action. If one believes therefore in a logic of events, in cause and effect, that a good tree bears good fruits, that the wicked suffer punishment for their misdeeds — either here or in the hereafter — he must admit that Romantic drama, which had as its motto to imitate nature and life, failed entirely to live up to its fundamental doctrine.

It is, of course, admitted that this logic of events is not always immediately apparent in real life, and that accidents occur. But it is precisely one of the chief merits of a book or a play — one that gives the greatest pleasure — that it shows us this hidden train of events, and points out all the links of the chain that connects the dénouement with the beginning. Also, if occasional accidents may occur in a play, there is certainly no such thing as habitual accidents, and no satisfactory work of art can be constructed on them.

In legitimate drama one expects a plot that has an aim and that works toward this goal. The characters of Hugo do not progress in this way. They have a certain life, they move about, they declaim and gesticulate, but often this action is mere turmoil and nothing is accomplished. For example, from the beginning we expect Hernani to do two things — to carry away Doña Sol and to take vengeance on the King — but no progress is made toward either, at the end of the first or second acts. In the third he is still farther away from these goals, and neither is attained in the end.

Hugo's heroes are the direct opposites of those of Corneille, who work out their own salvation by the principle of interior action according to certain motives of character. No better statement of this opposition between Classic and Romantic characters, nor perhaps clearer exposition of the Romantic weakness in this respect, can be found than the speech Hugo puts in the mouth of Hernani himself, words that accurately describe his rôle in the play:

"You believe me perhaps a man like all others, an intelligent being, who goes straight to the goal he has set. Undeceive yourself. I am only a moving force! A blind and deaf agent of funereal mystery! A soul of misfortune made out of darkness! Where I go I know not. But I feel myself driven by an impetuous breath, by an insensate destiny. I descend and descend, and never pause. If, sometimes, breathless, I dare turn my head, a voice cries to me, 'Go!' and the abyss is deep and red in its depths, with fire and blood. On the traces of my wild career all is broken and dies. Woe to anyone near me. Oh, flee! turn away from my fatal path."

This exposition, and criticism, of the Romantic hero is complete. Have we not a right to expect him to be an "intelligent being"? What human or other intelligible interest can be found in a "blind and deaf agent of funereal mystery" controlled "by an insensate fate"? This pessimistic hero, Byronic in character, is, beginning with Chateaubriand, traditional in French Romanticism. His fatalistic control is in reality the hand of the author — which Hugo calls " insensate."

Compared with this weakness, expressed in the passage quoted, in Hugo's conception of plot and character, which are fundamentals of drama, his other faults are of secondary importance, although one might note that his local color is too often in details that are non-essential, that his history is trivial or distorted, and that his tragic and terrible scenes, inspired doubtless by Shakespeare but developed in Hugo's particular manner, are frequently too harrowing and long drawn out, and are certainly not in agreement with French taste.

What can be commended has already been pointed out. In addition to a frequent note of sincerity and passion and a constant sympathy for the weak and oppressed, it is above all his splendid lyricism, his poetry and feeling, and the beauty and harmony of its expression. It is true that he is constantly turning aside in the strictly dramatic development of his plots and characters in order to create pathetic or moving situations to be exploited for lyric effect, but he does this with rare beauty and poetry. In that connection should be mentioned the one phase of dramatic construction in which Hugo may be granted real power. Within the limits of a single scene or situation he shows skill in exploiting all its lyric, and often even its proper dramatic possibilities, and in bringing it to an effective climax. It is only dramatic skill in details, such as language, dialogue, contrast and suspense, and it can not redeem his plays from their more fundamental faults, but it affords much interest, especially since such merits are readily and universally appreciated, while the faults may be apparent only through more careful consideration and reflection.

The Romantic theatre, then, as exemplified by Hugo, is important chiefly for its destructive work. The revolution against Classic convention and sterility was salutary and necessary, but, as with most revolutionaries, the chief work of rebuilding must be done by their successors. It is to be noted that nearly all of the specific innovations proposed have been incorporated in recent drama. Many of the faults of Hugo are characteristic of the Romantic school, which in general is too subjective, emotional and imaginative to succeed in the most impersonal and objective of genres, and some of these weaknesses will be more fully developed in treating the other Romanticists.

CHAPTER III

OTHER ROMANTIC DRAMATISTS

DUMAS, DELAVIGNE, VIGNY, MUSSET

ALEXANDRE DUMAS (1802–1870)

THE first development of popular and, strictly speaking, unliterary elements in the legitimate French theatre was touched upon in the treatment of Hugo, but their real advent is with Alexandre Dumas, that robust Napoleonic quadroon who elbowed his way so unceremoniously into literature, and who, the year before the appearance of *Hernani,* broke down the doors of the *Comédie* and brought in his melodramatic *Henri III,* followed by the crowd. Dumas is the real sponsor and popularizer of melodrama, and of popular drama, on the Romantic stage. It came to him legitimately from Pixerécourt,[1] the king of boulevard melodrama, without being abashed in his presence, as it might have been in Hugo's, over its lack of etiquette and good breeding, and without needing to cover its ungainly form with the mantle of poetry.

Everyone knows Dumas the novelist through his *Three Musketeers* and *Monte Cristo* and recalls some of his qualities. Besides, it is not easy to escape an author of some three hundred volumes, who first introduced factory methods into literature and dispensed it wholesale. In an early introduction to one of his plays he tells us how

[1] I have accepted Wright's statement (His. of Fr. Lit. p. 693) concerning the accent marks on this name.

he became a dramatic author. The son of a Revolutionary general who had negro blood, he was left without a sou at the age of twenty, and what was worse, with no education or training for earning a livelihood. On the strength of his sole accomplishment, good handwriting, he became an undersecretary to the Duke of Orleans at twenty dollars a month, and, with characteristic Dumas energy and audacity, set himself to reading and study in order to make his mark in literature.

His great dramatic awakening came through the performance of Shakespeare at Paris by the English troupe in 1827, and he relates this event with the usual Romantic fervor. In Shakespeare he saw all the dramatic geniuses rolled in one. " I recognized finally," he concludes, " that he was the man who had the most created, after God. From that moment my vocation was decided; I felt that the special mission to which each man is called was being offered to me; I had in myself that confidence which had been lacking until then and I struck out boldly toward the future."

Encouraged to emulation by these great creators, especially by the example of Shakespeare — and possibly by God's also — Dumas undertook heroic tragedy and wrote in verse a drama which, revised later, is published under the following title:

Christine

ou

Stockholm, Fontainebleau, et Rome
Trilogie dramatique en cinq actes, en vers
Avec prologue et épilogue

Strange to say, this play was accepted for presentation by the *Comédie!*

The appearance of *Christine* having been delayed, Dumas returned to the attack with a much stronger play, this time frankly in prose, *Henri III et sa Cour,* which the *Comédie* presented with startling success in 1829, a year before the appearance of *Hernani.* Although it was written in prose and was looked down upon as simple melodrama, its popularity was disconcerting and ominous for the Classic partisans.

As a historic drama, *Henri III* is typical of Dumas. Its local color and history are laid on with a lavish but not discriminating hand. We find a little of everything of the times: facts, follies and fashions. We learn the cost of theatre tickets, the latest games and oaths, and the recent style of turn-down collars. History is not separated from legend, and even magic and superstition seem accepted. Catherine de Medeci lays bare her most secret schemes for dominating the young King, schemes which, if ever formulated, were certainly never put into words. Dumas's history, then, is usually trivial and gossipy, the sort, as has been said, that is recounted of the great by valets and chambermaids.

Nevertheless there is underneath all this a plot full of invention and of sustained power and interest, which is conducted with great rapidity and skill, and which progresses with exciting interest to a breathless finish. Dumas is, in plot at least, a born playwright, and this quality explains largely his success. It is he, and not Hugo, who really popularized Romantic drama. Moreover, the subject of this play, illicit or immoral love treated with unconscious approval, is significant of Romantic philosophy and practice, although the real vogue and power of this theme were much more strikingly established in one of Dumas's subsequent pieces.

Henri III, despite its historic pretensions, is at heart popular melodrama, a little on its good behavior in its first appearance in polite society, and somewhat cramped in the severe confines of the *Comédie*. But, once introduced it quickly becomes familiar. A little later Dumas allows it to run riot in that stupendous play, *La Tour de Nesle*, which appeared at the Porte-Saint-Martin theatre in 1832. *La Tour de Nesle* is the father of all melodrama. Nothing has ever equalled it in pure melodramatic power, nor in success. It has been played everywhere, but in Paris alone unknown thousands of times, and, nearly a hundred years old, it still thrills the populace in the back-alley theatres.

Despite the non-literary quality of *La Tour de Nesle*, it is a significant play of Dumas, since we see here without disguise one of the important elements that he introduced into legitimate drama. This element, which is one of the secrets of Dumas's genius, is the strikingly popular character of his imagination, of his character creations, and of his whole conception of life. It is, as we shall see, the very essence of melodrama.

Historically, melodrama is the theatre of the common people, of those not trained to think, preferably of the credulous and ignorant. It portrays life fashioned to their tastes — life as they imagine it, and not at all as they have lived it or seen it. Its most fundamental characteristics are: first, a lack of literary or artistic merit; second, a desire to arouse or shock, to thrill with joy or to move to tears; and third, a capricious imagination without the restraint of experience and judgment, giving unexpected or improbable incidents rather than logical development of action. Its external signs, the manifestations of these characteristics, are well known. They are, above all, murders, duels, abductions, surprises, disguises and mysteries; they call for a special architecture of dungeons, cells, trap-doors, sliding-panels, barred windows and underground passages; and they demand as properties masks, hats and cloaks that hide the face, drugs, sleeping-potions and poisons. A profusion of these traits is a sure sign of melodrama, and it is obvious how frequent they are, not only in the plays of Dumas but in those of Hugo and the other Romantic playwrights.

Dumas's type of drama is based on a conception of life formed not by observation and experience but by imagination. Surely no thoughtful person ought to be mistaken as to the identity or reality of his character creations. These startling figures whom he launches into his breathless plots simply throw all probabilities to the winds, and, clothed with the merest fig leaf of possibility, depend on their speed to run the gauntlet of the realistic observer — and they usually get through. They are not true to real life and are even absurd, but they are remarkably typical of popular fancy in its mood of relaxation.

Dumas's manner of conceiving life was much dependent on exaggeration and antithesis, as it was in Hugo. Most often it rested on the assumption that all the vices belonged to the great and noble, in appearance, and all the virtues to the poor and humble. One example in many of this amusing type of logic is the speech of Buridan in *La Tour de Nesle*,[2] where he proves to the companion of his strange adventure that the masked women who had invited them so mysteriously to this orgy belong to the highest society. After each recital of the effrontery, perversion, and unrestrained debauchery of these women, he draws the conclusion: "*Ce sont de grandes dames.*" A few lines at the end will give an idea of his style: "You see well then that these are noble ladies. At the table they abandoned themselves to all that love and intoxication can have of impulse and unrestraint; they spoke blasphemies; they pronounced perverse speeches and vile words; they forgot all restraint, all modesty, forgot heaven and earth. They are noble ladies, the most noble of ladies, I assure you."

Such characterizations undoubtedly flatter popular imagination. Whether this be owing to a sense of social injustice or to some other cause, these assumptions are pleasing to the common people. If proof is needed, one has only to note the applause accorded today to the anarchistic orator, for whom every rich man is dishonest, every ruler cruel and wicked, and even every comfortable bourgeois base.

Dumas, then, as well as Hugo, and much more than Hugo in style, imagination and character conception, introduced popular psychology into literature and posed as a champion of the common people. In fact we might already have had, in his work, a theatre of social reform

[2] Deuzième Tableau, Scène V.

if he had been a moralist. This, however, he was not, but the spirit of didactic moralizing is rarely long absent from French genius, and Dumas had a son.

But Dumas was not only a popularizer of melodrama in the Romantic theatre, he was also the most powerful and influential creator of the contemporary drama of passion, a form that has long outlived the Romantic movement proper. The play which above all others popularized the drama of passion is *Antony,* a five-act, prose piece that appeared in 1831; it occupies a place in the drama of passion similar to that of *La Tour de Nesle* in melodrama. *Antony* is not a historical play but treats bourgeois life of the author's time. If this practice had been more frequent among the Romanticists, the drama would undoubtedly have been brought to earth and to the realities of life much earlier, but Dumas and his contemporaries only rarely chose such subjects, and it remained for his son and the next generation of playwrights to exploit all the possibilities of such a theatre.

This play is a breathless drama of guilty love, and is particularly remarkable for the audacity of its situations and of the character of its chief figure. Antony has been very aptly called the famous ancestor of a long line of infamous heroes. In only one respect, however, is he original; for the most part his qualities are clearly in line with his Romantic predecessors.

As a type or a general conception Antony is Byronic, and Dumas's motto beneath the title of this play, taken from Byron, is doubly significant as we shall see: " They have said that *Childe Harold* was I, what do I care! " Antony is also the proud illegitimate outcast, the Didier

of *Marion Delorme*. But in one quality, and that is
the backbone of his creation, he is Dumas himself. The
usual Romantic hero had been an irresolute creature,
exhaling his violence in words and led by fate to a pathetic death or suicide. But Antony is not a suicide;
he does not kill himself because he can not win an impossible love; he takes love by brute force and kills his
mistress to protect her reputation and honor!

The audacity of this dramatic character is precisely the
most prominent quality of Dumas himself; as suggested
by the quotation from Byron, he has created Antony in
his own image. The character is not an agreeable one
here, but as an instrument of drama, a will in action, it
is much superior to that of a Hernani or a Ruy Blas,
and when properly civilized later and divested of its Romantic nimbus, it is a most popular conception.

An analysis of Dumas's numerous other plays, usually
of the pretentious historic genre, written before the fall of
Les Burgraves, can hardly be justified. Autopsies so long
after decease are especially unpleasant, and are, besides,
not necessary in this case in order to determine the
cause of death. Dumas's plays were of a short-lived
race, and most of them died of old age while still young
in years. The three we have mentioned, *Henri III*, *La
Tour de Nesle*, and *Antony*, typify perfectly the chief
contributions of Dumas to the development of the theatre, namely historic melodrama, the psychology of popular imagination and the brutal drama of guilty passion.

Dumas's many faults, such as his negligent style and
his tinsel characters, are evident, and, moreover, are of
minor concern when an author is studied not for himself

nor for what has perished with him but to determine what
has survived. He was not a theorist as Hugo was, and his
robust good sense turned naturally to the chief possibility
of popular success in Romantic drama, an exciting story
or plot which would exploit the emotional character of
Romantic literature. Had he lived in the Naturalistic
period and had he been a realist — which he was not —
he would doubtless have been one of the first to fling to
the public that " bleeding slice of life " of which so
much has been said; placed as he was, he could only offer
them a " bleeding slice of imagination." This served
very well until they had tasted real blood.

CASIMIR DELAVIGNE (1793–1843)

Casimir Delavigne can hardly be classified with the
Romantic dramatists, since he is wholly a Classicist at
heart and largely so in practice; he might, in fact, be
presented, in his early manner in any case, as the best
example in his time of the drama which the Romanticists
were seeking to overthrow. He preceded Hugo, in date
and early popularity, with a few successful plays. These
plays are largely Classic in form, tone and style, and
have most of the faults that had come through imitation
and adherence to convention.

In his later plays, which appeared in the midst of the
Romantic movement, he endeavored, without lasting success, to combine some of the Romantic innovations with
the dignity and reserve of Classicism. The only play
of his that is perhaps worth reading today is *Louis XI*,
and this partly as a literary curiosity, and in contrast

with the work of the outright Romanticists. This historic drama, although based on careful study of the records, deforms history almost as much as do the plays of Hugo or Dumas. Only here the method and effect are exactly the opposite; the Romanticists magnified and distorted all they touched; by Delavigne everything is reduced and belittled. It is like looking through the wrong end of the telescope; such figures as Louis and Commines are rendered incredibly mean and petty.

Finally, Delavigne lacks the poetry of Hugo, and in his constant adherence to the *style noble* falls into deplorable platitude. He is one of the writers who prove that Classicism could not be maintained nor reformed.

ALFRED DE VIGNY (1797–1863)

Alfred de Vigny is one of the leading figures of the early Romantic group, (the *Cénacle*) and, although not primarily a dramatic writer, he took a very considerable part in the capture of the theatre for the new school. In fact, he was the leader of one of the three battles by which the national theatre, the *Comédie*, was won. His *More de Venise*, a translation of Shakespeare's *Othello*, which was played there in 1829, had a significance comparable to that of *Henri III* and *Hernani*. This was the first time a French author had dared to present a genuine translation of Shakespeare, and quite naturally this performance had a meaning and importance that were impossible for the English troupe of 1827, who spoke their own tongue. The play excited much controversy, was fairly successful, and undoubtedly aided in forming the

lines of battle. It should serve also as a reminder that
the new school looked to Shakespeare for its models,
and believed, at least, that it fought under his banner.

Vigny was of noble birth, from a well-known family
of Touraine which had fallen in its fortunes, and which
came, in the poet's early youth, to live in Paris. He was
by nature reserved and sensitive, with a melancholy that
developed gradually into a system of stoic pessimism.
With a real sympathy for those who suffer much in life,
of whom he was one, he is rarely expansive, and is
often called the poet of poets. One of his best known
works is the historic novel *Cinq-Mars*, and his strongest
writing is in the field of poetry, and particularly in that
of an epic-philosophic character. As a serious thinker
he excelled all the other Romanticists. In form and
style, in soberness and concentration, he has much of the
Classicist.

In addition to the translation of *Othello* and a considerable contribution, in this early period, to the theory
of Romantic drama, he has left only three original plays,
and of these only one, *Chatterton,* presented with great
success at the *Comédie* in 1835, is of such outstanding
merit and significance as to demand consideration today.

The hero of this play is, of course, the young English
poet, Chatterton, who cut short a life of great literary
promise by suicide at the age of eighteen. Vigny's
presentation of Chatterton is very simple. He is poor,
young, sensitive. He asks for a subsidy to be able to
continue his writings for mankind; he receives instead
a menial position and commits suicide.

In its style, its lack of color, its simplicity of plot and

practical conformity with the unities, and above all in its very conception as a subject, *Chatterton* is almost entirely Classic. On this latter point, the author's own words, which seem not only to approve the Classic point of view but to criticize the Romantic conception, are especially interesting as written by one who, a few years before, had proclaimed with Hugo the necessity of a drama that would present " a vast spectacle of life ":

" I believe, above all, in the future and in serious things; now that the amusement of the eyes through childish surprises makes everyone laugh in the midst of serious action, it is time, it seems to me, for the drama of thought."

" An idea which is the examination of a wounded soul should have, in its form, the most complete unity and the most severe simplicity. . . . The material action is of little importance. This is the story of a man who has written a letter in the morning and waits for the answer until evening; it arrives and kills him. But the moral action here is everything. The action is in this soul given over to black despair."

Here is a moral and mental drama, written in general conformity with the Classic rules. It would seem, then, to be an example of pure Classic tragedy; it is, in fact, a typical product of Romantic philosophy and, because of this, a thoroughly Romantic play.

Chatterton is really a thesis play of which the purpose is to uphold the rights of imagination and feeling in life as against the dominance of reason and good sense, and the appeal is imaginative and emotional, and very little rationalistic. Chatterton asks for a pension, gets a posi-

tion, and kills himself. His action is as little justified by
reason and good sense, by the ordinary rules of life, as
is the fatalistic pessimism of Hernani, " that blind and
deaf agent of funereal mystery driven by an insensate
fate."

The success of the play would seem due to two factors,
the Romantic vogue of such heroes and the absolute
conviction in Vigny's appeal. Vigny, in his sensitive-
ness, pessimism and suffering, is strikingly like Chatterton. Here was the one play above all others he could
write. Like Dumas in *Antony*, he could put himself into
the character, and this note of sincerity was recognized.
Any other explanation seems impossible, for the play
lacks the usual Romantic color, has a minimum of action,
and is frequently awkward in its dramatic technique.

What *Chatterton* seems to prove, then, is that the
essence of the Romantic drama is a conception of life,
or a state of mind: or better perhaps, considering its
pathological character and brief duration, we could call
it a state of nerves. It had its causes in history, but it
was transitory and little in accord with the permanent
genius of the French people. Just at this time, Hugo
and Vigny might successfully make sentimental appeals
for the individual against society, for feeling against
reason, but the usual attitude of French audiences is to
turn thumbs down on all pleas that are contrary to good
sense. The characteristic French rhetoric is intellectual
argument based on logic and reason. Consequently the
reign in France of purely lyrical and emotional drama
was strikingly brief and stormy.

Alfred de Musset (1810–1857)

In the theatre, Hugo is to be studied largely for the importance of his theory and Dumas for the influence of his practice, but Musset's plays can still be read for their own interest and charm. He was too young to play a rôle in the inauguration of Romantic drama, and his pieces, written to be read, were not represented until its decline, so he has hardly had an influence on dramatic evolution. With all that, his work is the most durable of the Romantic school, and, personal and original as it is, can be considered as the most characteristic product of Romantic philosophy combined with French temperament.

Musset is the perfect " enfant du siècle," that Romantic flower of passion and imagination grafted on the perennial plant of French realism; its fruit had the color and form of Romanticism, but the sap, savor and vitality came from a more native and hardier stock. He was born in Paris, was a member of the Romantic group in his early youth, but soon asserted his independence. He is known especially as the lyric poet of youth and passion, and, within this range, one of the greatest. In character, he was generous, impulsive and likeable, an eternal youth who lived in his emotions and worshipped love. His life was comparatively uneventful, except for his tragic *liaison* and quarrel with George Sand in 1833. This event colored all his remaining years and deepened his natural pessimism. In the last part of his life, especially, he turned to dissipation and produced little after 1840.

He wrote only one play, his first, *La Nuit Venitienne*, for presentation on the stage. It appeared in 1831. It has no outstanding merits, but its failure was probably due largely to the hostility toward the Romantic school. After this he refused to write for the stage although he continued to compose in dramatic form for publication. Altogether he has left some fifteen comedies worth mentioning, for the most part short plays published under the title *Comédies et Proverbes*. Most of them are written in prose but in tone all are idealistic and poetic. None of these plays was performed before 1847, and while the greater number have been staged since, and have become in some instances classics in the French theatre, this presentation is often held unfortunate, since acting takes away the atmosphere of fancy and poetry which is one of their charms.

Written as they were at the whim of the author and to fit no dramatic system, these plays represent an unusual variety of moods and categories. A few, such as *Il faut qu'une porte soit ouverte ou fermée* or *Un Caprice*, are nothing more than witty dialogues, airy trifles made of nothing. However, they are expressed in a style so beautiful, a style suggesting Marivaux but infinitely more natural and simple, and are such perfect examples of the fine art of Parisian conversation, that they have become classic French curtain-raisers and have invited frequent imitation. Others, such as *A quoi rêvent les jeunes filles* and *Il ne faut jurer de rien*, are hardly less light in tone and in the play of fancy and humor, but are, at the same time, remarkably keen psychological expositions. The two mentioned are particularly notable for their insight into the heart of the young girl, showing its romance, its innocence, and its purity. There is much of the feminine in Musset's intuitions, and in the characterization of the young woman especially, he is almost unequalled on the French stage. Rostand has modeled strikingly his *Romanesques* on Musset's *A quoi rêvent les jeunes filles*.

However, the plays on which rests Musset's chief dramatic fame are dramas of love, its ecstasies and tortures, its surprises and tragedies. Perhaps his masterpiece is *On ne badine pas avec l'amour*, which is a direct reflection of his experience with George Sand. It is highly poetic, rising to tense emotion, and terminating in tragedy, and it is at the same time relieved by humorous and burlesque strokes that would furnish worthy pencil sketches to put in a Shakespearean gallery. It is hard to find anywhere, except in Shakespeare, truth and fancy blended in an atmosphere more charming, and few dramas, written in a tone of high idealism, bring nearer to us the eternally poignant problems of love. Also we have here, most pointedly expressed, Musset's own philosophy of love and life: " One is often deceived in love, often hurt and often unhappy; but one loves, and when he is on the brink of his grave and turns to look behind, he says to himself: I have often suffered, I have sometimes been deceived, but I have loved. It is I who have lived, and not an artificial being created by my pride and my *ennui*."

This apotheosis of love, consciously proclaimed here

by Musset, represents in fact the attitude of the whole Romantic school; love is their constant theme and its divinity is never questioned.

Musset had the unusual quality of being able to put himself quite sincerely into more than one of his dramatic characters in the same play — even into those that seem opposites. In the play above he pleads the cause of Camille as sincerely as that of his own image, Perdican. Another notable instance is in *Les Caprices de Marianne*, where the two Mussets, Célio and Octave, his good and evil angels, turn by turn plead and banter with love and death.

Not all of these plays which lay bare the human heart in its passion of love end in death. One that does not end as tragedy is *Le Chandelier;* but the danger and suffering combine to form a drama hardly less poignant.

Musset is the only one of the French Romanticists whose plays seriously suggest Shakespeare, and this is in qualities quite his own and not a result of imitation. One of the dramas most resembling Shakespeare's is *Lorenzaccio*, his only ambitious, five-act, historical tragedy. Its hero, Lorenzaccio (the evil Lorenzo), is a cousin of Alexander, the tyrant of Florence. To free the oppressed city Lorenzo decides to kill the suspicious and closely guarded ruler, and, in order to have access to him and find opportunity, he assumes the rôle of a cowardly profligate, a libertine and a drunkard. Here lies the tragedy. The love of this life of debauchery seizes him and holds him, and, too late, he finds that his assumed character has become his real one. He carries out his intention, as his last claim to virtue and respectability, but he does it realizing that the sacrifice is in vain, that Florence will pass under another tyrant, and that his own life is ruined.

Musset is in this play, as always, giving us largely his own life and experience. After his *liaison* with George Sand, in order to forget his sorrows, he plunged into a round of dissipation, and, although he often reformed for a time, this vice more and more fixed itself upon him. The play is animated and colorful and shows a real power of historic reproduction.

Another play more characteristic of Musset and no less suggestive of Shakespeare is *Fantasio*, a fine mixture of fancy and reality, folly and wisdom, wit and philosophy. No more charming illustration of these qualities can be found than in the conversation of Fantasio and Spark at the beginning of this play, nor is it easy to cite a scene which more strikingly depicts certain psychological states characteristic of the period. Musset's ability to divide himself into two opposing characters who toss the cue to each other in fascinating repartee is nowhere better seen:

FANTASIO.

"Alas! all that men say to each other is the same; the ideas that they exchange are almost always alike in all their conversations, but inside those separate machines what recesses, what secret compartments! It is a whole world that each carries in himself, an unknown world, which is born and which dies in silence! How isolated are all these human bodies. . . . What a wretched thing man is! Not to be able even to jump from the window without breaking his legs! To be obliged to play the violin ten years in order to become a tolerable musician! To have to learn in order to be a painter, in order to be a stable-boy! To learn in order to make an omelette! Come, Spark, I feel like sitting down on the stone wall, watching the river flow by and counting one, two, three, four, five, six, seven, and so on until I die."

SPARK.

"I can understand nothing of this perpetual struggle within yourself. As for me, when I am smoking, for example, my thought is changed into tobacco smoke; when I am drinking, it becomes Spanish wine or Flemish beer; when I kiss the hand of my mistress, it enters through the tips of her slender fingers, to run through my whole being in electric currents; I need only the perfume of a flower to divert me, and of all that universal nature contains, the slightest object is sufficient to change me into a bee and to make me flit here and there with a pleasure that is always new."

But one must read the entire scene to appreciate the variety of its fancy and the brilliancy of its wit.

The plot is a simple one, based on the masquerade of Fantasio in the rôle of the King's jester, but the conclusion is significant. To save the unhappy little princess, Elsbeth, from marrying a man she does not love, Fantasio will break a treaty, cause a war, and bring ruin and misery on thousands. For Musset love is the only thing in the world. He returned to this theme again and again, and in doing so was only quoting his own heart.

The popularity of Musset's pieces is undeniable and has been strikingly universal; even the extreme realists, violent enemies of Romanticism, have had little but praise for his work. This appreciation is easy for one who reads his plays, for they seem today as fresh as ever;

the difficulty is to point out adequately the precise reasons for their durability.

In the first place, he has confined himself to the field which Romantic and subjective drama was most competent to cultivate, an intimate study and exposition of the human heart in the passion of love. To do this, his own heart was not only an instrument of remarkable delicacy and capacity for recording all the tremors of love and passion, but he had a frankness, sincerity and lucidity, perhaps unequalled, in laying bare these secret records of the soul. Racine undoubtedly made a much wider analysis of human passions and presented it in a drama of more sustained intensity, while Shakespeare's was not only wider but is translated into a variety of realistic action that is incomparable; but Musset suggests both these masters and neither is Musset's superior within his specialty.

Another merit, of which the full value can be appreciated only by reading him, is the purity and charm of Musset's style. It is Classic in its simplicity, and yet it uses all the liberty and resources won by the Romanticists. One quality is ever recurrent and always delightful; in situations where we expect to find, and where other Romanticists seek for, the word or expression that would be fine, striking, or picturesque, Musset surprises us by the revealing power of the simple, natural phrase. It is in fact a frequent touch of realism that is exceedingly important in holding his characters near to earth and maintaining our contact with them. To this extent Musset is a realist. This trait perhaps explains in part the approval he has had from realistic writers, and it certainly identifies him with the long line of French masters of the simple and precise phrase, from Pascal and Racine down to the present day.

Finally, Musset's freedom from the mold of a dramatic system has been a great factor in his durable popularity. Dramatic fashions often change quickly, and antiquated styles are easy objects of ridicule and aversion. Musset's are too slight to invite criticism. This does not mean, however, that he was without a dramatic art; it is in fact most sound, only it was not hampered by the conventions or exigencies of the acting stage. His character drawing is really superior, strikingly so for the haste with which these sketches must often be made in his short plays.

But it is in his plots especially that we find the highest art which conceals itself. At first glance, perhaps, nothing seems more capricious, more carelessly motivated, than the plots of Musset's plays. Certainly this action carries no suggestion of the exciting, tumultuous stream of Dumas, that sweeps its breathless victims to destruction. In comparison, it is rather the winding brook, that turns here and there to water a fern or flower, that murmurs gaily down the slopes, and spreads out in placid pools, but none the less it has an object and a goal, to which it tends as irresistibly and as naturally as water seeks its level; and Musset's characters also, lured by their pleasures, are sometimes, before they are aware, carried over the falls to destruction.

Viewed in the light of later history, two features of the Romantic movement in the French theatre are outstanding: it was primarily a rebellion with the usual exaltations and excesses of revolutions, and, in its emotional and imaginative characteristics, it was destined to be short-lived, since the dominance of these qualities conflicts with the racial and permanent traits of rationalism and realism that determine so largely French genius. The disorder, inconsistencies and improbabilities of Romantic drama had been under fire from the beginning. With the failure of *Les Burgraves* in 1843, the check was complete. Hugo left the theatre. Dumas was already turning largely to his immense historic novels, and beyond the dramatization of some of these, rarely appeared on the stage after this date. And the ardor of many Romantic partisans had cooled.

The date of 1843 may be taken, then, as the official end of outright Romantic drama, since it is further marked by the appearance of Ponsard's *Lucrèce*, inaugurating a reaction against the Romantic theatre that was notable enough to be called the School of Good Sense. However, it is not to be thought that all this dramatic activity aroused by Romanticism was suddenly stopped; the stream was only deflected and modified. In reality, it is here divided; the main current, realistic prose drama, impelled by the Romantic doctrine that art should imitate all nature, the good and the bad, followed the direction indicated by Dumas in treating contemporary life and manners. Combined with the "well-made play" of Scribe, it has passed through the Realistic Social drama of Augier and Dumas fils to come down to the present day as the chief form of French dramatic activity. We shall return to this main stream in the later chapters. For the present we shall trace the more direct, although less important, current of the Romantic drama written in verse, which, deflected and corrected by the movement called the School of Good Sense, has descended, through the various representatives of French poetic drama in the second half of the nineteenth century, to its best recent exponent, Rostand.

CHAPTER IV

THE SCHOOL OF GOOD SENSE AND LATER VERSE DRAMA

PONSARD, AUGIER, BORNIER, COPPÉE, RICHEPIN

FRANÇOIS PONSARD (1814–1867)

A TREATMENT of the School of Good Sense headed by Ponsard calls for two preliminary reservations: it was not a school and Ponsard was not the head of it or of any other dramatic movement. The period in question is merely one where the current of drama makes an important turn, and the work of Ponsard serves as a significant landmark. The chief causes for this reaction against the Romantic theatre are found in this drama itself.

Exterior causes hastening this reaction were the growing spirit of materialism and realism in the society of the period, and the revival of interest in the seventeenth century Classics, marked by the appearance of the great tragic actress Rachel and explained by the national tendencies of the French toward rationalism, order, realism and good sense. The French at this time were entering on an era of great commercial activity and scientific development, and these conditions of society are reflected in their philosophy and literature. They will be more fully developed in connection with the realistic prose drama, of which they are determining characteristics, but it is well to remember that they influenced verse drama also, by greatly limiting it and by modifying its character. The part of Rachel in reviving the Classics may be open to question, since the reaction was naturally due, but her influence at the *Comédie* was very great.

Ponsard was a provincial who had studied law at Paris. After a few years of uninteresting law practice in his native city, he relieved the tedium by writing a drama, *Lucrèce*, and brought it to Paris at the psychological moment. He was surprised himself at the success of his play and the importance given him as leader of a new movement, and when we read *Lucrèce* today, this seems still more surprising to us. The play is Classic in subject and in its adherence to a number of the conventions, but some of its qualities, such as style, poetry and inspiration are probably due more to Ponsard's inability to follow the Romantic practices than to a desire to avoid them. But, after all, it was his admirers largely who made this necessity for Ponsard into a virtue.

The popularity of *Lucrèce* gave Ponsard a reputation that outlasted his lifetime. The following appreciation, taken from so sound a critic as Jules Lemaître twenty years after the dramatist's death, is characteristic of this esteem:

" The revival of *Le Lion amoureux* has shown us once again that the honest Ponsard, so often criticised, is a good, solid dramatic author, one of those who speak best to the honorable instincts of the people, one of those who are able the most skillfully, and at the same time, the most naïvely, to teach it simplified history, to give it the noblest and clearest lessons of virtue, to develop for it the finest traits of morality in action, and finally, after a happy ending, to send it home, satisfied, tranquil and replete with good sentiments for which it is grateful. . . . During his lifetime the public did him the poor service of contrasting him with Hugo and inaugurating him chief of the School of Good Sense. This was a little ridiculous, and nevertheless, if Hugo remains, in the theatre as elsewhere, an incomparable lyric poet, the real truth is that a drama of the worthy Ponsard is in no way more tiresome, on the stage, than *Marion Delorme* or *Le Roi s'amuse*. On the contrary, despised Good Sense, here is your revenge. The fact is we love, terribly, good sense, we bourgeois of Paris and the provinces. This taste is an old racial trait." [1]

The last part of this passage is especially significant. Undoubtedly it does call for an overwhelming maximum of common sense — and a corresponding minimum of poetry — to prefer Ponsard to Hugo, even if the former is a soothing, bed-time moralist. Ponsard's dramatic reputation proves conclusively the virtue acquired with the French by conforming to good sense, just as Hugo's does the danger in violating it.

Ponsard is best known for his *Lucrèce,* although he wrote other worthy and successful plays, of which the most notable are *Charlotte Corday* and *Le Lion amoureux*. In these he has turned to French national history; we find him, in fact, availing himself of most of the innovations of the Romanticists, without any of their excesses or brilliancy. In *L'Honneur et l'Argent,* he

[1] Lemaître: *Impressions de théâtre,* vol. 2, p. 49.

even wrote verse drama dealing with the society of his day in one of its notable aspects, commercialism.

Altogether the pieces of Ponsard are significant as noting the trend of the times, but his own merit was greatly over-rated. He is really colorless and uninspired. He won his place in popular favor and in the history of the stage partly because the French, just at this time, were more exasperated by the un-French faults of Romanticism than concerned over positive merit or originality. But he was not the first writer, or man, to succeed, in France or elsewhere, by means of correctness and decorum, and doubtless he will not be the last. To be correct is, everywhere, a wonderful means of success. Perhaps the fury of the radical intellectualist against the " bourgeois " in literature is more than half caused by his dread of the moment when he will be forced into the inexorable mold of tradition and respectability; a fate he rarely escapes, even if it come only as the final *Sottise* (Stupidity and Death) which seized upon the poor Cyrano.

Emile Augier (1820–1889) [2]

The mature and really serious work of Emile Augier is to be found in prose drama, in connection with which he will be more fully treated, and only his youthful indiscretions were committed in the School of Good Sense. However, he was rather long in reaching the age of reason and seven of his early plays — before *Le Gendre de M. Poirier* — are written in verse.

[2] See Chapter VIII for more complete treatment.

Augier's first play, *La Ciguë,* followed Ponsard's *Lucrèce* at the Odéon in 1844, and aided materially in establishing the fiction that there was to be an Indian Summer of Classicism. It is a pleasing little imitation, placed in Greece, conforming to the unities, and well written. His next, *Un Homme de Bien,* is less good, particularly because of a certain ambiguity of purpose and characters. In his third, *L'Aventurière,* Augier attains his maximum merit as an imitator of the Classic genre.

L'Aventurière, decidedly more ambitious than the first two, has been variously judged by the critics, some putting it among Augier's best plays. It seems difficult to justify such praise. It undoubtedly suggests Molière and other great Classicists, if that be a certain merit. It suggests also their long line of imitators. *L'Aventurière* is in fact a striking, but none too happy, combination of Classic and Romantic elements; the characters live, act and talk as do those of the Classic drama, but their tears and sentiment are Romantic. It even comes perilously near to being another sentimental rehabilitation of the courtesan through love, in the style of *Marion Delorme.* Only the unity of time saves us, by hurrying Clorinde off the stage before she is able to take the final vows of Magdalenic chastity.

Augier's next verse play, *Gabrielle,* in 1849, brought him real fame, and is decidedly interesting, especially so as an example of all the conflicting cross-currents that are to be found at this dividing and turning point for the different streams of French drama. Here Augier's Classic fever is waning, but his Romantic temperature is higher, and there are ominous complications of realism. *Gabrielle* observes the Classic unities and logic, and assumes the moralistic attitude and language of the realists. Its Romanticism is in its moral; it attempts to prove that it is more poetic and romantic to be good and married — and wash the dishes — than it is to figure in the usual dramatic triangle.

Perhaps it seems something of a paradox to assert this of a play that is avowedly written as an attack on the Romantic philosophy which deified immoral love, but it is clear that Augier is still so imbued with the Romantic spirit that he resorts to Romantic arguments. There were stronger appeals than the poetic character of married life which might have been made to Gabrielle to save her home and virtue, and probably no author of good sense and judgment — which Augier decidedly was — ever ended a play with a line more unfortunate than " O père de famille; ô poète, je t'aime! " It is a striking testimony to the conflicting currents of Realism and Romanticism in the young writers of the day.

Augier's next three plays of his verse period do not add greatly to the value or significance of his first work, beyond proving him a writer of charm, although the last, *Philiberte,* is a delightful picture of the heart of a young girl.

Altogether the verse plays of Augier, written from 1843 to 1852, the dates of the fall of the Romantic theatre and of the inauguration of the Realistic school, offer the finest examples of the conflicting tendencies of this transitional period. Augier was fond of Classic literature and his early success in, and identification with, the School of Good Sense led him to adhere for a time to that style. But he was not a poet, either dramatic or lyric, although he wrote pleasing verse and his verse plays are much more interesting to read to-day than are those of Ponsard. He was really a realistic moralist, as had been shown in *Gabrielle*, where only the hindrance of verse and the lingering influence of Romanticism had prevented him from being the creator of the Realistic school, instead of leaving that honor to Dumas fils. With the appearance of the latter's *Dame aux Camélias*, Augier drops at once, and without effort, his Classic and Romantic trappings, and his verse, and takes his place as one of the leaders of Realistic Social drama.

HENRI DE BORNIER (1825–1901)

Bornier has sometimes been called the last of the Classicists. It is perhaps true that he represents more perfectly than any other verse dramatist of his generation, certain qualities that are characteristic of Classic drama, but this is not due to any conscious imitation; these qualities are natural with him. Besides, he was by affiliation quite as much a Romanticist.

Bornier received a sound education in the classics, and during the greater part of his life was director of the Arsenal library at Paris. He was then to an unusual degree a man of books and study. His life was uneventful. In addition to a few volumes of poetry and novels, Bornier is the author of several plays. His real fame, however, rests on one piece, *La Fille de Roland*, which had an enormous and well merited success, and which has maintained its interest. Since it is quite representative of Bornier in his other plays, as well as typical of a number of verse dramas written in the second half of the nineteenth century, it is worthy of special attention.

La Fille de Roland does not conform to any of the Classic rules that were under direct attack by the Romanticists. In subject matter, color, style and verse, it has used all of the Romantic innovations, all in fact except the mingling of the tragic and comic; it is serious and elevated throughout. However, it is primarily a mental or moral crisis, developed logically according to the principle of interior action, and above all its characters are free agents, working out their own fate by force of will; it has after all the heart of Classic tragedy. It has also some of the external qualities of Classicism, such as sobriety and rhetorical eloquence rather than lyricism and sentiment, but these are less fundamental.

Its great and durable success is due first of all to genuine merit, but also to a combination of circumstances. The subject is a happy one dealing with heroic French epic poetry, in which legend and history are sufficiently confused to allow the author a free hand. It is moreover a subject admirably adapted to the genius of the dramatist, in its elevated moral tone and epic heroism; and finally it was presented at a time, just after the war of 1870, when its fine and ardent patriotism aroused tremendous enthusiasm. At this moment particularly it was natural that such passages as the following one should strike responsive chords:

> "O France! douce France! ô ma France bénie!
> Rien n'épuisera donc ta force et ton génie!

Terre du dévoûment, de l'honneur, de la foi;
Il ne faut donc jamais désespérer de toi,
Puisque, malgré tes jours de deuil et de misère,
Tu trouves un héros dès qu'il est nécessaire!"

But the play has many eloquent and beautiful passages and scenes. The characters are perhaps at times a little too epic and superhuman, which makes it difficult for us to enter fully into their struggles, but on the whole the appeal of the drama is one of the noblest.

The character of this appeal and its success furnish an important lesson on one feature of French drama. Realistic as the French are, they have also a decided fondness for the heroic, provided the appeal is made in good taste and form, without offering matter for ridicule. Classic drama proves this point, as does their entire history. They are, moreover, charmed with rhetoric and moved by the well written tirade to an extent incomprehensible to Anglo-Saxons. The heroism and patriotism, and the eloquence and good form in which these are expressed, in *La Fille de Roland* are powerful factors in its success.

La Fille de Roland is modified Romantic drama; without the Romantic school it could never have been conceived or written. In spite of this, it is Classic tragedy to the extent of being built on the great principles by which Corneille inaugurated this genre, and this has been accomplished not by any attempts at imitation but in conformity with the author's native genius, and with the natural taste of the French. It is an interesting model of historic verse drama, after the reaction of good sense and reason had eliminated the melodrama so characteristic of the Romantic period. The completeness of the reaction in this play is still perhaps exceptional, but it marks an evolution that is natural to French genius, and, in this respect, Bornier was certainly not the last Classicist; there will always be such Classicists in France. The French prefer ordered eloquence to unrestrained lyricism, and a moral or mental problem to a vast spectacle of life.

François Coppée (1842–1908)

François Coppée is a Romantic dramatist of the second generation, one not unaffected perhaps by the reaction of good sense and one living in the midst of realism, but a Romantic dramatist none the less. A Parisian, born of humble family and forced at an early age to earn his living, he always retained his sympathy for simple life and common people. The volume of his work is considerable and falls into several categories, but his fame is greatest as a lyric and as a dramatic poet. Despite his other work, he wrote a greater number of successful verse plays than any other French author of his day.

His really significant dramas may be classed in two groups: in the first he is above all a Romanticist and a disciple of Hugo and Dumas père, and in the second he is primarily the idyllic and lyric poet in pieces that recall Musset. In the first class are to be placed his more ambitious efforts, for the most part five-act, historic tragedies, such as *Severo Torelli*, *Les Jacobites*, and *Pour la Couronne*, and in the second are found especially a number of one-act plays, of which some have already become classics of the French theatre, such as *Le Passant, Le Luthier de Crémone, Le Trésor* and *Le Pater.*

In Coppée's longer historic pieces, we are inclined to see not only the outright Romantic playwright, but even something of the Romantic melodramatist, especially in subject matter. *Severo Torelli* is so extreme and horrifying in its premises and situations that only a Shakespeare could have fully mastered it; *Les Jacobites* has much of the violence and some of the crime of *Le Roi s'amuse;* and even in *Pour la Couronne,* probably the best of his tragedies, the Romanticist's love of striking situations has led him to create a dramatic dilemma from which there is no escape without considerable damage to poetic justice.

This last play may be taken as a fair example of the class. In *Pour la Couronne,* Michel Brancomir, dominated by his young wife, is about to betray to the Turks the country he had so gloriously defended. His son, Constantin, is forced to kill him to save his country and his father's fame, and then tormented by remorse, Constantin allows himself to be accused of the intended treason and dies in disgrace. It is throughout an interesting and moving drama, but the third act especially, in which the father is killed, is notably effective. However, Coppée has done here what Hugo and others did so often; in order to create a strong situation, he has allowed himself to be enticed into an *impasse.* Constantin is entirely noble and sympathetic, but after the killing of his father he can neither live honored, with his own consent, nor die dishonored, with the consent of the audience.

As we have seen, dilemmas of this sort are frequent

in Hugo and are usually exploited for their immediate pathetic and lyric effect; Coppée has exploited this one dramatically — and magnificently — but the rest of his play is badly compromised none the less. A very similar situation is to be found in *Severo Torelli*. The practice is obviously due to the desire to find a strong, overwhelming situation, and proper consideration has not been given in advance to the possibilities of liquidating this situation satisfactorily; in its inspiration, at least, this is a usage of melodrama.

With all this, Coppée is very far from having all the faults of Hugo's drama. Most of the absurdities and impossibilities of the latter have been eliminated. Coppée's plots and situations are, in general, properly motivated and do not rely on surprises and accidents. His characters especially are not the fatalistic Byronic types, nor are they simply built on antithesis, vacillating and moving in a circle. On the contrary, they are as a rule consistent, strong-willed and masters of their own fate, even in the terrific storms by which the author surrounds them. Coppée's dramas are consequently much changed from their Romantic prototypes, although not all of the possible modifications dictated by good judgment have been made. His is rather the work of Hugo corrected by Corneille, who was himself half a Romanticist in taste and spirit; it is an improvement dramatically over Hugo's plays, but while many faults are eliminated, some are applauded.

It is probably the short plays of Coppée that will live longest. *Le Passant,* associated with the first great stage triumph of Sarah Bernhardt in 1869, has been a model

for one-act lyric dramas since its time, and the others
mentioned above have been favorites with some of the
greatest actors of the French theatre. It is not that
these modest pieces are remarkable in their psychology
or thought; doubtless such types as those found in *Le
Passant* and *Le Trésor* are now somewhat discredited;
nevertheless, these little plays are flowers of sentiment
and lyricism, and, although floral fashions change as do
others, a true flower of nature is always beautiful. They
are entirely genuine and even most characteristic of
Coppée's genius.

In all the plays of Coppée the spirit of democracy and
the interest in humble life and people are apparent. This
popular element began with the Romanticists but is here
much more in evidence, and Coppée has been called the
realistic poet of the humble. Such passages as the following are numerous:

> "Non! mais j'ai bien assez réfléchi pour savoir
> Que tout droit en ce monde est doublé d'un devoir.
> Pour avoir trop usé de l'un sans remplir l'autre,
> Ceux qui portaient des noms fameux comme le nôtre
> Sont tombés, et leur plainte est perdue en l'écho
> De ce canon vainqueur qui vient de Marengo. . . .
> Moi qui dois désormais borner ma perspective
> Aux trois ou quatre champs de blé que je cultive
> Et demander ma vie au labeur de mes mains,
> Je fais très bon marché de tous mes parchemins." [3]

In any case, there is nothing of the aristocrat in
Coppée, and this is to be seen in the motives of his
characters. It is interesting to note the successive trans-

[3] *Le Trésor,* scene I.

formations of the aristocratic ideals in dramatic heroes. The Cid struggles over *points d'honneur* which are almost feudal, and in *Hernani* these points are Romantically chivalric, where they are not purely fantastic. Gérald's honor, in *La Fille de Roland*, involves primarily moral righteousness and Christianity. In *Pour la Couronne*, the dominating motive of Constantin is patriotism, rationalized and justified by the social welfare, by the desire to save the country and the people from the cruel reign of the Turk. It is a noticeable evolution toward realism in that most uncompromisingly chivalric and idealistic element of French character and of French literature, the *point d'honneur*.

JEAN RICHEPIN (1849–   )

Although Coppée's work extends into the twentieth century and links with the present generation, there is a temptation at this point to carry this development of verse drama still further in the direction of realism and of popular poetry and sentiment. As such a representative there is perhaps no one who has a better claim to our interest than Jean Richepin. He has had some notable stage successes in the field of verse drama, and in large part for qualities that are natural to it, poetry and idealism, rather than for merits that may be found in spite of the verse form.

The pieces of Richepin are of an astonishing diversity; in fact with him variety and disorder seem to be the rule, sometimes even in the same play. He has written blood-and-thunder melodrama in such a play as *Par le Glaive*,

From a French production of *Le Chemineau*

and made a moving picture farce out of the historic Don Quixote. However, in *Le Flibustier* and *Le Chemineau* he has not only done something different — that he does regularly — but also something important enough to invite the serious attention of the critics, as well as the enthusiasm of an audience.

Le Chemineau is perhaps his best work and stands nearest center in his genius. It is an evocation of what is most idyllic and poetic — in imagination naturally — in the life of a tramp. It has already been mentioned in connection with Coppée's *Passant* that the fashions in Bohemians and other, similar poetic creations change decidedly — naturally since they are so little formed on reality. In this play Richepin has almost popularized with the Parisians the knight of the freight-rods and wheat fields. Doubtless since Fenimore Cooper sent over his noble red-skins, no greater hoax has been played on French audiences, nor has been more universally enjoyed by them. However, there should be no question of reality here; whatever merit the play has lies elsewhere.

This merit is obviously the poetry. As in the case of George Sand's idyls of peasant life, this joyous poet, like some Hindu fakir, has often, from a mere mustard seed of fact, grown a whole flowering tree of imagination and poetry. Take for example the following description of the kingdom and riches of the wanderer:

" Mais dis-leur donc, tu sais, quand ta tête se monte,
Tout ce que tu m'en dis, à moi, de tes beaux jours
Vécus sur la grand'route et que tu vis toujours!
Dis-leur donc que le gueux, mendiant une croûte,
A contempler les champs qui bordent la grand'route

En fait son patrimoine en s'en réjouissant;
Dis-leur que des pays, ce gueux, il en a cent,
Mille, tandis que nous, on n'en a qu'un, le nôtre;
Dis-leur que son pays, c'est ici, là, l'un, l'autre,
Partout où chaque jour il arrive en voisin;
C'est celui de la pomme et celui du raisin;
C'est la haute montagne et c'est la plaine basse;
Tous ceux dont il apprend les airs quand il y passe;
Dis-leur que son pays, c'est le pays entier,
Le grand pays, dont la grand'route est le sentier;
Et dis-leur que ce gueux est riche, le vrai riche,
Possédant ce qui n'est à personne: la friche
Déserte, les étangs endormis, les halliers
Où lui parlent tout bas des esprits familiers,
La lande au sol de miel, la ravine sauvage,
Et les chansons du vent dans les joncs du rivage,
Et le soleil, et l'ombre, et les fleurs, et les eaux,
Et toutes les forêts avec tous leurs oiseaux! " [4]

If the composition and style of the whole maintained
the beauty and merit of the above passage, there would
be much less doubt about admitting the work of Richepin into a sketch of French drama. Unfortunately this
is not the case. In incident, as well as in style, the
author constantly descends to the most common and
vulgar.

The side of greatest interest in his dramas, therefore, in
the evolution of the verse play, is the one that reflects the
popular element. Assuredly, in this five-act, verse drama,
represented in a national theatre in 1897, we are a long
way, not only from the kings and nobles of Classic
drama, but also from the bourgeois of the Romantic; and
high style has descended in the form of the *mot propre*,
not merely to dig in local soil, but sometimes in the dung-

[4] *Le Chemineau,* act V, scene III.

hill. Perhaps, after all, it is well to remember that there are limits beyond which we are hardly justified in going, even in the search for gems of poetry.

In the last half-century, then, of history of the poetic drama following the downfall of the Romantic school, we see some of the diverse tendencies that are to be expected in the readjustments succeeding a great upheaval. We note especially Augier, in his early period, hesitating among the conflicting currents of Classic, Romantic, and Realistic drama. Ponsard sought definitely to reëstablish something in the Classic genre, and with Bornier, we find the climax of what was natural and genuine in this tendency to return toward Classicism. However, with Coppée, we come to the more normal course of development after the brief reaction of the School of Good Sense had spent itself, and we see that later poetic drama must, after all, be built up from the Romantic school. The solid foundations laid by Corneille were not destroyed, and doubtless also the new constructions will resemble the old — art is too fundamentally an expression of national life to change over night — but they will be built with Romantic materials, and in the greater freedom of Romantic laws.

The small number of authors and plays necessary to mention in this half-century of poetic drama emphasizes the slight volume of the verse stream, especially when compared with the numerous, significant prose plays. Verse drama of this period would seem pale indeed were it not for its sudden burst of brilliancy at the end of the century in the work of Rostand, whose glory for a time overshadowed all his contemporaries, not only those who wrote in verse but the prose dramatists as well.

CHAPTER V

EDMOND ROSTAND (1868–1918)

IN the attempt to evaluate the qualities and permanent worth of Rostand's poetic drama, after his death and after his work has been clarified by a quarter-century of world-wide popularity and discussion, it is fairly clear that all the important problems of this investigation are to be found in one play, *Cyrano de Bergerac*. His other pieces are most significant in tracing the source and destination of evolutionary tendencies, in showing the final lapse of certain leanings, and in underlining and amplifying the more fundamental articles of the poet's faith and experience so as to make them stand out before our eyes as a coherent and fixed philosophy of life, but the summit of his achievement is *Cyrano*. To state the problems of Rostand's position, then, in French drama, one has only to consider *Cyrano;* to solve them, all of his plays are not too much.

In the numerous articles which followed the appearance of *Cyrano,* we are able, sweeping aside the mass of the injudicious, which are the result of hostile prejudice or blind admiration, to find a few explanations of the great success of this play that are worthy of serious mention. Its freshness and salubrity pleased especially, coming at the precise moment when all were sickening of the sordidness and pessimism in the Naturalistic movement. To many it seemed a skillful combination of everything that had been most popular in French drama for three centuries, a sort of artistic patchwork quilt using all the favorite French colors. To some the secret of its success lay in its inexhaustibly gay humor, that pleases an audience seeking amusement, and in an agreeable emotion and sentiment not deep enough to be disturbing or painful, combined with the type of popular imagination based on antithesis, best exemplified in Dumas père and Hugo.

No doubt some of the popularity of *Cyrano* is explained by each of the causes mentioned above, but all taken together do not account for its quarter of a century of continued success. The revulsion against the Naturalistic stage was as short-lived as the Naturalistic movement itself, but its passing did not affect the favor of *Cyrano*. The composite character of the play, its alleged national *mélange*, is in material and color made from the Romantic drama, and is far from being typically French; in fact, quite as often it conforms to Spanish, Italian, or English taste. Finally, this humor and wit and this careful dosage of emotion, sentiment and imagination to flatter the palate of the audience, give an excellent characterization of the theatre of a Scribe or a Sardou, who takes the audience's taste as sole guide and writes for the moment, to please, and who pleases for the moment only, but these qualities can not account for the twenty-five years of *Cyrano's* popularity — played the world over — and for its continued acceptance as a piece of literature. All the reasons above could explain only an ephemeral popular favor. Our problem is to determine whether this striking success is simply the *bouquet d'artifices* of Romantic drama, the last brilliant flare of a spectacular movement, or the steadier flame of a masterpiece, lighted by the regularly transmitted torch of French national genius.

Edmond Rostand was born at Marseilles, and was consequently one of those ardent southerners, come to Paris, who have contributed markedly toward raising the temperature of French literature; he even claimed a trace of Spanish in his blood, which, considering its bright Provençal tinge, hardly needed this additional color. He belonged to a wealthy family, cultured and devoted to the arts, especially to music and literature, and, except for his uncertain health, he had every encouragement and opportunity to cultivate the profession of poet, to which he early turned. His higher education, ending with a law course, was carried on at Paris, and it was there that he began his dramatic career.

Rostand's early volume of verse, *Les Musardises,* which had charm and promise, was hardly accorded all the praise it merited, and doubtless his first play, *Le Gant rouge,* a farce comedy, has not received all the criticism it · deserved, owing to the fact that it was not printed. His real reputation began with the representation at the *Comédie,* in 1894, of *Les Romanesques.* This three-act comedy was a decided success, and gave the promise of a new dramatic poet in France.

Les Romanesques is a charming play in itself, with poetry and fancy, but it is more interesting still as an example of the early influences to be found in the young

poet's work. It is first of all inspired avowedly by
Romeo and Juliet, showing the Romanticists still looking
to Shakespeare as their model. But it is more directly
based on Musset's *A quoi rêvent les jeunes filles* — a
Musset brought down to date and familiarized a little
by passing through Coppée, and made more intricate by
rhyming with Banville. However, this does not mean
that the play is a mere imitation; it is entirely the
author's own. Few writers have shown a greater number
of influences, for he had other literary ancestors still
more potent and all his atavisms are clearly marked.
But these strains are combined in Rostand into a perfectly harmonious whole which resembles no one else.

It is in his next play, *La Princesse Lointaine,* in 1895,
that we find Rostand much more complete, with all his
Provençal intensity and enthusiasm, and with a part,
at least, of his philosophy already formed. The subject
of this play is the touching legend of the troubadour,
Joffroy Rudel, who loves the unknown princess and who
makes his pathetic voyage in order to see her before he
dies. The dominating note of the play is the high, almost
ecstatic idealism of this love between Joffroy and Mélis-
sinde, made more dramatic by the momentary weakness
and failing of the latter and of Bertrand, Joffroy's companion. This philosophy of love, placing its supreme
merit and power in idealism and renunciation, is a fixed
faith with Rostand and a corner stone of his dramas. It
is worthy of note here that the poet even dares, in the
words of the monk, Trophime, to stamp this love with
divine approval. Answering the physician's doubts as
to God's part in this quest, he says:

" Car il gagne tout, c'est du moins ma pensée,
A toute chose grande et désintéressée;
Presqu'autant qu'aux exploits des Croisés, je suis sûr
Qu'il trouvera son compte à ce bel amour pur! . . .
L'important, c'est qu'un cœur nous batte dans le torse! . . .
C'est pour le ciel que les grandes amours travaillent! " [1]

It is interesting to compare this philosophy with that of the early Romanticists, such as Musset. With them also, love is a supreme power, but their love is passion. Here and elsewhere in Rostand it is etherealized into a pure ideal.

La Samaritaine, which appeared in 1897, is in some respects the least satisfactory of Rostand's plays. Although in form and dramatic technique it is probably superior to its predecessors, the attempt to give a purely scriptural scene, with Christ and the Woman of Samaria as the chief characters, is obviously most difficult. The play can hardly be said to offend religious reverence but it does perhaps offend religious taste. Particularly is Christ made too much a Romantic poet. However, in its treatment of the kind of love already mentioned this play also is significant, especially in its attempt to identify human love and divine love. Note the words of Jesus to Photine:

" Non, tu ne dois pas avoir honte.
Comme l'amour de moi vient habiter toujours
Les cœurs qu'ont préparés de terrestres amours,
Il prend ce qu'il y trouve, il se ressert des choses,
Il fait d'autres bouquets avec les mêmes roses:
Car c'est à moi que tout revient. . . .
Je suis toujours un peu dans tous les mots d'amour." [2]

[1] Act I, scene II.   [2] *La Samaritaine,* 1er tableau.

The early plays of Rostand, taken together, hardly furnished an adequate prophecy of his admirable *Cyrano*. Even when studied in the light of fulfillment, in which all prophecy gains significance, they account at the most for Rostand's inheritance from all Romanticism, his ardent southern temperament and enthusiasm, and his exaltation of ethereal love and of idealism in general. There would still remain unaccounted for that which is most French and national, the soul and character of Cyrano himself; and this is the soul of the play, if we are to believe in its immortality — and if we do not, it is at least its breath of life.

Cyrano de Bergerac is a five-act, heroic comedy, which appeared at the Théâtre Porte-Saint-Martin in 1897, with its title rôle written especially for the great actor Coquelin and played by him. It had at the time, and has had since, a popularity surpassing any play of the last half-century. It has been performed thousands of times in France and with equal success in other countries; it has even been this year, 1924, the most decided theatrical triumph of the season in New York. What is still more significant, the sales of the French text have been counted in hundreds of thousands.

The first performance of *Cyrano* has been almost universally compared with the appearance of the *Cid* and *Hernani*, but the comparison is really misleading. The latter plays mark the inauguration of new schools; *Cyrano*, if it serves in any way as a landmark, would indicate the survival and culmination of Romanticism. The mere fact that all three attracted much attention means little and can be asserted, in varying degrees, of other plays that are not highly significant.

The subject was a happy choice for Rostand; in fact, it permitted a rare affinity between author and theme that can occur but once with a writer without resulting in mere repetition. In the hero, Cyrano, Rostand has dis-covered a perfect character for the expression of his Romanticism, his southern temperament and his intense idealism, and in the period of Louis XIII, with its mix-ture of heroism and super-refinement, he has found the ideal setting and atmosphere for his style and qualities as a writer.

Cyrano de Bergerac is, first of all, a historical drama, based on the life and writings of that highly romantic and original contemporary of Molière. If at times Cyrano seems in the play fantastic to the point of the impossible, the fault is not Rostand's, but is rather that of Cyrano's biographers and of legend, if it is not due to the truly novel character of this original figure. Ros-tand has read and absorbed his sources, and has really utilized them to an astonishing extent. For example, he has so saturated himself with the works of Cyrano that the vocabulary of the play is almost as much that of the seventeenth as of the nineteenth century poet; the two combine admirably and both tend toward the *pré-cieux*. For once this super-refinement and over-elabora-tion of style, which is regularly Rostand's besetting sin, fits so perfectly his subject that it must be considered an artistic virtue. In the many-sided presentation of Cyrano as a poet, musician, pseudo-scientist, philosopher, duelist and buffoon, Rostand is entirely justified by his sources;

Maude Adams as Duke of Reichstadt in *L'Aiglon*—1901

and even Cyrano's rôle as a lover, the one essential
invention of fact by the author, is suggested in at least
one passage of his biography.

But, after all, the chief value of historic drama, as such,
is not in its faithful adherence to historic fact but in its
power of historical evocation, which is in reality an illusion comparable to the illusion on which drama is itself
based. Its effectiveness lies further in the ability to use
this historical illusion as a background or atmosphere in
which to depict the characters, who must always be primarily contemporary to be comprehensible, and who can
not really be anything else since they are created by a
contemporary. Judged by these criterions, the merit of
Cyrano de Bergerac is striking, but since it is an impression of ensemble the play must be read in its entirety
to appreciate this.

Since *Cyrano* will be fully analyzed in order to bring
out the ultimate value of Rostand as a dramatist, there
is no need to consider it further for the moment, beyond
calling attention to the fact that those critics who predicated a new drama in France on this work were evidently
dazzled by its brilliancy and wonderful success, since it
is obviously not a new kind, but is at most the perfection
of a genre already well known. What excellence it has
beyond this is due to the genius of the author. *Cyrano*
brought Rostand every honor and raised him to a pinnacle
of fame beyond which he could hardly hope to mount.
The fact that he did not fall from this eminence too
disastrously in his next plays confirms considerably his
right to a high rank.

However, *L'Aiglon,* in 1900, is far from being a masterpiece the equal of *Cyrano*. It is again historical, with the son of Napoleon as its chief hero, and is a more elaborate and ambitious attempt than the preceding one. No doubt, one of the chief weaknesses of *L'Aiglon* is inherent in the subject. The main character, in actual life, did nothing on which to base a play, and this fact is too well known to allow the author sufficient freedom to invent a drama. The pretended conspiracy then is only a parade and no one takes it seriously.

Moreover, we see here that some of the qualities of the author must be classed as faults rather than merits in drama, particularly his astonishing facility in improvisation and adornment. In *Cyrano*, with its *précieux* atmosphere and characters, these qualities were an essential part of the play. In his other pieces they tend to smother the real drama with too much richness of decoration.

In spite of this, *L'Aiglon* is not a mediocre work. The one possible theme in the play that could really be made dramatic was Napoleon's prestige and glory. The dramatist has evoked this to a marvelous degree. Its impressionism is magnificent, but in this aspect it is rather a drama of ghosts and visions. Its stage popularity has naturally fallen below that of *Cyrano*, but in any other comparison could be called great, and *L'Aiglon* is still revived with success. Sarah Bernhardt had in it one of the triumphs of her later career.

Between *L'Aiglon* and the next play, *Chantecler*, there is a period of ten years, and during this time a new influence had entered the poet's life and was to become a large factor of his future work. Because of ill health, by which he was continually threatened, Rostand, during these years, had withdrawn himself largely from work and excitement and had gone to live on the beautiful country estate that he had created in the south of France. Here for the first time he seems to have been deeply touched by the influence of the country and nature. Until then, the life of his plays had been drawn almost entirely from books, from history and legend, and of course from the imagination inspired by these sources. There is hardly evidence that he was aware that real nature existed, for that which is found in such plays as *Les Romanesques* might as well be from a painted stage curtain. But his next play is drawn from the country entirely and deals solely with animal life — not a human being appears in *Chantecler* — and the observation of nature has furnished not merely the figures of this play but all the concrete or external action, the plot and details; only the ideas are human.

This striking reflection of an influence has already been mentioned in connection with his first play, where the part of Shakespeare and Musset is clearly evident. Also, as we shall see in his other works, the whole Romantic school can be found blended in him. However, he is never simply a mirror; the soul and motive of the picture, whatever be its form and color, come from Rostand. *Chantecler*, for all its difference in setting and inspiration, has the same lesson and philosophy as *Cyrano*.

Owing to many causes, but particularly to the fame of its author and its long period of preparation, no play was ever so widely advertised and awaited with such breathless curiosity as *Chantecler*, which was performed at the Porte-Saint-Martin in 1910. Moreover, this curiosity was intensified by the originality of the play's composition. For a poet known especially for the lyric beauty of his thought and language and the romantic conception of his dramatic characters, for his high idealism in short, to attempt to put all these qualities before a twentieth century audience with barnyard fowls and animals as his interpreters, seemed a challenge to failure, if it were not a huge burlesque. In fact the burlesque side was so evident that it was exploited by nearly every little theatre of Paris before the play appeared.

The conditions mentioned suggest the serious obstacles that *Chantecler* had to overcome on representation, and explain much of the character and extent of its success on the stage. The inherent difficulties involved in the conception of the play, especially, can not be too strongly emphasized, for in spite of Rostand's almost superhuman ingenuity — and often also because of it — they greatly affect the impressions produced by the piece on the stage. Rostand has really given in *Chantecler* a great poem, second in his work only to *Cyrano,* and like it worthy to be ranked among the classics of French literature, but it was, on the stage, only a success of curiosity. The average spectator saw merely its unique or spectacular sides, or at most its surface wit and satire, and its real and deeper meaning is revealed solely to the serious student of literature or of life. And this situation was aggravated by the richness of the poet's fancy and the brilliancy of his wit. *Chantecler* is like one of those beautiful fields of wheat topped by poppies that delight the eye of the traveler along French roads; the rich color of the flowers hides the solid grain beneath.

The chief animal characters of *Chantecler* are, of course, symbols for human beings, but they are not consistent symbols; that is to say, animals in form with human attributes, or humans masked as animals. They are sometimes human and sometimes animal. In the more serious — and rarer — passages, they are human only, but most often the abundant imagination of the poet, caught by some animal trait, attaches itself to a merely animal analogy and refines it through all the degrees of playfulness, wit and cleverness to a quintessence of affectation. This super-refining quality of the poet is constantly leading him from the straight road of drama into the flowery paths of pure fancy. This fancy of Rostand is like Roxane, who still remained the *précieuse* in the balcony scene and who kept repeating: *C'est le thème, brodez, brodez.* In *Cyrano* this super-refinement had its place but here it is frequently disconcerting to the audience and trying even to the reader.

The plot of *Chantecler*, without its embellishments, is very simple. Chantecler, the cock, is the king of the barnyard, admired by all. His song has a secret importance known only to himself; it is his crowing that brings the light. All life is dependent on him. We see him in the first act, in his simple happiness, laughing at the fears of the watchdog, Patou, who warns him against the cynicism of the Blackbird and the affectation, pretension and exotic fashion of the Guinea-hen, the Turkey and the Peacock, which threaten to demoralize his kingdom. He is hated especially by the night birds, because he announces the dawn.

The Hen-pheasant appears and, charmed by her beauty,

Chantecler is induced to attend a tea party of the Guinea-hen, where, through a plot of the owls, he is to be insulted and killed in duel by the Game-cock. The plot works out as intended, except that Chantecler, about to be overcome but given new courage by his rôle as protector of the weak, when the Hawk appears, attacks his opponent again and is overwhelming him with blows. The latter, in attempting to use his razor spurs, cripples himself and flees. Then Chantecler turns on his faithless admirers, denounces with bitter invective the snobbery of the Peacock and Guinea-hen, outscoffs the Blackbird himself, and scorning the inconstant hens, flies away with the Hen-pheasant to the free life of the woods, leaving behind all his troubles and duties.

The last act is in the forest. Chantecler is loved but is not wholly happy, thinking of the duties he has left behind. The Hen-pheasant wishes his whole life, she is jealous especially of his devotion to the Dawn, his mission, and she plots to bring about his disillusion. She finds her opportunity while Chantecler is under the spell of the voice of the Nightingale. He is overcome with grief when it is killed by a poacher. Then she covers his head with her wing so he can not see the approach of Dawn and shows him that the sun rises without his crowing. His despair at first is great but, as a new Nightingale appears to sing, he regains courage; he will continue to announce the Dawn whether he is necessary to it or not. One may be mistaken as to his importance but he must not abdicate his mission and duty.

The Hen-pheasant at first refuses to accompany him,

in his return to the barnyard and his duties, but, in an attempt to save his life from the poacher, she is caught in a net, and the play ends with her waiting for the hand of the man who will bring her to the barnyard into captivity.

The characters of *Chantecler* are sometimes only animals, so one must not expect a human significance in all of their actions. However, they do frequently have a human rôle and its meaning and application to modern society are in most cases quite evident. The most important actors, and those in which this symbolism is most serious, are the Hen-pheasant and Chantecler.

At times Rostand would seem to have identified the Hen-pheasant with the woman of advanced ideas. For example, in the first act he says in speaking of her: " It sometimes happens that she finds the male too well dressed, in his gala attire. She sees him more beautiful than herself and she ceases to lay and to hatch. Then nature gives her the purples and golds, and, proud and superb Amazon, she flees, preferring rather to have the blue, the green and yellow, all the colors of the rainbow on her back, than to have young pheasants beneath her grey wing. In short, she renounces the virtues of her sex; *she lives*."

But taking the rôle of the Hen-pheasant as a whole, it would seem a mistake to identify her entirely with this type. She is more properly a representative of woman in general — of the feminine in life — with all that this may mean of beauty, seductiveness and influence either for good or for bad. Her power over Chantecler is not always pernicious, but it is also evident that the author wishes to point out that woman may be a real danger for man's more serious mission and duties.

Obviously Chantecler does not represent any restricted type but stands for the genius of the French nation as a whole. He is the harbinger of light who points out the way, as France has so often done in history. He has the chivalry and the *esprit* of the French people, and especially marked are his patriotism, attachment to the soil of France and aversion to foreign fads and fashions. In short, he represents the virtues of the French people, what is best and most characteristic in them.

Chantecler hardly has all the eloquence and oratory of *Cyrano* but it fully equals it in lyric beauty; striking passages of this character abound. One of the most perfect of these is the hymn to the sun, sung by Chantecler in the first act, beginning:

> " Toi qui sèches les pleurs des moindres graminées,
> Qui fais d'une fleur morte un vivant papillon,
> Lorsqu'on voit, s'effeuillant comme des destinées,
>   Trembler au vent des Pyrénées
>   Les amandiers du Roussillon,
> Je t'adore, Soleil! ô toi dont la lumière,
> Pour bénir chaque front et mûrir chaque miel,
> Entrant dans chaque fleur et dans chaque chaumière,
>   Se divise et demeure entière
>   Ainsi que l'amour maternel! " [3]

No less notable for its lyric beauty is the dialogue, filled with love and poetry, between Chantecler and the Hen-pheasant, in the second act, where he tells her his secret and brings the dawn, while a climax of lyricism, feeling

[3] Act I, scene II.

and musical expression, beyond which perhaps Rostand never rose, is found in the song of the Nightingale, in the fourth act, set off as it is by the strange refrain of the Toads. As perfect in its grace, feeling and reverence as in its form is the prayer of the small birds in one of the most charming scenes of the play, beginning:

> "Dieux des petits oiseaux!
> Qui pour nous alléger mis de l'air dans nos os
> Et pour nous embellir mis du ciel sur nos plumes,
> Merci de ce beau jour, de la source où nous bûmes,
> Des grains qu'ont épluchés nos becs minutieux,
> De nous avoir donné d'excellents petits yeux
> Qui voient les ennemis invisibles des hommes,
> De nous avoir munis, jardiniers que nous sommes,
> De bons petits outils de corne, blonds ou noirs,
> Qui sont des sécateurs et des échenilloirs. . . ."

and ending:

> " Si dans quelque filet notre famille est prise,
> Faites-nous souvenir de Saint François d'Assise
> Et qu'il faut pardonner à l'homme ses réseaux
> Parce qu'un homme a dit: ' Mes frères les oiseaux.' " [4]

Perhaps more striking still, at least in harmony of sound and sense, is the song of the Owls, resembling, in its succession of soft syllables, the muffled, downy beat of the wings of these night birds:

> " Vive la nuit souple et benoîte
> Où nous volons d'une aile en ouate,
> Où, quand tout dort,
> Grace au mutisme de notre aile
> La perdrix n'entend pas sur elle
> Venir la mort!

[4] Act IV, scene I.

Vive la nuit commode et molle
Où l'on peut, lorsque l'on immole
    Des lapereaux,
Ensanglanter la marjolaine
Sans avoir à prendre la peine
    D'être un héros! " [5]

But, beautiful as are the many passages that might be cited, the deeper value of *Chantecler* lies in its philosophy of life. It is the piece in which the poet has put the most effort, the most thought and the most of himself. He has himself said: " *Chantecler* is a poem rather than a play . . . a symbolic poem in which I have used animals to evoke and develop the sentiments, passions and dreams of men. . . . My cock is not, properly speaking, a dramatic hero. He is a character which I have used to express my own dreams and to make live, before my eyes, a little of myself."

Chantecler is the man who, confident in his youth and strength, feels himself more powerful and important than he is: he meets adversity and temptation, measures the inconstancy of fortune and friends, and finally has the grievous disillusion of recognizing that his place and mission in life are infinitely less than he believed. But he is also the man to whom experience and sorrow give strength and courage rather than despair, and who returns chastened to his work and duty, without having lost either the joy of life or its faith.

" There must always be a nightingale in the forest,
And, in the soul, a faith so habitual
That it returns there even when killed." [6]

[5] Act II, scene I.   [6] Act IV, scene VII.

Above all, Chantecler is not a hero of romance far removed from common life. His history and his soul are those of the most humble, and so can be his idealism.

" When one knows how to see and to suffer, one knows all.
In the death of an insect one sees all disasters.
A circle of blue suffices to see pass the stars." [7]

Chantecler may be properly considered as the last dramatic message of Rostand. His *Dernière Nuit de Don Juan,* although practically finished before the war, was never entirely completed. Rostand died in 1918, and *Don Juan* did not appear until 1921. Although it takes an original point of view in presenting a very familiar stage character, and lends itself to a magnificent dramatic spectacle, this play can hardly rank among the most significant of Rostand's dramas.

Cyrano de Bergerac is the supreme dramatic achievement of Rostand. It is, moreover, the piece in which culminates the only distinct school of poetic drama that existed in France in the nineteenth century. It deserves, then, special consideration from both of these points of view.

It is, first of all, a Romantic drama. If it had appeared a half-century earlier, its evolution and place in dramatic development would have seemed easy to fix — at first sight. Coming as it does after a full generation of realistic literature, and with its author brought up in the Naturalistic atmosphere, it appears, in its brilliance and vigor, a strange phenomenon. Is it simply a flower of pure Romantic stock, blooming by some strange accident,

[7] Act I, scene V.

in the wintry field of bleak realism after lying dormant for fifty years, or is it, after all, a modified product of its species, showing the improvement of cultivation and the influence of the climate and soil in which it is grown?

The Romantic elements of *Cyrano* are unmistakable. In it Rostand conforms to practically all the theory of the Romanticists — but he also excels most of them in practice.

One of the important features of Romantic drama was local color — in historic drama this color should be the evocation of the spirit and atmosphere of the age represented. In this respect, the play is superior to any of the Romantic productions. With marvelous skill, the author makes live before us, in rapid, magic strokes, the turbulent audience that stood in the pit, the prankish page who fished up bourgeois wigs from the upper gallery, the foppish marquis who sat on the stage to show his court prerogatives and the ribbons and lace on his costume, and the *précieuses,* or romantic blue-stockings, such as Roxane and her friends, who peeped through their masks from the boxes. We are back in the seventeenth century, with its heroism and bombast, with its brave soldiers and bragging bullies, with its wigs and ruffs, with its clever women and witty men, its masks, its romance, its duels, with all the brave show of the most brilliant city, court and country of the epoch. And this color and history are not on the surface but come from the heart of the work. The plot of the play is made to depend on the preciosity, or super-refinement, of Roxane, and whether or not Rostand has brought to life the real historic Cyrano — a matter of absolutely no importance

— he has placed him, as conceived, in the only atmosphere he could breathe and against a background that is both real and artistic. In doing this, he has much surpassed the usual Romantic practice. He does not choose some famous figure and deform it, as Hugo and Dumas often did, but he takes a comparatively obscure one and illuminates it, and at the same time lights up a whole page of interesting history.

In its far-reaching effect, perhaps the most important innovation of the Romantic school was the mingling of the kinds: the combining of the sublime and the grotesque, or of the tragic and the comic, and the introduction of the lyrical element into drama. In these respects, *Cyrano* is truly a Romantic play. The comic side, and particularly its gaiety, wit and humor, are too obvious to call for specification. What is more interesting is that some of the best French critics have been inclined to see in this the chief merit and appeal of the play. However, this would be accepting a quality that is expressed in detail and on the surface as superior to one that is in the heart of the drama. It would be, moreover, equivalent to saying that *Cyrano's* merit is purely transitory, good for an evening's entertainment, and that it possesses no serious appeal that can be carried away and returned to, after the novelty is passed, with pleasure and profit.

Cyrano is primarily a drama of elevated motives and this serious quality forms its lasting appeal. It is, above all, a play based on a single character and the chief motives of this character are honor, independence, and self-sacrifice, all factors of serious drama, and all most fundamental. On the first of these motives there is no need to insist. It is the key to Cyrano's character, as it is to that of most French dramatic heroes. It is the motive of his duels and other exploits, it is the sentiment that seals his lips on his love for Roxane, when Christian is killed, and it is his strength, in the end, to draw his sword against the approach of death in order to preserve his glory intact. It should be noted also that his is the traditional and national French honor: the *point d'honneur* of the Cid, feudal in its punctiliousness; the honor of Bayard, chivalric in its delicacy; and the honor of Roland, sublime in its hopelessness.

Cyrano's independence is as strongly drawn as his honor, with which, moreover, it is closely united. Also, it is this quality which gives him his chief dramatic strength and differentiates him absolutely from the traditional Romantic hero, who is the pawn of fate and events, from a Hernani falling at the King's feet for pardon, or from a Ruy Blas changing his coat of prime minister for his valet's livery at the voice of his master. Never, perhaps, has this spirit of independence been more eloquently expressed than at the end of Cyrano's famous tirade against subserviency, where he states his own ideals:

> " Mais . . chanter,
> Rêver, rire, passer, être seul, être libre,
> Avoir l'œil qui regarde bien, la voix qui vibre,
> Mettre, quand il vous plaît, son feutre de travers,
> Pour un oui, ou un non, se battre, — ou faire un vers!
> Travailler sans souci de gloire ou de fortune,
> A tel voyage, auquel on pense, dans la lune!
> N'écrire jamais rien qui de soi ne sortit,
> Et modeste d'ailleurs, se dire: mon petit,

Sois satisfait des fleurs, des fruits, même des feuilles,
Si c'est dans ton jardin à toi que tu les cueilles!
Puis, s'il advient d'un peu triompher, par hasard,
Ne pas être obligé d'en rien rendre à César." [8]

If this declaration were only the oratory of a Romantic
hero, it would mean little, but we find that it is a code
lived up to throughout the play.

Cyrano's self-sacrifice in his love for Roxane is no
less a motive in the drama and furnishes occasion for
most of the emotion of the play. He himself has stated
perfectly this rôle in his death scene, when told that
Molière had copied from him one of his greatest successes:

> "Oui, ma vie
> Ce fut d'être celui qui souffle — et qu'on oublie!
>   (A Roxane)
> Vous souvient-il du soir où Christian vous parla
> Sous le balcon? Eh bien! toute ma vie est là:
> Pendant que je restais en bas, dans l'ombre noire,
> D'autres montaient cueillir le baiser de la gloire!
> C'est justice, et j'approuve au seuil de mon tombeau:
> Molière a du génie et Christian était beau! " [9]

This sacrifice and the idealization of an impossible love
have already been referred to in *La Princesse Lointaine;*
it is a favorite theme with Rostand.

Like Hugo and other Romanticists, Rostand was a
lyric poet and has introduced lyricism into his plays.
There is, however, a notable difference when compared
with Hugo. The latter constantly sought to create lyrical
situations, often at the expense of his plot and character

[8] Act II, scene VIII.   [9] Act V, scene VI.

development. Rostand has maintained the lyrical element subordinate, and has used it only when it is in place and in order to add to the dramatic effect. Take, for example, the scene of the fife-player in the fourth act, where the Gascon company, exhausted with hunger and privation, threaten to revolt, and where Cyrano makes one of the strongest appeals that can be made to men, the appeal of childhood recollections and music.

" Approche, Bertrandou le fifre, ancien berger;
Du double étui de cuir tire l'un de tes fifres,
Souffle, et joue à ce tas de goinfres et de piffres
Ces vieux airs du pays, au doux rythme obsesseur,
Dont chaque note est comme une petite sœur,
Dans lesquels restent pris des sons de voix aimées,
Ces airs dont la lenteur est celle des fumées
Que le hameau natal exhale de ses toits,
Ces airs dont la musique a l'air d'être en patois!

.   .   .   .

Ecoutez, les Gascons. . Ce n'est plus, sous ses doigts,
Le fifre aigu des camps, c'est la flûte des bois!
Ce n'est plus le sifflet du combat, sous ses lèvres,
C'est le lent galoubet de nos meneurs de chèvres!
Ecoutez. . C'est le val, la lande, la forêt,
Le petit pâtre brun sous son rouge béret,
C'est la verte douceur des soirs sur la Dordogne.
Ecoutez, les Gascons! c'est toute la Gascogne! " [10]

Recited with the accompaniment of the slow, intense southern music, this is as effective dramatically as it is beautiful lyrically.

It is very largely the lyrical passages in *Cyrano* that should decide one of the most disputed questions in

[10] Act IV, scene III.

Rostand's poetry, his ability to evoke deep and sincere feeling, love or passion. No one denies him the gift to express graceful and agreeable sentiment and emotion, but it is often claimed that he does not have the deeper power. No doubt the highly etherealized and idealistic love that Rostand portrays by preference has contributed to form this opinion. Also, in *Cyrano* there is much intentional super-refinement. However, it is precisely in this play that Rostand has himself invited this test of his ability. In the well-known balcony scene, where Cyrano forgets Christian and speaks his own love to Roxane, the poet explicitly disavows, in sincere love, the elaboration of exquisite similes and highly alembicated sentiment. Here then, if anywhere, his words should express real feeling. The passage is too long to quote in its entirety, but the lines at the end are representative.

"Oh! mais vraiment, ce soir, c'est trop beau, c'est trop doux!
Je vous dis tout cela, vous m'écoutez, moi, vous!
C'est trop! Dans mon espoir même le moins modeste,
Je n'ai jamais espéré tant! Il ne me reste
Qu'à mourir maintenant! C'est à cause des mots
Que je dis qu'elle tremble entre les bleus rameaux!
Car vous tremblez, comme une feuille entre les feuilles!
Car tu trembles! car j'ai senti, que tu le veuilles
Ou non, le tremblement adoré de ta main
Descendre tout le long des branches du jasmin." [11]

In the above passage, where the poet wishes to be most direct and simple, there are perhaps more elaboration and refinement of style than we are accustomed to associate with the expression of the deepest feeling. Cer-

[11] Act III, scene VI.

tainly such style is far removed from the agonizing phrases of a victim of the heart in Dumas's *Dame aux Camélias,* or from the disconnected, passionate cries of a victim of the dramatist in Sardou's *Patrie,* but this may be none the less the natural language of a lyric poet. We should hardly expect him to make love in the language of the butcher or the baker, or even perhaps in the same style as that of the doctor or the banker. We can not apply here the criterions of realistic literature. Shakespeare certainly knew the true language of feeling, and moreover, possessing every key in the gamut of human expression, could strike the most realistic or even brutal note, when he wished, and yet the style of Shakespeare in an exactly similar scene has the same qualities. One has only to read three lines of Romeo's speech to be reminded of this fact:

> " It was the lark, the herald of the morn:
> No nightingale: look, Love, what envious streaks
> Do lace the severing clouds in yonder east: — "

The connection of Rostand's drama with Hugo's is too obvious to need comment, but there is one fundamental difference between these two authors: Rostand is a dramatist and Hugo is not. In demonstrating this fact from *Cyrano,* all the secondary factors of dramatic ability, those of detail or those which may be contained in a single scene, will be discarded. Hugo also could be effective within those limits, although it is doubtful if anything in Hugo can be found as perfect and sustained dramatically, without the false notes of melodrama, as the final act of *Cyrano.* In this last act, where Rostand has

thrown the idealistic net of time, of nature and of religion
over the stage, to soften before our eyes the more cruel
lines of grief and terror in this tragedy of sacrifice and
death, we have an almost perfect piece of sustained
dramatic artistry. The quiet of the convent, the religious
music and the autumn setting combine perfectly in a scene
that is thoroughly dramatic and always appropriate. Such
little touches as that of the falling leaves, symbolizing the
imminent death of Cyrano, fit perfectly into a harmonious
whole.

> "Comme elles tombent bien!
> Dans ce trajet si court de la branche à la terre,
> Comme elles savent mettre une beauté dernière,
> Et malgré leur terreur de pourrir sur le sol,
> Veulent que cette chute ait la grâce d'un vol! " [12]

But admittedly the more fundamental elements of
drama are to be found in the creation of characters and
their translation into action in a play, and, back of these,
in the author's conception or philosophy of life, of which
character and action are the products.

Hugo's characters are inconsistent, the products of antithesis, controlled by the arbitrary hand of the author,
under the mask of blind fate, and his plots are as illogical
as his dramatic figures. Cyrano is a consistent character,
acting in every crisis in accordance with dominating motives, and coming to the end which we should expect the
sum total of these qualities to produce. With his Quixotic honor, his keenly sensitive spirit of independence,
which prevents his accepting the slightest favor or help,
and with his exalted ideal of sacrifice, we anticipate his

[12] Act V, scene V.

lack of worldly success, his death in poverty and his failure to win the woman he loves. Also, it is most important to note that in putting the real drama in the soul of Cyrano, developed by motives contained in this character, Rostand returns to the Classic practice initiated by Corneille of making drama interior, and creating dramatic heroes who are masters of their own fate.

There is, to be sure, antithesis in Cyrano's character — there is antithesis in the characters of Hamlet and of the Misanthrope — but it is not the author's basic conception. It is not *because* Cyrano is a poetic genius that he is a failure; it is not *because* he is made grotesque by a large nose that he is a tender and spiritual lover.

Whether in strict agreement with fact or not, Rostand has made him a poetic lover and a genuine hero, and has used his wit to keep sentiment from becoming sentimentality, and his sense of humor and irony to prevent Quixotic bravery from appearing as pure boasting and bravado. When Cyrano, moved by his hopeless love for Roxane, is about to weep, he is checked by the humorous thought of tears running down his big nose, and we are saved from the pit of pathos. When he stages his spectacular duel against the hundred men, he forestalls the charge of mock heroics by calling himself a " Scipio, triply nosed "; when in the end his independence and honor are exalted into hallucination and he draws his sword on the spectres of Cowardice, Stupidity and Death, he falls to the earth with a smile and a jest for his *panache*. And it is precisely this conception of the character of Cyrano that makes him most national and offers him the greatest promise of being immortal among French heroes.

Walter Hampden in *Cyrano de Bergerac*—1923

Reckless bravery is a favorite quality in heroes of all times and countries, but there is something in Cyrano that is essentially French: his sense of the uselessness of the sacrifice and the light-heartedness with which it is made. As a symbol of these qualities, at least, his *panache* is truly and traditionally French and not simply Gascon; it is the plume of Henri IV about which every Frenchman rallies.

The native good sense of the French is not duped by forlorn hopes, but their desire for the approval and admiration of their fellows, their social instinct, drives them to such exploits, and their irresistible racial gaiety enables them to jest in the face of death. Seek in French heroes of legend or literature at all times and you will find these same qualities of hopeless but light-hearted courage and Cyrano is one of the most recent of these national symbols.

Cyrano's bravery has gained a battle of which the credit goes to another; his talent has given success to Molière; his wit and sentiment have won the woman he loved for a friend, and his honor has enabled him to keep up the generous but useless sacrifice; and finally his independence, in an age of flatterers, prevents worldly success and brings him in poverty to death. But these noble qualities and these misfortunes are in themselves not so much the reason for his popularity as is his manner of exercising the first and of enduring the second.

The one word that best describes this manner, or better this ideal, is the word that Cyrano adopts as his guide to life: to be *admirable*. This undoubtedly includes for the French a certain amount of display — to wish to be

admirable is to seek to be admired. When Cyrano breaks
up the play of Montfleury and reimburses the players, by
throwing his purse on the stage, Le Bret reproaches him
for an act that has left him penniless; he replies, " Ah,
but what a fine gesture it was! " The Frenchman often
plays to the gallery, but his bravado is genuine and he
can maintain it in the face of death. This is the case of
Cyrano. It is not simply that he is willing to die like a
brave man, as hundreds have done before, but that he
dies like a Frenchman, with gaiety in his heart and a
jest on his lips. As he himself says:

"I should like to die, some day, under a bright sky,
Uttering a witty word, for a fine cause!
Oh! pierced by the sole noble arm that exists,
And by an enemy that one knows to be worthy,
Far from a bed of fever, on a field of glory, to fall,
With the point (sword and witticism) in my heart at the
    same time as on my lips! " [13]

A part of this prayer was denied him, and he was
struck down in ambush, but his philosophy was undis-
mayed. When, in his delirium, he draws his sword on
death, he cries: " What do you say? It is in vain? I
know it! But one does not fight in the hope of success!
No! no! it is finer when it is useless." And he dies with
his plume unsullied and with the jest, the point, on his
lips.

Rostand's drama belongs to idealistic literature — the
only kind exactly suited to verse. To this extent it does
not deal with real life — or rather with everyday physical life, for it is just as real to think, to imagine, to have

[13] Act IV, scene III.

aspirations, ideals and enthusiasms as it is to eat, to make money, to marry and to be divorced. However, it is not Realistic literature in the accepted sense and hence it can not be judged entirely by realistic criterions. It is more proper to ask if it is artistic, beautiful, noble or poetic than it is to determine if it is practical, probable, typical or informative.

Not a little of the criticism passed on *Cyrano* has been conceived from realistic points of view, which is not surprising perhaps in this realistic age, but such standards are none the less inapplicable in this case. To condemn the play as immoral or insincere because Cyrano and Christian deceive Roxane, thereby implying that it sets an example that is dangerous, would be equivalent to condemning most of myth and romance. On such basis one might cite for malicious murder Jack of the Bean Stalk for deceiving and killing the Giant, or banish for cruelty the " Old Woman who Lived in a Shoe " for whipping her children and sending them to bed without supper. Hero worship, romance and sentiment are natural. Like all faculties of the mind, they may be overindulged in, but no more so than the practical and materialistic. And it is after all perhaps finer, and less easy, to be a Don Quixote and tilt at windmills than a Sancho Panza who thinks only of a hot supper at the next inn.

But *Cyrano*, although it does not reflect a real situation, nor exploit a social theory, may none the less pass a judgment on life. In final analysis, Cyrano's philosophy is a practical one; it is moral contentment and riches. He does not give a code for material existence but he offers a moral philosophy that is complete, and that is not unaware of the struggle in what we call real life. The sadness of realism has touched this philosophy, and we see here the influence of Rostand's age. Cyrano is a *raté;* he admits failure in the worldly sense. But he lives his own life, according to his own cult, and dies with a smile of contented honor.

Rostand's philosophy, in rejecting the pessimism of materialism and taking refuge in moral contentment, is even more fully confirmed in *Chantecler*. It might seem as if the poet had turned expressly from the idealistic field of romance to the humble life of the barnyard in order to impress the practical side of his philosophy. For the lesson of *Chantecler* is the same as that expressed in *Cyrano:*

> " Sois satisfait des fleurs, des fruits, même des feuilles,
> Si c'est dans ton jardin à toi que tu les cueilles."

And this doctrine of moral contentment, in refusing to be carried away by the rage for material riches and worldly success, is not only practical, but is the only one that is in the reach of all. Perhaps also it should be noted — for this shows how thoroughly Rostand is a humanist — that this philosophy is the particular lesson of literature and the humanities. The appeal of *Cyrano,* then, is honor, bravery, romance and sentiment, admirably blended with a spice of comedy and humor, and touched only with the sadness of realism.

In Rostand is found the most recent prominent representative of poetic drama, and his work is clearly a development from the Romantic movement, and is perhaps its most perfect achievement. However, it is especially notable for the reform that has been accomplished by the inevitable assertion of French genius in eliminating the inconsistencies of character and action of the early school, and by the reëstablishment of interior and moral action.

Whether or not his work marks the culmination of this genre, it belongs to the realm of prophecy to say, but it is safe to predict that the French, with their love of the heroic and elevated, and their fondness for rhetoric, are not likely to abandon entirely poetic drama.

Nevertheless, French literature since the middle of the nineteenth century has been prevailingly realistic, corresponding to the influences of the age. It is to the realistic prose drama, then, of this period, that we shall turn to find the main stream of the French theatre and to see more abundantly exemplified the chief traits of French dramatic genius.

CHAPTER VI

SCRIBE AND THE WELL–MADE PLAY

EUGÈNE SCRIBE (1791–1861)

THE number of people who are really romantic is limited in any society or age, perhaps particularly so in France. During the Romantic period, the young artists, poets and idealistic lovers went to applaud *Hernani* and *Henri III,* and the scholars and the conservatives, the Classicists, went to hiss, or stayed at home to write criticism. The crowd — the butcher, the baker and the tired bourgeois and his wife — went to see Scribe; and, since this last group is not only much more numerous than the first, but is wealthier and healthier, the theatrical popularity of Scribe far outlasted that of Hugo or Dumas.

Scribe, like Romanticism, is one of the sources of the modern French drama. At the beginning of the nineteenth century, the old character comedy developed by Molière and preserved by his imitators was without life, largely on account of the same causes that killed Classic tragedy: the exhaustion of the types to which this comedy confined itself and the sterility from two centuries of inbreeding and imitation. Scribe created a new sort of comedy. His work in this genre is similar to that of Dumas père in Romantic drama: both introduced popular elements and through these attracted the crowds. Dumas brought on the stage popular and adventurous imagination and intense passion. Scribe gave an intrigue and suspense to satisfy the curiosity, and aspirations adapted to the after-dinner mentality of the comfortable little bourgeois. To do this, Scribe took what the French called *vaudeville,* a form half-way between a play and a musical comedy, but too insignificant to be either, and developed it into a real comedy of intrigue, or even into tragicomedy, historical comedy, or serious drama.

In reality Scribe restored a comedy of intrigue rather than created it, for certainly Beaumarchais and others wrote comedies of intrigue. But the theatre constantly repeats itself, quite as much as any other branch of history does, and at least Scribe's form was particularly adapted to the needs of his time. It was realistic, matter-of-fact, ingenious rather than imaginative, and fitted to modern settings.

Eugène Scribe, the son of a Parisian merchant, was educated in law but was early attracted to the stage by a call that was intelligent and determined, even if not idealistically inspired. He wrote at least a dozen plays before he uncovered a vein of success, and about four hundred more before he exhausted it. As a playwright simply he is perhaps the most successful in history, and his pieces brought him an enormous fortune. He was elected to the French Academy in 1836.

He was a typical bourgeois of the narrow sort, without any of the breadth and liberal philosophy of Molière, and with a purely materialistic conception of life. This would seem a poor equipment for a writer — and it is for an author of literature — but for a playwright it was admirably adapted to the aim to which he limited himself. In the decidedly commercial and materialistic epoch of French society in which he lived, he was able to give the bourgeois class, lately come into wealth and importance, a theatre of easy amusement that accorded with their philosophy of material comfort and smug respectability. Scribe's dramatic career lasted from 1815 to 1861, and, although his plays are often signed by a collaborator, he seems usually to have done most of the work himself; in a few only is the hand of another author evident.

Scribe's first stage success was *Une Nuit de la Garde Nationale,* in 1815, a one-act vaudeville. What astonishes us to-day, in reading it, is the insignificant character of this vaudeville skit and the reasons for its popular success. Much of the favor must have been due to the numerous verses sung in each scene to popular airs — at least these seem as silly and uncalled for as the songs which are so strangely applauded in vaudeville today — but doubtless it was also owing to the choice of a subject which was just then of public interest. One of the large factors of Scribe's unfailing popularity was his intuition in exploiting the theme of the day, or at least in choosing a subject that appealed to the particular foibles or tastes of his generation. But, with all that, the merit of this early vaudeville is incredibly slight; we do not wonder that Scribe had to write four hundred plays to elevate this form into the dignity of real comedy.

For a number of years Scribe was the official playwright of the Gymnase theatre, where this evolution from vaudeville into comedy was very gradual. His process consisted in a reduction of the place and importance of the songs and in a decided extension and strengthening of the intrigue, which involved a lengthening of the play as a whole. It was not until he began to aspire to the dignity of the national theatre, the *Comédie,* that we have the best examples of his work. In these he eliminates the verses entirely and attempts more than one of the ambitious forms of drama.

No enumeration of Scribe's plays is necessary today. While many of them may still be read with an interest of curiosity, owing to their clever intrigue, only a few of the best survive in any sense. *Bertrand et Raton,* in 1833, is one of the first and best of his so called historical comedies. History here, as is usual with Scribe, only furnishes him with a few names and ideas for a play, and in no way interferes with his invention, nor does it probably add to, or subtract from, the audience's interest in the piece. In this comedy, Scribe is usually given credit for the creation of one of his characters that is most nearly original, Bertrand. Perhaps relatively he does stand above most of Scribe's chessmen, but his absolute originality and merit are still not great.

Le Verre d'Eau (1840), another historical drama, is widely known and is one of his most ambitious and worthy plays. *Adrienne Lecouvreur* (1849), to which a collaborator, Ernest Legouvé, contributed something, is probably his most appealing play in its tone and sentiment, as it is also one of his best in style, and it has had world-wide popularity. Finally, one should mention *La Bataille de Dames* (1851), in which the particular excellence of Scribe, his technique and unrivalled invention in intrigue, offers its finest example.

Scribe was also the composer of a number of opera libretti that are well known, such as *La Dame Blanche, Fra Diavolo, Robert le Diable* and *Les Huguenots.*

The recent reactions against Scribe's type of play have been so extreme that it is perhaps hard to do him justice. In fact, he appears always to have been, for the critics, a great resource for caustic or witty copy, so that it might seem that no one has really approved his work — except the play-goers. As to the qualities that may make a play literature, this criticism is fully justified. His style and language are often negligent and usually commonplace, and his thought and ideas are borrowed and mediocre. Even in wit, of which he really seems to have had the French writer's usual liberal endowment, he takes no chance of missing his auditors and prefers the quips and jests that have never failed fire.

However, it is in his conception of life and character that the criticism is most serious. In a naïvely sincere passage of his speech on his reception into the Academy, Scribe seems to claim that life and the theatre have no connection. Nevertheless, his own conception of the theatre, of life, and of history was exactly the same for each, and can be described by one word, petty. Perhaps the best exposition of this idea is the often quoted one in *Le Verre d'Eau* where, in the character of Bolingbroke, he expounds his philosophy of history.

" BOLINGBROKE. One should not despise the small things; it is through them that one comes to great ones! You think perhaps, as everybody does, that political catastrophes, revolutions, the fall of empires, come from deep, serious and important causes. That is an error. States are dominated or led by heroes, by great men; but these great men are themselves controlled by their passions, their whims, their follies; that is to say, by what there is, in this world, most petty and wretched. Do you know that a window of the Trianon palace, criticized by Louis XIV and defended by Louvois, gave rise to the war which devastates Europe at this moment! It is to the wounded vanity of a courtier that the kingdom has owed its disasters; it is to a more futile cause still that it will perhaps owe its safety. And without going further — I who am speaking to you, I, Henry Saint-John, who until twenty-six years old was looked on as a fop, a giddy fellow incapable of serious occupation — do you know how I suddenly became a statesman, a member of parliament and a minister?

ABIGAÏL. No, indeed.

BOLINGBROKE. Well, my dear child, I became a minister because I knew how to dance the saraband; and I lost the power because I had a cold. . . .

ABIGAÏL. And what can you do?

BOLINGBROKE. Wait and hope!

ABIGAÏL. Some great revolution?

BOLINGBROKE. Not at all, a mere chance, a whim of fate — a grain of sand that will overthrow the victor's chariot.

ABIGAÏL. Can you not create this grain of sand?

BOLINGBROKE. No, but if I find it, I can push it under the wheel. Talent is not to replace Providence and create events, but to profit by them. The more futile they are in appearance, the more, according to me, they have importance; great effects produced by small causes, that is my system." [1]

To take very seriously this passage would be absurd if it did not describe so well not only Scribe's usual exposition in his historical dramas, but also the ordinary train of life of all his plays; and if it were not moreover an almost perfect description of the usual conduct of his

[1] *Le Verre d'Eau,* Act I.

plots. The dramatist is always pushing a grain of sand under the car of his dramatic characters, so that their journey might be thought of as a series of exciting mishaps or derailments. Only, the audience, being warned so constantly to watch for the grain of sand, thinks of it as a part of providence and not the result of accident.

Scribe's characters are all stock properties — each with qualities according to label; his statesmen are all clever, his soldiers are all courageous, his young girls are all pretty and rich, and his widows — he specializes in widows, just as he does in second hand wit — are clever, courageous, pretty and rich all together. These stock characters serve perfectly his purpose, which is to carry out the plot. What they lack to make them convincing — besides originality — is sincerity. All the battles of Scribe are sham battles. His characters never really hate each other, nor are they ever deeply in love with each other. They pretend to be, but we can not take them seriously. We feel confident that the rivals are not going to kill each other or themselves, and in the end we see that we were right; the most deserving wins the beautiful heiress and the other gets the hand of a young and wealthy widow, and is entirely contented. There is no unreasonable aspiration in his plays. The aims of life are a rich marriage, money and comfort.

Naturally, Scribe's characters are quite respectable. But respectability and morality are purely matters of keeping up appearances, and, in fact, his worthy bourgeois are sometimes thoroughly immoral, although doubtless such a charge would have greatly surprised both them and Scribe.

This budget of Scribe's deficiencies as a dramatic author is so heavy, and covers so many items, that it must have been balanced on the credit side by a merit of striking value to explain his preponderant influence on the form of modern drama. For this influence is incontestable, and in almost all recent systems of drama, or in reforms anywhere that rest on technique and construction, Scribe has been either the model or the antagonist. This merit of Scribe is to be found in the perfecting of plot and action into what is called the *pièce bien faite* (the well-made play).

Scribe has attained to this interest and perfect enchainment in plot largely by the use of two devices of drama: suspense and motivation by means of suggestion. In the matter of suspense — in his inexhaustible invention and in his clever use of it — Scribe was a dramatic genius probably unequalled in the history of the theatre, and he is perhaps more than anyone responsible for this distinguishing trait of modern, compared with early, drama. In any case, he so enlarged and popularized this factor of suspense with French audiences that it must needs be accepted as fundamental by his successors.

The particular method of his employment of suspense has already been indicated, in treating his conception of life; it consists of a series of minor crises, developed regularly by petty causes, by his grains of sand. His matchless cleverness is to be seen, not only in the placing of these grains but in the resources of his invention in righting the car of his actors, shifting it to a new track and guiding it forward to another spill, in this exciting obstacle race.

To carry out his system, the author usually requires at least two figures who are rivals, and who will be as clever and as specious as he is himself. For this contest must seem real enough to be exciting, and at the same time the accidents must not kill or prevent anyone from entering the home-stretch in a neck and neck finish in order to receive at least a second prize. Good examples of this sort are to be found in his *Verre d'Eau* and his *Bataille de Dames*. In the first play, during the contest between Bolingbroke and the equally clever Duchess, the car of the latter, without counting minor swerves, is upset by actual count at least a half-dozen times before its final overthrow — this time not by a grain of sand but by a glass of water — and in the second play the suspense is not only keener but the crises are even more numerous.

Scribe's motivation of the plot and action in his plays calls for special examination. In so far as it is the natural working out of basic motives in his characters, it is, of course, highly commendable, and is only the interior action on which all modern drama is, or should be, founded. We demand logical, or at least intelligible, action based on the characters, and we condemn a plot that is illogical, inconsistent and disconcerting. Scribe's plays avoid these faults and conform, in appearance at least, to these proper demands.

However, Scribe's characters are rarely sufficiently solid to bear the weight of the action, and, far from being masters of their fate, are usually unable to stand alone. Hence they become mere pawns of the playwright, and much of this action, seemingly so logically enchained, is not inherent in the situation or in the characters, and it is often made to seem natural and logical purely through the force of suggestion in the minds of the auditors. He hinges the most important developments on pure accident, but we have been so carefully prepared to expect this accident, or our eyes have been so persistently attracted to the spot where something should occur, that, when it comes, it seems only a part of the natural train of life. In fact, we come so entirely under the spell of these suggestions that no small part of our pleasure is our curiosity to see the particular manifestations of Scrib-esque Providence, which he has so adroitly prophesied, and which at the time seem a part of the divine order of things.

This plausible but artificial rationalizing of the dra-matic action is found constantly in Scribe, in minor de-tails as well as in capital events. An example of this sort is the killing of the cousin of Bolingbroke in *Le Verre d'Eau,* and the latter's succession to the fortune. It is a capital event, but was in no way inherent in this play. Nevertheless, by our knowledge that this cousin was the only obstacle, and by Masham's frequent mention of an impending duel with some one who had insulted him, it has the appearance, when it occurs, of being an integral part of the plot. The aspect of this method that is most interesting to note just here is that the dramatist has in mind only his audience and not the realities of life; his psychology is purely one of suggestion and the rela-tionship of thought images, and not that of inherent cause or of the real logic of events.

It is this same point of view that has dictated the

dramatic character of the playwright's language and style and the implied or prescribed action that is necessary in interpreting his plays. Some of the greatest dramatists seem to have created their characters with certain autonomous motives, to have placed them in a prescribed situation in life so they can not wander at random, and then to have contented themselves with recording the actions and words of these persons who work out their own fates. Scribe does not take a situation in life; he writes all his plays in the theatre. His characters are not real persons; they are only imaginary actors, and the playwright sits in a stall of the theatre so that he can have the auditor's point of view. His visualization and his auscultation, so to speak, of these dramatic puppets, of which he pulls the strings, are perfect. Every entrance or exit is carefully planned, every step is measured, and every gesture, smile and grimace given proper light and perspective. Speeches are short, judged for their carrying effect and never overloaded with meaning.

Above all, these plays are written to afford a maximum of action and expression. Take a scene chosen almost at random in *La Bataille de Dames*. It covers but seven short pages, and could hardly require that number of minutes in acting, yet in this brief time a single character, the Countess, changes tone, and doubtless underlines it with gesture or facial expression, no less than fourteen times, recording, among other emotions, cordiality, jest, good humor, curiosity, amusement, irony, anger, mockery and determination. Here we see one of the important practical merits of Scribe's pieces. His plays are written to be acted and they offer effective rôles for the actor, and interesting scenes for the audience. In these respects, Scribe is undoubtedly on firm ground, since plays must be acted and must appeal, and certain conditions and restrictions must be observed for their success, but it is significant to note again that this excellence is created from the relatively narrow point of view of the play-goer, and not from the broader one of a thoughtful observer of life.

The faults and merits, then, of Scribe's plays are outstanding. His theatre is devoid of serious ideas, strong characters and artistic style, all important factors in determining the permanent worth and literary value of a play. To offset these weaknesses, he had an exceedingly clever dramatic technique in plot and action, perfectly adjusted to the demands of an audience seeking amusement. It is evident that this excellence, necessary as it may be, can not compensate for his deficiencies. Good plot may demand a high quality of invention, but possibly because, in itself, it suggests no fertile analogies in life and is not thought-provoking, it does not have a permanent value comparable to a strong or original dramatic character, which always invites comparison with our own character or with the characters of others, and offers a lesson in life.

But the value of Scribe's particular merit, secondary as it is unless combined with other qualities, should not be depreciated; it is really necessary to the life of the theatre. The drama must be played to live, and on its success in performance depends its degree of vigor and development. Scribe cultivated precisely those qualities which make for success, and it will not do to condemn this by calling it the commercial theatre. The theatre must succeed commercially and popularly or it will not succeed in a literary or artistic way; it will be dead. Those who attack the commercial theatre should think only of a means for giving it the higher values without impairing its popularity. Scribe made his comedy widely popular in France and, at the same time, created a form that was transmittible and even exportable, and in which could find place some of the merits which he so conspicuously lacked.

It is often said today that Scribe imposed his form on his successors, and that his influence has been pernicious. This is hardly a fair statement. If his successors adopted his form, this was certainly because it best suited their needs, and the fact that his plays had wide vogue and influence on the drama in other countries proves there was more strength than mere Parisian tradition in this adoption. That the form of Scribe may have later hardened into a tradition, and have been imitated in its most doubtful features, is but the natural development. The Classic form had the same history.

The adaptability of Scribe's form is certain. The merits that it had, those of order, clarity, probability and good sense, are all characteristic French virtues. It is true that it was empty of the higher values, but for that reason exactly it could contain them. Its careful plot could be made to rest on strong characters and these could become symbols of real life, and illustrate a worthy philosophy. It needed, then, only a realist and a moralist to supply such elements, and those qualities are rarely long absent from French genius. They are found in Scribe's successors, Dumas fils and Augier, who before he had passed from the stage had filled his empty form and offered to the public a more substantial drama, without loss of interest and popularity. Scribe, in his perfect technique of plot, showed that the theatre could succeed without ideas. Really he builded better than he knew. The younger Dumas sometimes proved that Scribe's form could still succeed with ideas, even of the most didactic sort.

CHAPTER VII
DUMAS FILS AND REALISTIC SOCIAL DRAMA

DUMAS fils launched Realistic drama with his *Dame aux Camélias* in 1852, and his last important play appeared in 1887, the same year in which the Théâtre Libre inaugurated a partial reaction against his form of drama. These thirty-five years, sometimes called the period of Dumas fils and Augier, mark an important epoch in French dramatic history. Not only were many excellent plays written during this time but the forms of drama created then have, with only minor modifications, continued down to the present day and are still the prevailing types in the French theatre. Moreover the influence of these models has been very great on the recent drama of other countries.

This theatre is known as Social drama, or the Comedy of Manners (the French *Comédie de moeurs*), and some of its special varieties are the Problem Play or the Thesis Play, and the Useful Play. It is realistic, which separates it from Romantic drama, and it is sometimes called the Theatre of Ideas to distinguish it from the plays of Scribe.

Realistic Social drama opened a new field for the French theatre; it turned from the exhausted character comedy of Molière and the empty comedy of intrigue of Scribe to a serious study of man as influenced by his en-

vironment, and particularly in his connection with the
social problems of the day. It is a study of the individual, then, rather than of a universal type and it is
based on contemporary society, which it constantly reflects. Also this was a time when the theatre claimed
for itself the widest province and the most complete liberty; when it concerned itself with the things of life
that touch us most nearly, with private and public morals,
with social reforms, with politics and even with the laws
and statutes. It is the epoch when the theatre comes
into closest touch with the social sciences. Moreover, because of these characteristics and through these assumptions as to province, Social drama has brought up for
renewed discussion some of the fundamental questions
concerning the purpose of the theatre: whether its primary purpose is to amuse or whether its province is to
instruct and reform, and whether it should be held as
art for art's sake or should have a utilitarian aim.

The purpose of this chapter will be to call attention
to some of the general causes that lie behind Realistic
Social drama, to trace its affiliation with the preceding
forms of the theatre from which it was developed, and especially to show its exact character, its varieties and its
tendencies in the plays of Dumas, who was its chief creator, and who more than anyone else dominated its development throughout the period in question.

In its highly temperamental and emotional aspect, the
Romantic movement in France may be thought of as a
symptom and product of the Revolution, and hence a
passing state of nerves which for a relatively short time
stimulated powerfully feeling and imagination. But the

French are by nature rationalistic, and their good sense was bound to bring them back quickly to a literature of observation and realism. The moralistic strain also, or at least the intellectually moralistic, is an integral part of French literature, consequently it was only natural that the French theatre should turn quickly to the study of serious problems in life, in this instance to Social drama.

However, there were material and social conditions that contributed to this return to realism and explain in part the character of the theatre at this time. The period of the drama of Dumas and Augier is largely that of the Second Empire, and this was an era of striking material prosperity and commercial development in France. It was the time when Paris and other large cities were extensively reconstructed, when speculation was rife and when a whole new class of French people acquired wealth. At no other time perhaps was French society so affected by money and by materialistic conceptions, and these conceptions influenced notably the Realistic theatre. The middle and lower classes rose higher in the social scale, and made their influence felt in the realm of art.

The final form of government was not yet wholly settled, the kettle was still boiling a little and occasionally bubbling over, following the great explosion of the Revolution, but clearly democracy was to remain as the chief content of the cauldron after expelling the upper layers of society, which had so long kept it hidden; and the connection between democracy and the realistic and social literature of the second half of the nineteenth century is obvious. If a democracy is not absolutely essential to the development of realistic literature, it is certainly the condition of society in which the sort of realism we find at that time most naturally flourishes and has the widest appreciation.

We see, then, the commercial spirit of this epoch, and note that French literature was no longer dominated so completely as formerly by a cultured class. These conditions affected profoundly the drama of Dumas and Augier, and of their successors, and they explain further a part of its peculiar interest and value for us. It was the period when the state of French society in many ways most nearly approximated our own today, and we constantly find, in Augier especially, the same problems of life as those with which we are now struggling.

Concomitant with these material and social influences were others that concern more particularly the character and processes of thought. The dominant philosophy of the day was the positivism of Comte, which turned away from the purely metaphysical systems to a study of the natural and physical phenomena that are found in the sciences, in order to explain on this basis human life and society; especially great was Comte's contribution toward creating the social sciences. The particular application of this philosophy to literature and history is best seen in the determinism of Taine, whose well-known method of attempting to explain all literary movements and products of the individual mind by the three factors, race, environment and period (*la race, le milieu et le moment*), has entered so largely into literary history.

It is on the principle of environment especially that the theory and practice of Realistic and Social drama largely rest, not only in this period, but even more so later, for the maximum influence of positivism and determinism had not yet been reached. Man was no longer classed in a few great types, as in character comedy, with traits of character that are universal and almost abstract, but was looked upon in the infinite variety of the individual, affected and largely determined by the surroundings and society in which he lived; and this conception not only gave endless new subjects for the drama but stressed especially the importance of social and physical phenomena.

Positivistic philosophy was largely based on scientific knowledge and the period in question was marked by the great development of the experimental sciences — it is the period of Pasteur. Consequently the methods of investigation employed in the laboratory came to affect considerably those of literature. This was especially true later, when a whole theory of realism, Naturalism, was built up on this predicated analogy between scientific and literary methods, but already in the plays of Dumas we find scientific influences and pretensions.

All the general causes, then, tended toward realism and furnished the conditions favorable for the development of the Realistic Social theatre, but the particular character of this drama, its form, principles and literary endowments, is determined by its inheritance from the preceding forms of the theatre from which it naturally grew.

Romantic drama, although idealistic, was the most fertile source of the Realistic Social theatre; it emancipated it from former systems and rules and furnished it with its chief doctrines and often with its themes. It was, above all, the Romanticists' innovation in mingling the kinds, and their insistence that all sides of life should be represented in the drama, the common and the base as well as the noble and elevated, that were of the greatest consequence in the Realistic theatre. These practices were carried forward to their logical conclusion by the Realists. Their plays are pieces that may be either comedies or tragedies, or an equal balance of both, and in which certainly the base and seamy side of life finds sufficient place. In fact, later, the Naturalists, the would-be successors of the Realistic dramatists, turned almost exclusively to this field of sordid life, tempted perhaps also by its possibilities for an easy success in scandal. It is needless to say that the language of such a theatre was prose, and that all the reforms of style proposed by the Romanticists were utilized.

The chief ambition of the Romanticists, to give France a national historic drama, was in itself a long step toward creating the Realistic Social theatre. Dumas the elder had already, in such a play as *Antony*, come to treat the contemporary history of the individual, and the younger Dumas needed only to substitute observation and realism for the elder's imagination, and to introduce a serious moral aim into what had been mere adventure and passion, to inaugurate the new kind.

But the younger Dumas, and to an extent Augier also, did not turn away from the traditional theme of Romantic drama, irregular or illicit love. It was even the surest popular appeal in most of their plays. However — and the difference of philosophy is really absolute — they looked on such love with the eye of a moralist, as a danger to be fought rather than a god to be worshipped. Much of Realistic Social drama, then, proceeded directly from the Romantic school, modified only by the commercial, scientific and realistic spirit of the age.

Scribe's contribution of the form and technique of his well-made play to his successors has already been mentioned, and its adaptation by them was not difficult. Naturally it fitted perfectly the love intrigue, in which he also had used it. Much of the action, which with Scribe was made to appear logical by means of skillful suggestion in the minds of the audience, could be legitimately based on the stronger characters of his successors. It is no doubt true that these more genuine characters and broader ideas occasionally strained or broke some of Scribe's conventions, and no less true unfortunately that these characters and ideas were often not allowed this liberty and were unduly cramped, but, on the whole, the suspense and the clever plot and action of the *pièce bien faite* were made to do genuine service in presenting real life and thought. Without this interest in plot the more serious moralistic and didactic appeals of many of these plays would never have reached a popular audience.

Finally Realistic Social drama did not inherit from the theatre alone; in this case at least, it benefited largely from the novel. Balzac had already, before 1850, powerfully renewed the novel and brought it far along the road of realism. In doing this he had turned to the life of his own day, and especially to the manners, appetites and vices of all classes of society, with unusually good measure for those, such as the petty bourgeois, who had received so little attention in earlier literature. Above all, Balzac had stressed the importance of environment, both social and physical. It will be recalled that the fundamental conception of his great series of novels, *La Comédie Humaine*, is based on this important idea. This series has volumes on Parisian life, on provincial life, on country life, on military life, not to mention several other categories, and its chief effect is to show how character, manners and morals were modified by surroundings or *milieu*.

In the execution of his plan, Balzac stressed the materialism and commercialism of the times and gave unusual space to details of a concrete and physical nature, one of the chief features of Realistic literature. Furthermore he brought the scientific conception into literature, or more exactly he made use of certain sciences, such as physiology and medicine. The drama at this period went to school to the novel, with Balzac as the master.

Bearing in mind, then, only the cardinal points in this evolution, we can see in a broad way what Dumas fils inherited and utilized from his predecessors. Before Dumas, the comedy of character, as well as Classic tragedy, had become sterile through servile imitation. The Romanticists had overthrown Classic tragedy without adequately renewing it, and the place of Classic comedy had been taken, in public favor, by vaudeville, greatly developed by Scribe, in which the sole interest and merit are in plot and intrigue. Taking advantage of the doctrine of Romanticism which advocated the combination of comedy and serious drama, Dumas fils has put the content of Balzac, the study of contemporary social problems, into the form of Scribe, the *pièce bien faite*. His comedy, then, arouses curiosity by the plot or story and has the deeper interest that comes from the social question treated, and he has further suffused and warmed this with an intense emotional power drawn from the drama of passion which he inherited from his father. The more original elements that he added to this composition, and especially his contributions as a realist and a moralist, are best understood by a detailed study of his life and dramatic career.

ALEXANDRE DUMAS FILS (1824–1895)

More than any other French dramatist of the nineteenth century, Dumas fils was a creator. On most of the roads followed by the French prose drama for the past seventy years he was a pioneer; he even discovered a number of the bypaths into which the theatre has since been occasionally enticed. His restless and independent mind, his self-confidence, and his very lack of background and tradition made him a prolific initiator of new forms, and in most of these his undoubted dramatic gift scored a sensational success. It was inevitable that this originality and this success should impress powerfully his contemporaries and successors. In countries outside of France even, it is surprising how many of his innovations have been followed and exploited during the past fifty years, often without his being given due credit for them, perhaps because so many have been taken second hand, from contemporary French playwrights.

Alexandre Dumas fils was the illegitimate son, recognized and brought up by his father, of Alexandre Dumas, the famous novelist and playwright. He lived his whole life at Paris. While quite young, he began to write novels but soon turned to the stage, and all of his work that has any great importance is dramatic.

The one fact of Dumas's history that is most important in explaining his work was his position in life as an illegitimate child. In his early youth this brought him some painful experiences, and undoubtedly led to a certain bitterness in his attitude toward society, especially when he criticises the conventions and prejudices that bear upon the mother and child in such cases as his own. This experience was also potent in directing his mind to the study of immoral love and its dangers. He has devoted himself to this subject more than any other of the really significant French dramatists.

He was brought up by a good-hearted but prodigal and careless father, in a reckless, dissipated, pleasure-loving group in Parisian society. In due time, something serious in his own character revolted against this life, and he saw all its sins, miseries and falseness. But he is too prone to judge the whole of French society by that one little corner of Paris. In more than one of his plays, he attempts to show that debauchery and libertinism are undermining the morals of all French life, so that, in reading him, at times we almost forget, as he certainly does, that there are honest French people, uncontaminated, and that these make up in France, as elsewhere, the bulk and backbone of the nation.

His lack of a serious education also often betrays him in the discussion of important social problems. However, he was aggressive, determined, capable of great exertion, and gave the most serious and long-continued effort to the writing of his plays. His mind was quick and keen and he was *au courant* of all the questions agitated in his generation. In short, his attitude and mind were largely those of a keen journalist. In addition, he was a man of society, witty, a fine conversationalist, and did not forget that the theatre *must* entertain, whether that be its chief aim or not.

Dumas fils has some of the qualities of his father, particularly a powerful imagination and a love for the unusual. Hence we find him so often choosing subjects that excite or shock, and at times creating characters who are most interesting and striking, but not always true to life, or at least not typical. Nevertheless he had other qualities to offset these. He was, of all that with which he came in contact, a remarkable observer, and he saw more readily a bad motive than a good one. He seems to lack, in most of his plays, the indulgence and charity which have become so prominent in recent writers on social problems. He still believed in individual guilt.

As a rule, the value of Dumas's plays depends much on the balance which he was able to maintain between these qualities just mentioned. Occasionally Dumas the observer is overpowered by his imagination and love for the striking; the elder Dumas gets the upper hand, and we have a play or a character notably false to life.

Finally Dumas's most marked trait is that he does not observe and write *merely* to give us a picture or to amuse us but that he always points the moral. In fact he nearly always chooses his point of view and paints the picture for the sole purpose of teaching the lesson decided upon in advance. In his purpose and mission at least, he is a

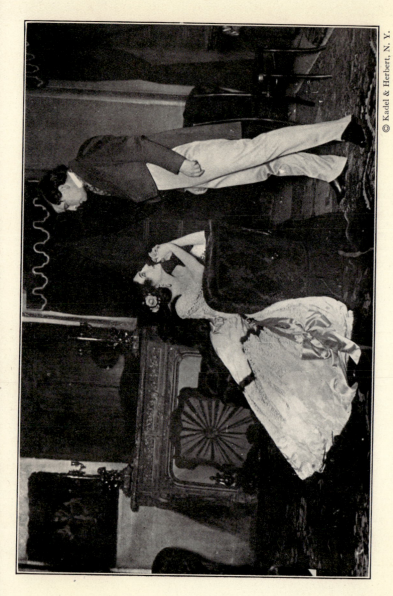

© Kadel & Herbert, N. Y.

Ida Rubenstein in a modern production of *La Dame aux Camélias*

social reformer, a preacher on the stage, who believes he is called to save man from his many vices. His real interest is in this mission and not simply in literature or in the theatre.

His first play, *La Dame aux Camélias*, finished in 1849 but not played until 1852 on account of difficulties with the censor caused by its realism, was written when he was quite young, in haste, and with no preconceived theories, being in fact adapted from an earlier novel that he had composed following the vein of the Romantic school. In one respect it is an epoch-making play. This life of the courtesan, so often and so falsely portrayed by the Romanticists, is here drawn from personal experience and observation, and presented with a fidelity to actual conditions hitherto unknown on the stage. In spite of its theme and tendency then, this play is the beginning of the modern Realistic drama.

His second significant play, *Le Demi-Monde*, in 1855, is perhaps his masterpiece and is written with a much firmer dramatic art. Dumas here undertakes the serious study of an important social question, thus inaugurating Social drama, and also, for the first time, takes a conscious stand on the subject of immoral love, a stand which he maintains all his life.

Dumas's *Question d'Argent*, in 1857, cannot be considered among the most important or characteristic of his pieces, but it has a certain interest in evaluating his dramatic work. It is one of the very few plays he wrote not based directly on immoral love; in theme it is more in the usual field of Augier. Dumas is clearly not sufficiently equipped to write a profound study of the money question, but it is interesting to see how skillfully he has popularized his discussion of the problem. In no other play does his witty and clever dialogue show to better advantage. The character of Jean Giraud is also of decided merit and, although imperfectly drawn, proves the capability of Dumas in this feature of drama, a power rarely realized completely owing to his absorption in his themes and plots.

This piece is also one of the best examples to show the dual interest inherent in combining a Balzac study and a Scribe intrigue. Dumas usually succeeds better; here the separation is often clearly marked.

Dumas's third really significant play likewise created a new genre, and the one with which his name is most closely associated, namely the *pièce à thèse,* or Thesis Play. This is *Le Fils Naturel,* in 1858, written to show that the laws and conventions concerning the illegitimate child are harsh and unjust and should be changed.

It is at this time that we find Dumas declaring that the mission of the dramatist is of the highest, that it is even sacred, since it has power over human souls. Undoubtedly this mission assumed by Dumas is sincere and his intentions are commendable. But one may very well question whether the stage, to which people, after all, go primarily for amusement, is a place to propose legislation or to preach the Gospel. Furthermore as we shall see, the Thesis Play and the utilitarian stage, here inaugurated, have been a constant temptation for the theatre to depart from the path of literature, of art, and even of truth into that of propaganda and social reform.

It is impossible to treat adequately in a brief chapter

the great variety of Dumas's plays, but the potential significance of certain pieces can perhaps be appreciated by noting their themes and tendencies, since the leads they suggested or opened up have been more fully worked in recent drama.

Un Père Prodigue, in 1859, based on the character of his father, is of no special importance in his work other than to suggest by its title the lack of taste and delicacy of the author, which is evident in a number of his plays and probably in none more strikingly than in the next, *L'Ami des Femmes,* which appeared five years later. But this second play is more remarkable as being one of the pioneer attempts in what might be called formal psychological drama. The psychological study is sufficiently pretentious and, as always with Dumas, very clever, but its serious value may be questioned. The hero, De Ryons, is a sort of psychologic Sherlock Holmes, specializing in running to earth clues in feminine emotions. Dumas's audience did not think this chase led to anything of value, and it might be mentioned that recent audiences have shown the same attitude toward somewhat similar, although abler, studies in some of Curel's plays.

None the less, Dumas returned to the charge with another play of pseudo-scientific import, *L'Etrangère,* in 1876, in which medical science, and particularly physiology, furnishes the chief ammunition. He attempted to give a psychological and physiological explanation for his characters. Perhaps he would have succeeded better — others have done so since — if his characters and his scientific training had both been nearer normal. As it is, the chief interest of the attempt is curiosity in the exhibits of his laboratory *préparateur*. Brieux has entered the same field with his *Damaged Goods* (*Les Avariés*); only with Brieux the gravity of the Doctor and the grewsomeness of his skeleton closet frighten us a little. Here we are at most amused by the medical professor's little wiggling vibrios.

Dumas returns nearer home, and closer to us, in *Les Idées de Mme Aubray*, a sociological study, based on forgiveness and Christian charity. Here Dumas's sympathy for the wronged mother and illegitimate child was so great that he has given the play unusual emotional appeal. His characters doubtless belong in a social Utopia, but they are sincere, on Dumas's part, and touch us by this quality.

In two plays, *Une Visite de Noces* and especially *Monsieur Alphonse*, Dumas has almost, if not quite, anticipated Becque and the later Naturalists, in creating the *Comédie Rosse*, the " tough comedy " that flourished with the Théâtre Libre. The only flaw in his claim to this doubtful honor is that these plays portray a few worthy and sympathetic dramatic figures to offset the contemptible rôles of the leading characters.

A play that deserves special consideration, as an example of the extremes to which his moralistic aim sometimes carried Dumas, is his *Femme de Claude*, in 1873. It is a drama animated by patriotism, and no doubt the dramatist's imagination was abnormally aroused by the recent Franco-Prussian war; its puritanism is as stern as that of John Knox and its symbolism is inspired by the evangelist Saint John. This, however, represents only an occasional aberration of Dumas, and his last two plays,

Denise and *Francillon,* show a return to his former manner and subjects, without adding anything to them of special value.

Of the several plays, then, in which he turned the drama in new directions, there are doubtless three that stand out for the importance of the forms they created. These are *La Dame aux Camélias, Le Demi-Monde,* and *Le Fils Naturel.* In the first of these, he struck again the realistic note which was to lead the drama back onto the firm ground of observation, after its bewilderment in following the noisy and illusory fanfare of Romanticism; with the second, he opened up the new and vast field of the *comédie de moeurs,* where human nature is studied in connection with, and as affected by, its social environment; and with the third, *Le Fils Naturel,* he created a new model, the *pièce à thèse,* or Thesis Play, with which his name is most closely associated. The importance of the forms these three pieces inaugurated warrants a more detailed consideration of the plays themselves.

The theme of *La Dame aux Camélias,* which is the poetization or redemption through love of the courtesan, and its effect, which is to magnify largely the importance of love and passion in life, need no comment other than to remind the reader that Dumas took an exactly opposite stand on this question in his later plays. The attitude here is that of the Romantic school, and the genealogy of Marguerite Gautier from Manon Lescaut and Marion Delorme is obvious. It is easy, then, to explain the origin of the work and its philosophy. What is difficult is to account for the great and enduring success of the play.

In this respect, *La Dame aux Camélias* has always

been the despair of the critics. The more they have in-sisted on finding it weak and unhealthy, false to life, and imperfect in its dramatic construction, the more per-sistently it has continued to live and to inspire its audi-ences with its nervous and vibrant vitality.

It is not that the critics are wrong in what they have found to blame in it. It is often puerile. The scenes are sometimes thin and ragged, and certainly some are out of date. The life it portrays is doubtless none too true, and even if it were true is worth little enough; its merit in this respect is its striking external realism. It has no philosophy to speak of, and is so far below Dumas's later standards of dramatic construction that he might very well have written it in a dream.

But with all that, it is, or ought to be, one of the finest object lessons in existence, to the critics as well as to others, to show in what consists one of the greatest dramatic resources. It has the power to reach and move an audience, — and an audience of the most varied sort. In fact, take away the critic's pen and shut him in with the thousand others for an evening, and he also will be moved and grow pale in the scenes between Mar-guerite and Armand, at the ball after their rupture, and will fight against tears in the final act of Marguerite's death.

Probably Dumas's greatest credit in the history of the French stage is his part in creating a theatre of ideas. Here, however, is a living proof that he, himself, did not need ideas to succeed as a playwright. In fact, this play shows why he did so regularly and so strikingly succeed in spite of his ideas. No dramatist ever preached more to his audiences than Dumas. Usually this would have been fatal and all his logic and all the skill and suspense of the *pièce bien faite* would hardly have saved him. *La Dame aux Camélias* explains how the born dramatist, with his father's instinct for all that holds and moves an audience, was able to carry on his nervous shoulders the triple burden of the moralist, of the preacher, and of the social reformer.

The drama has many weapons with which to win over its hearers, but none is so sure to conquer large numbers as passion. The dramatic thrill that is most general and most frequent is the thrill of deep emotion or feeling. Read the climactic scenes between Armand and Marguerite in the third, the fourth, and the fifth acts of this play as a proof. Admit that these persons are Romanticists or even neurotic sufferers. There are, none the less, situations in life when the emotional soul, be it love, longing, grief, despair, seems to rise to the lips and radiate its power. Dumas has known how to find those occasions and to translate *realistically* this emotion into words and dramatic scenes. It is not easy to find another play which shows more clearly the power of passion and feeling in the drama and demonstrates more conclusively that this quality may cover a multitude of dramatic sins.

Le Demi-Monde is probably Dumas's most important play. With it he inaugurated Social drama, a realistic study of the social problems of his day as he saw them manifested in the society of Paris with which he was acquainted. Moreover, in this play he shows clearly what his own attitude is to be toward the kind of social questions which almost exclusively interested him. He is no longer a follower of the Romanticists. Although obsessed quite as much as they were by the all-absorbing theme of love and passion, his philosophy is exactly the contrary of theirs. Marguerite Gautier, so sympathetically painted in *La Dame aux Camélias*, and known by so many aliases in Romantic literature, has here become Suzanne d'Ange, incapable of real love, heartless, an adventuress endeavoring to break into honorable society. She is judged and condemned by the sternest of moralists. Her attacks on honest society must be thwarted by all means, even, it would seem, by the most dishonorable.

However, *Le Demi-Monde* is not to be praised simply for creating Social drama and for illustrating the philosophy of its author. It has other good qualities and less common ones. Those mentioned above would alone hardly give it the honor, usually accorded, of being Dumas's masterpiece. It is, from the dramatic standpoint, one of his best constructed plays, the one perhaps in which he has put the largest number of his many striking merits as a dramatist and observer, and the fewest of his several faults as a thinker and moralist.

The dramatic technique of Dumas has been described as pouring the contents of Balzac's novels into the mold of Scribe's comedy. Both of these elements have an undeniable merit. With the first Dumas creates a theatre of ideas; or, more exactly, he restores thought to it after it had been emptied by passing through the hands of Scribe. The merit of the well-made play, to a certain extent at least, for the rigid application of its technique may be objected to, is no less certain. Drama is action, and if this is to mean anything and to interest an audience, it

must be action with a purpose and goal; it must have
a plot.

The chief weakness in Dumas's drama is not in either
of these two elements but in the difficulty of combining
the two so that the dual purpose may not mar the unity
of the play. This fault is sometimes found in his
pieces. The moralist occasionally halts the action to
preach, or to expound his theories; the showman frequently holds up the performers while he explains the
significance of their actions. In *Le Demi-Monde* this
dual purpose is rarely, if at all, apparent. The play is
most strongly knit. The attempt of Suzanne d'Ange to
break into honorable society, her cleverness and courage
and our more or less natural sympathy for a fight against
odds form the plot and hold the interest; and it is this
same attempt and its frustration that make the social
problem of the play.

It is not the intention to claim that *Le Demi-Monde*
is not open to some criticism. It is, but for the most
part this criticism is not fundamental. It is true that
Olivier de Jalin is the beginning of the long line of rea-
soners and preachers on the stage. But he is here first
of all an actor in the drama, and there is really little
to show that he will become unbearable later in the rôle
of de Ryons or Rémonin. A worse accusation against
Olivier is that the author has been unable to make him
as honorable and sympathetic as he intended. Much as
we may sympathize with his purpose to save his friend
from a heartless and unworthy adventuress, we are unable
to approve his methods. Even more, we quite deny his
right to throw stones, and when, in the end, his friend

calls him " *le plus honnête homme que je connaisse*," we openly revolt.   However, we should not forget that the play is after all primarily about Suzanne d'Ange.

Of all Dumas's plays, probably the one most characteristic of his manner and interests is *Le Fils Naturel*. In the first place, it deals directly with the subject of the illegitimate child, which, because of his own irregular birth, more constantly than any other subject preoccupies him.   However, this drama is mainly significant and interesting in the work of Dumas because it represents, as the first and most perfect model of his thesis plays, the final and inevitable phase of Social drama, not only in the hands of Dumas, but in those of nearly every dramatist who has essayed this genre.   It is perhaps not sufficiently recognized that the Thesis Play is an almost certain terminus on the road of Social drama, if it be not the precipice over which its authors often fall.

Certainly no one would think of denying the powerful renewal that came in the drama, as well as in the novel, through the study of man affected by his physical and social *milieu*.   The analogy, also, with the aims and methods of natural science, by which the drama was considerably influenced, is generally recognized.   None the less, it is easily possible to carry this analogy too far and to assume that the scientific spirit and method are equally applicable in literature.   This mistake has been made, in theory at least, by the extreme realists, by the Naturalists of the novel, such as Zola, and by some of his counterparts in the drama, such as the extremists of the Théâtre Libre.   These theorists overlook the fact — to mention but one difference — that the detached and dispassionate attitude of the scientist, who studies a rock or a plant in his laboratory, is entirely impossible for the dramatist, who studies the human heart; in other words, who confesses his soul and the souls of his hearers before a thousand of his fellow men, and for their delectation. Even could he, by the impossible, attain to this scientific detachment, it is certain that it would be before empty seats. A drama, a study of humanity, must warm by its emotion and its sympathy; the degree of coldness of the audience records its failure or its success.

Social drama, such as Dumas wrote, dealt with the important social problems of his day, with marriage, divorce, immorality, illegitimacy, and in general with many questions that come closest to life. Naturally the dramatist, as well as the audience, had his opinions and convictions on such questions. Under these circumstances, it is too much to expect him to be always judicial, an impartial seeker for the truth. He is making a plea before a jury, and his success is to move them and touch their sympathies. Writing, then, on a social question on which he has strong convictions and prejudices, he is tempted, inevitably, to make a plea, to maintain a thesis. Social drama tends naturally to the Thesis Play.

This inherent situation in Social drama and this inevitable state of mind of the dramatist have created the utilitarian theatre and the propaganda play. Admittedly, no one held such a conception of the mission of the theatre more strongly than Dumas fils, or did more to popularize this view.

" The theatre," he says in the Preface to *Le Fils Naturel*, " is not the goal; it is only a means to the goal.

Moral man has been determined. Social man is yet to be defined. A work that would do for good that which *Tartuffe* has done against evil would be superior to *Tartuffe*.

" Let us then, through comedy, through tragedy, through the drama, through burlesque, in whatsoever form suits us best, inaugurate the utilitarian stage, at the risk of hearing rail the apostles of Art for Art's sake, words absolutely devoid of sense. Any literature that does not aim at perfection, moralization, idealism, in short at the useful, is weak and unhealthy, born dead. Pure and simple reproduction of facts and of men is the work of a scribe or a photographer, and I defy anyone to cite a single writer consecrated by time who has not had for purpose the improvement of humanity."

But the rôle of Dumas as a moralist and reformer is too well known to need further comment here. What has not been so clearly recognized, perhaps, is that Social drama tends naturally to become the Thesis Play, and that the Thesis Play is, by definition largely, and by practice certainly, a plea more or less one-sided. However, as one may see with *Le Fils Naturel* as an example, this does not mean that such plays may not be the most moving and effective of dramas.

When *Le Fils Naturel* is looked at critically, we can see that all the virtues and merits have been put on the side of the mother and son, and that all the wrongs and antipathetic qualities are charged to the account of the father and his family. No doubt that is the reason why the play may arouse our sympathy and move us to indignation even, without our feeling in the end entirely satisfied that the last word has been said. Certainly, when we once accept the data of this play, the *donnée,* we find it hard to escape the conclusions of the author. His faultless logic and intense dramatic movement carry us along to the dénouement without a chance, or perhaps even a desire, for escape. It is only if we have the curiosity to return to the point where we were swept into the stream that we become aware how carefully the ways were oiled for our downfall.

It might be expected that the utilitarian stage and the propaganda play, so widely popularized by Dumas, would find a sympathetic reception in America. We are probably inclined, nationally, to the utilitarian in art, as elsewhere, and the success of this form with us is abundantly exemplified in recent years. Every movement, in fact almost every society or organization, be it ever so far removed from literary interests, has had its propaganda play. Whether this gives promise of good drama or not, it is, at least, a striking testimony to our fondness for the dramatic genre, just as it is also evidence of the far-reaching influence of French models.

Dumas was far from being a simple realist. He really escaped from the Romantic fold through being a moralist. But this quality of a moralist, which controls him at all times, may not only carry him into realism, but through and beyond it into the realms of imagination and symbolism. The indignant preacher may dwell on his subject until he becomes the inspired, or perhaps the mad, prophet. Nowhere is this clearer than in tracing the development of Dumas with regard to the one character he has so constantly pictured, the courtesan, from her appearance in his first play to his supreme vision of her in *La Femme de Claude*. Marguerite Gautier was borrowed from Romantic fiction and merely staged realistically by Dumas. Before his next play, the moralist had had time to consider her character seriously and he pictures her in her true light, as Suzanne in *Le Demi-Monde*, cold and self-seeking, although still with the paint and charm of her butterfly stage in Marguerite. In *Un Père Prodigue*, she is Albertine, with the paint rubbed off, not only selfish but mercenary; all pretense of love is dropped. She ruins men with indifference to secure money to maintain her effrontery. In Suzanne and Albertine we have the most realistic conceptions, and perhaps Suzanne is truer to life than Albertine.

In Césarine, the wife of Claude, we find the preacher turned prophet and seeing visions. The courtesan has become a symbol of evil, magnified, a monster of the Apocalypse, threatening destruction to all France. This is not an exaggeration, as will be seen from Dumas's own words in the preface to this play, where he explains his vision of this subject. He looks down at Paris and sees it as " a great melting pot where God makes his experiments."

" I was at this point in my observations, and I was asking myself what would become of us and whether we should not, in the end, be asphyxiated by these poisoners of our atmosphere, when I saw an enormous bubble appear in the cauldron; and there came forth, not simply from the scum and smoke but from the basic matter of the contents, a colossal Beast, which had seven heads and ten horns, and on its horns ten

diadems, and on its heads hair of the color of the metal and
alcohol which gave it birth.

   •   •   •   •   •   •   •   •   •

"At certain moments, this Beast, which I thought to
recognize as the one seen by Saint John, gave forth from
all her body an intoxicating vapor, through which she appeared
radiant as the most beautiful angel of God, and in which came,
by thousands, to sport, to tremble with delight, to scream with
pain, and finally to evaporate, the anthropomorphic animal-
cules whose birth had preceded hers.

   •   •   •   •   •   •   •   •   •

"This Beast could not be sated. To go faster, she crushed
some under her feet, she tore some with her claws, she ground
some with her teeth, she stifled some beneath her body.

   •   •   •   •   •   •   •   •   •

"Now, this Beast was none other than a new incarnation
of woman, resolved to revolt in her turn. After thousands of
years of slavery and helplessness, in spite of the conventions
maintained by the theatre, this victim of man had wished to
overcome him, and thinking to break the bonds of her slavery
by breaking those of modesty, she had risen up, armed with
all her beauty, all her cunning and all her apparent weakness."

This remarkable passage, we must remember, was written by the same hand which drew Marguerite and her
companions so realistically that their prototypes were
identified by all Paris and the censor refused to pass the
play. It was such plays as the one based on this vision
and *L'Etrangère* that caused the Naturalists to attack
Dumas's realism, and that led Zola to say that Dumas
used observation and reality only as a spring-board from
which to leap into the realm of theory and imagination.
The accusation is not wholly true, for these are not his

most characteristic plays, but such flights of theory were always temptations to Dumas.

Dumas himself would have wished to be judged by his moral effect, although it is certain that his influence is primarily dramatic. Some of the tasks he set were: to reconstruct the family code on the basis of justice, equality and love, and to free the woman and child from unfair laws. He attacks the importance of money as vitiating marriage, and all lack of morals that endangers family life. He wishes to reform the prejudices and laws that seem to him unjust, particularly those concerning marriage and divorce, and he uses the stage as a tribune to propose these reforms. In doing this, Dumas often saw only one side of the question, and his attacks are sometimes unjust and his remedies insufficient, but they are always presented with dramatic force, and with a logic that is hard to refute if once we accept the premises.

Dumas's character drawing is subordinate to other interests. In fact, this situation is somewhat inherent in Social drama, although we see in a writer such as his contemporary, Augier, that this subordination is in no way necessary. One character, or rather type, which Dumas has created, is of special interest. This is the reasoner, the moralist of the drama, found in most of Dumas's pieces. It is, of course, Dumas himself, showing his actors and pointing out the lessons of the play. Substantially the entire spiritual life of Dumas can be found in this character.

His women are usually fragile, if not deceitful, and good women are rare in his plays. One might say that he has at least popularized, if he has not created, the modern type of the *femme troublante*. His men are perhaps no better morally than his women, being most frequently egotistic, if not odious. Of course, much of this is inherent in his subjects, which for their presentation most often demand the idle, dissipated or pleasure-loving classes.

Dumas's dramatic art is exceptional, and his plays are among the best constructed of the modern stage. Everything leads straight to the dénouement, which, according to his own words, should be as inevitable as the answer to a mathematical problem. This faultless, and doubtless over-logical construction has been attacked, particularly by the writers of the Théâtre Libre, about 1880–1890, but it is yet to be proved that it is wrong, except in over-emphasis.

In judging the final value of Dumas's plays, we must say that they do not present any very complete picture of French life. But what he does give is highly dramatic. His plays are moving — perhaps, also, they irritate and exasperate us with their faultless logic, which does not always satisfy and convince. His greatest contribution is to be found in the works of his contemporaries and successors. If his own work has not always lived, much of it does survive in the writings of others, and it is only after considering some of these, and particularly Augier, that we can fairly pass judgment on the real value and possibilities of this drama of which he was the chief creator.

However, while reserving judgment on many of the possibilities in Dumas's drama, we may draw conclusions at once on some outstanding features. He brought drama back to realities, recaptured it from imagination and impulse, restored it to its traditional French guardian, rationalism, and endowed it with serious thought and purpose.

These are inestimable services which outweigh all his faults, of which some at least are obvious and important. He relied too much on logic and not enough on experience, he turned the drama decisively toward propaganda, and his dramatic success in treating immoral love aided in forming a school where any second-rate author could master the triangle play and find a market for his talents.

CHAPTER VIII

EMILE AUGIER (1820–1889)

EMILE AUGIER is sometimes given an equal credit and a prior date to those granted to Dumas fils in inaugurating Realistic Social drama. It would be ungrateful to question this claim to honor for a writer who has at least rendered the cause services equally great, if the assumption did not seem to obscure the particular genius of Augier and find contradiction in the dates and real qualities of his plays. Dumas was certainly the pioneer who first explored the realistic field and raised the flag over these new outposts of drama. Not only did Augier lack Dumas's native audacity, but his greater acquaintance with, and affection for, the earlier established forms of the theatre held him back. However, it was he who consolidated most of the positions chosen by Dumas. With his wider experience, his richer training, and especially his breadth, poise and unalterable good sense, he judged and completed the work of his colleague; some of these outposts he rejected as too dangerous, others he reconstructed, and practically all he strengthened, so that if these systems of drama have lasted down to the present day, much of the credit is due to Augier.

It was not until two years after the appearance of *La Dame aux Camélias* — and five after its composition — that Augier gave his first outright realistic drama, *Le*

Gendre de M. Poirier, in 1854. Up to that time all his significant plays had been in verse and in the style of the School of Good Sense. No doubt *Gabrielle* is realistic in its details of every-day life, but both its verse form and its adherence to the unities hamper its necessary freedom as a realistic play. Its real significance is its attack on Romantic philosophy; and Augier's verse plays that followed this one during the next four years prove that he might, like Ponsard, have continued longer in this reactionary genre, if it had not been for Dumas's illuminating success in his realistic picture of contemporary society. Augier himself confirms this originality of Dumas both by following his example with *Le Gendre de M. Poirier* in 1854, and by attacking his early philosophy with *Le Mariage d'Olympe* in 1855.

Our main effort, then, should not be to discover a pioneer of the Realistic Social theatre in Augier, but on the contrary to appreciate in him the finest and most finished product of that school, and at the same time one of the best and most genuine French dramatists of the nineteenth century, whose sincere, virile and solid plays, national in every line, are one of the real assets of French literature and are worthy of appreciation and emulation everywhere.

Augier has been too little known in America and other countries. As has frequently been the case later, we have imported flimsier and more questionable authors and pieces, and then have criticized French morals and literature with these as a basis. Such criticism may be warranted, but before we can use it to set up a superiority of Anglo-Saxon taste or moral standards, we must explain

why we pass over the more solid and worthy pieces for
the more sensational plays. Augier has had no such
public hearing in this country as Dumas, or even as
Sardou and Bernstein. Yet among his plays are several
of the nearest genuine masterpieces of nineteenth century
realistic French drama, and every one of his twenty-five
acknowledged pieces can be read today with pleasure
and interest, and often with the maximum profit for their
insight into the life and ideals of the French people.
Moreover, the moral standards they set are as high, as
sincere, and as truly national as any we can predicate as
criterions by which to judge other literatures.

Whatever may be our explanation for this and similar
neglect on our part — none can fully justify it — it will
probably rest on the general principle that the themes
and qualities of Augier's dramas are more completely
national and less exportable that those of certain other
dramatists. His plays are deeply rooted in French soil
and life and their subjects deal with the fundamental
French virtues. They are defences of the home, the
family, the sanctity of marriage and sound morals against
the pernicious effects of money, luxury and immorality,
and they illustrate the commoner French qualities of
labor, economy, sobriety and democracy. Naturally such
plays do not offer many startling headlines for the posters
of theatrical managers, and their adequate appreciation
calls for some knowledge of French life, but they are worth
the effort. Moreover, these plays deal with a period of
history when French society faced many problems similar
to our own today, and the reader of Augier's pieces will
constantly be impressed by their contemporary interest.

Augier was born at Valence in the south of France, but at eight years of age came with his family to Paris, where his father bought a notary's practice. He was of good bourgeois stock. At Paris he received a sound education, especially in the classics, and was a solid and even brilliant student. He then entered the law school, and, after his studies there, was placed in a lawyer's office to complete his reading — which he did in the field of literature and the drama.

His contact with gay or Bohemian life, with which Dumas was so familiar, is evidently slight, although one of his biographers relates how the young law student and two of his friends made a figure in these circles about this time, possessed of one dress suit, which they wore by turns, and a single, inalienable gold coin.

From an early age he was drawn to the theatre, and before leaving college had written plays, which he later destroyed. His first published play, *La Ciguë*, represented at the Odéon when he was only twenty-four, was quite successful, and from that time he devoted himself entirely to the stage. Nearly all of his plays were well received. It is especially to be noted that his life was a happy and uneventful one. When asked to give his autobiography, he stated that he was born in 1820 and since then nothing had ever happened to him.

Unlike Dumas he had no grudge against society. The key to his character, however, is his liberal bourgeois spirit. This stands for order and stability and explains his championing of the family as the base of society. The bourgeois is notable for his support of religion and established government, and we note Augier's hostility to the monarchist party. He has some of the restrictions of the bourgeois, but no one of his time saw more clearly the faults and vices of this class. The bourgeois class represents good sense and balance, and Augier avoids extremes; it holds stubbornly to its opinions, is not fond of abstract speculation, and clings to general ideas — those of the majority — and Augier reflects all of this in an enlightened way. In short, he was of the same race as Molière, of the school of good sense and good humor, with conservative leanings, and a liberal spirit.

Augier's dramatic career ran as smoothly as his life, since it was not marked by any startling event or metamorphosis. It is true that his work has been classed in three periods — since all Gaul was divided into three parts few French writers have escaped a similar fate — but to say that he had a verse period, a period of Social drama, and a period of Political-Social satire is very misleading. There is only one real division of his work. His first eight plays are, with one exception, written in verse, and the Classic influence in them is sufficiently marked to include them in the so-called School of Good Sense.

His significant work in the field of realistic prose drama begins with *Le Gendre de M. Poirier*. This play, for which a certain credit must also be given to Jules Sandeau, since it is founded on his novel, *Sacs et Parchemins*, is Augier's masterpiece, and has often had the honor of being called the model comedy of the nineteenth century.

The theme of the play is the uniting of the two classes, the nobility and the bourgeois, an important problem in France after the Revolution. Augier has treated it with

surprising breadth. The Marquis de Présles has the
courage, refinement, and liberality of his class, but also
the vices — its idleness, its arrogant pride and its contempt for the positive interests of life. The bourgeois
in M. Poirier is industrious; he has amassed a fortune
by honest diligence. He has common sense and good
intentions, a desire for the welfare of himself first, but
of society also. But he is vain, and his ambitions make
him ridiculous. He is, moreover, too materialistic, and
too narrow. The climactic scene of his clash with his
son-in-law shows the master hand of Augier.

GASTON. " Come in then, Hector, come in! Do you know
why Jean Gaston de Presles received three crossbow bolts at
the battle of Ivry? Do you know why François Gaston de
Presles was first in the storming of La Rochelle? Why Louis
Gaston de Presles had his ship sunk at La Hogue? Why Philip
Gaston de Presles captured two flags at Fontenoy? Why my
grandfather was killed at Quiberon? It was so that M.
Poirier might some day be knighted and become a baron."

THE DUKE (*aside*). " I understand."

POIRIER. " Do you know why, Sir Duke, I have worked
fourteen hours a day for thirty years? Why I have earned, sou
by sou, four million francs, while depriving myself of everything? It was in order that the Marquis Gaston de Presles,
who wasn't killed either at Quiberon, at Fontenoy, at La
Hogue, or anywhere else, might die of old age on a feather
bed, after having spent his life doing nothing." [1]

Augier has resolved his problem by reforming Gaston
and uniting the two classes through the young noble's
marriage with Poirier's daughter, Antoinette; in which
solution the author has been well inspired and largely

[1] Act III, scene III.

justified by recent history. His argument would be that woman is best fitted to unite, in her sympathies, both classes, having less prejudice and less stubbornness, perhaps, and in any case more adaptability, a natural elegance and capacity for rising to any social position. Fortunately, Augier has not tried to reform M. Poirier, who stands as a master portrait in dramatic literature.

Le Mariage d'Olympe, in 1855, is a somewhat delayed reply to Dumas's *Dame aux Camélias,* and is an indignant protest against the rehabilitation of the courtesan, or her admission into an honorable family, a protest so violent that it ends by killing her on the stage — which also killed the play. It is certain that such acts of violence will always be difficult of acceptance in France, and this accounts for the play's failure. However, despite some strong scenes, it is doubtful if the critics are justified who put this among the best works of Augier. Above all, it lacks his usual balance — owing doubtless to its controversial inspiration — and this in its basic conception of character. Suzanne d'Ange, who is Dumas's own apology for Marguerite Gautier, is a much more reasonable conception. What reason is there to believe that if Olympe were given a respectable position in society she would not have maintained it, at least in appearance? There is really, then, little justification for the *nostalgie de la boue* by which she is supposed by Augier to be affected. The author's thesis in this play was due to his extreme susceptibility when family honor was menaced, and to his strong reaction against the philosophy of the courtesan redeemed by love. But Olympe is as extreme as Marguerite, and Augier has a large enough balance of merit and good sense to assume an occasional mistake of this kind, without his standing being affected.

Augier's *Ceinture Dorée,* in 1855, treating marriage and tainted fortunes, is an interesting and worthy play, giving a good picture of the unscrupulous father, but it is not among his finest dramas. The next one, however, *La Jeunesse,* in 1858, is both in theme and characters one of the author's most vital plays — and this despite the fact that Augier has again returned to verse, with a realistic subject, and that one can find marked objections to the plot and dénouement. In this piece he not only depicts an unforgettable clash between the idealistic love of youth and the realistic experience of age, but also puts in opposition the simple, contented life of the country with the feverish excitement and luxury of the city. It is, in fact, a strong plea for a return to the soil and to the simple life, and is today, in its motives, one of the most modern of Augier's plays, touching subjects that appeal to youth everywhere.

Les Lionnes pauvres, in 1858, written with Edouard Foussier, is similar in tone and characters to *Le Mariage d'Olympe,* but it is specifically a protest against the danger to morals found in the luxury of Augier's time. It is a strong play, but not agreeable reading, the depths of depravity being touched. In fact, it is so many shades darker than the author's usual optimism allows, that we naturally suspect the hand of his collaborator, more than is generally the case. Sometimes these collaborators seem to have done little more than sign at the end. *Un beau Mariage,* by the same two authors, deals with Augier's most frequent theme, money and marriage, and although clever and interesting, is not the most significant of such pieces.

Beginning with *Les Effrontés* in 1861, there is a trilogy of political-social dramas, of which the other two members are *Le Fils de Giboyer,* in 1862, and *Lions et Renards,* in 1869. Not only are these pieces on the same general themes, but the author dares to repeat the same characters. The three plays read together give an impression of dramatic power that is indubitable — in many ways they are among the strongest of Augier's work. However, it is in these that we see some of the restrictions of the bourgeois in Augier; his prejudice against the Jesuits and the royalists makes it difficult for him to maintain the balance or fairness which in general is his most striking merit. Also, quite naturally, the change in parties and politics has caused some parts of this work to age rapidly. Of these plays the most perfect is doubtless *Le Fils de Giboyer,* and in the character, Giboyer, who is found also in *Les Effrontés,* the dramatist has again hung an original and strikingly life-like picture in the gallery of drama.

This last merit is also the outstanding one of the *Maître Guérin,* in 1864. As a dramatic character Guérin yields to none of Augier's creations, and, of all, he is drawn with the greatest fullness of line and detail. Because of this, critics have often placed *Maître Guérin* alongside *Le Gendre de M. Poirier,* as a masterpiece. As a strong dramatic portrait such evaluation is justified, but in other respects this play not only falls below *Poirier,* but several others of Augier as well. Above all, it lacks unity and simplicity of plot. On the other hand,

it rises nearest, both in conception and effect, to the
character comedy of Molière, and Guérin, himself, could
be acknowledged without loss of prestige by the great
master of comedy.

La Contagion, in 1866, is an attack on cynicism, and is
obviously a play into which the author has put some of
his inmost convictions. It is interesting to note the many
striking parallels to be found in theme and ideas between
this play and Rostand's *Chantecler.* Both dramatists evidently felt most deeply on this matter of skepticism.
Paul Forestier, in 1868, another relapse into verse, is
hardly up to the author's usual standard of this period,
and the same might be said of *Jean de Thommeray,* in
1873. The latter play, following the war of 1870, is
intensely patriotic and recalls Dumas's *Femme de Claude,*
in tone and purpose.

Augier's last two pieces, *Mme Caverlet,* in 1876, which
deals with divorce and is one of Augier's rare outright
thesis plays, and *Les Fourchambault,* in 1878, a domestic
drama, are both interesting and up to a high standard.
In fact, Augier, with his usual moderation and good sense,
stopped writing in the full maturity of his dramatic power.

Except in some of his verse plays, where the realistic
thought is often not in accord with the verse form, Augier's
style is admirable: correct, adapted to his characters,
idiomatic and even racy. A special merit is the author's
rare power in using the *mot propre* without being vulgar.
He is less keenly witty than Dumas, but is more naturally
so, and especially is more humorous.

In technique, Augier adopted the *pièce bien faite* as the
basis of his plot, but again he differs notably from Dumas.

In general, his plots are less breathless and the characters do not seem so driven by the action. This is one of the absolute merits of Augier, that he has, on the whole, been able to defend the independence of his characters both against the narrowness of the well-made play and the encroachments of a social thesis. His action uses suspense as did Scribe's and is perfectly balanced, but it is genuinely motivated in its characters and is less exciting, but more natural, than the plots of Dumas.

Augier's constant themes are money and marriage, or, since he treats marriage largely as affected by money or luxury, we might fairly say that the influence of money is the center of nearly all of his plays. His justification for this theme is not only the great rôle that money plays in modern society, but its particular importance at the time he wrote. In the period of striking industrial expansion of the Second Empire, the sudden wave of commercial prosperity, with its flood of newly acquired riches and luxury, threatened to sweep away or demoralize the racial virtues of honest labor, economy and morality, despite the anchors of home and family. Dumas also defended the family, but against a much more restricted peril, passion and immoral love. This distinction accounts for much in the different character and appeal of the plays of these two writers. The drama of passion of Dumas is undoubtedly of readier appeal — its emotion is in the range of all. Augier's subjects are often soberer, but their import is wider and much more serious.

There is even another distinction that is important between these two authors as moralists. Dumas's morality

is that of the converted sinner turned preacher. His
language and figures, then, are of the evangelist, colored
by the fire and smoke through which he has passed; they
are frequently picturesque and sometimes lurid, but are
often warped by an overheated imagination. Augier's
morality is innate. Its expression is quieter and more
natural, and more effective in its unconscious assumption
of the cardinal virtues. Above all, it is never merely
theoretic; it is the inherent age-long morality of honorable people. This distinction, perhaps a trifle exaggerated, has been keenly expressed by a *bon mot* of Augier,
himself, who, when asked what he thought of the moral
code of Dumas, replied: "*J'aime mieux l'autre.*"

The above distinction suggests the really fundamental
difference between these two authors, which affects not
only their moral conceptions but their whole work: action,
plot, characters and life. Dumas relies continually on
logic and formal reasoning; Augier tempers his logic by
real experience and good sense. Both of these attitudes
are dominated by racial French qualities, only Augier's
is much better balanced and is truer to the usual French
rationalism.

Dumas was really a one-sided genius. His rigidly
logical conclusions are often brilliant, perhaps even irre-
futable, but, unfortunately, sometimes existent only in
reason and impractical in experience. Many things seem
logically most obvious and urgent and are still impossible.
The rat orator in La Fontaine's fable demonstrated conclusively the need to bell the cat; what he lacked as a
real savior of his race was the reflection of experience.
Augier wastes no time belling cats.

The only fundamental principle that has been seriously attacked in Augier's plays is his philosophy of optimism. As for the element of this which is due to the practice of the *pièce bien faite,* it seems just to admit that Augier's dénouements were occasionally given an optimistic twist to fit the Scribe form. But even this is partly inherent in the kind of drama Augier wrote. His theatre deals prevailingly with characters whose principles are sufficiently sound to carry them safely through the tests to which they are put. To believe such characters exist in life is optimism, and it is a philosophy. To see only hopelessly weak, vicious or immoral characters is a philosophy also, pessimism. Augier is frankly an optimist, but he is also a sensible one, and it is hard to see a reproach in this.

The surest test of the higher value of a dramatic author is to be found in his characters, which give the measure of his insight into life and of his philosophy. Augier has without question left the richest gallery of dramatic portraits of any French playwright of the nineteenth century, and this in a form of the theatre which seems, at first thought at least, to lead away from the comedy of character to realistic details and social problems. Obviously this is a supreme accomplishment.

It should be noted that Augier's characters stand up under the double test: they are both types and individuals. They are not mere abstractions, nor are they so exceptional as to be unrepresentative.

The Marquis de Presles and M. Poirier, as representatives respectively of the nobility and of the *bourgeoisie,* have become classics. Poirier especially is a picture of the bourgeois of which every line is worthy to be engraved and preserved unchangeable. Nowhere else, within so narrow a space, has a more perfect idea been given of one of the strongest elements of the French race: its common sense, its industry and economy, its stubborn force and its stability; and also its exasperating routine. Of course no one would expect a single portrait to depict a whole class, that begins just above the peasant and laborer and rises to include the most cultured and most eminent men of France. Also Augier has given many other representatives of this class, in various stations and situations. But one might say that Poirier is the frame, the chassis, on which he constructs them all: Verdelet, Roussel, Charrier, Vernouillet, Maréchal, Tenancier, Guérin and how many others! Strip them of the coverings requisite for their special model, their trimmings and their color, and you will find the lines of Poirier on which they are built.

Maître Guérin is one of Augier's most completely painted characters, and the result has justified the effort. Guérin is a notary and a rascal, who always manages to cheat his clients and stay within the letter of the law. Why be a lawyer otherwise! In reality he is much more than that; he is a nineteenth century Harpagon. He worships money as much as Molière's miser did and goes as far to have it. Like him, he has lost all feelings, even those most nearly inalienable — family affections. His wife and his son leave him, and he remains impenitent, scarcely touched by this catastrophe. There is but one essential difference between the conceptions of Molière and of Augier, and this is the fundamental one between

Character Comedy and Social Comedy. Harpagon is stressed in the universal traits of a miser, his pure love of money, his passion to handle it and gloat over it. Guérin is a product of his age and environment. He wishes money for its power, and he gets it by dishonest speculation rather than by usurious and fraudulent interest. Also, instead of putting it in a strong box and burying it, he buys a château and a title — there are so many opportunities open to the bourgeois of the nineteenth century that were not available in the seventeenth.

What is interesting is to note how much Guérin has in common with Poirier. There is the same strength, the same practical sense, the same cunning in making a deal, and the same vanity and lack of delicacy. The one great difference is that Guérin is an outright scoundrel while Poirier is not consciously dishonest.

But Augier has created a character more original and more a product of his age than Guérin. This is Giboyer, who appears in two plays, *Les Effrontés* and *Le Fils de Giboyer*. Giboyer is a porter's son, who by chance has been given a higher education, and who does not have the necessary strength of moral fiber to rise and establish himself firmly against the handicap of poverty and the lack of influential friends. He is one of the problems created by higher education. It is not this education, of course, that is responsible for his lack of principles, but it may increase his power to harm. He sells his pen, his talent, and his convictions to the highest bidder of a venal press. He misleads the public by doctrines that he disbelieves and detests, because he needs money. He even descends to journalistic blackmail.

Giboyer is really a sinister feature of his times, and of our own day. He is found not only in the press but in politics and business. He is the political editor who is hired for his effective sophistry, but he might be the clever lawyer engaged to manage a shady business deal.

The most life-like touch in Giboyer's character is his love and sacrifice for his son. He is not wholly bad, and in reality all this prostitution of his talent and principles is due to the desire to provide for his son, to educate him and to make him an honorable man.

This has raised an interesting question. Critics have often treated Giboyer most kindly and claimed that he was at heart sound. Such views seem purely sentimental and emphasize the warning to be found in this character. If he were more obviously a scoundrel, Giboyer would not be dangerous. But his private virtues do not atone for the harm he does, and are even the cause for it. Parental affection does not justify vice, venality, blackmail, and the moral and political perversion of the people. Giboyer is only a sympathetic rascal — one of the most dangerous sort.

Wholly sympathetic characters, both men and women, are numerous in Augier's plays and are thoroughly well drawn. In his young women and girls, especially, he has an insight and understanding that are rare with French dramatists, and in which he can be compared with Musset. Philiberte, in the play with this title, is a sympathetic and entirely charming example of the young girl, and in such characters as Antoinette, in *Poirier,* he has shown his ability to draw with a few strokes young women who have poise, feeling, idealism and real strength.

A feminine character of a different sort, and which does not seem to have attracted all the attention it deserves, is that of Mme Huguet in *La Jeunesse*. The realism, sound psychologic insight and strong lines of this creation are superb, and should put this among Augier's most significant plays. Mme Huguet is the mother of Philip, the young lawyer of ordinary ability, who is in love with his dowerless cousin, Cyprienne. The mother had, herself, married a man of small fortune and mediocre talent, and her life had been the long struggle of an energetic woman to aid her husband to rise and to keep up appearances, in a social circle more ambitious than the one in which she had begun.

Philip has been trained by his mother's precepts, and such is his character that when he is offered the choice between a rich marriage without love and a long struggle in narrow circumstances with Cyprienne, he hesitates. On the one hand he has as example his sister, married to a farmer and content with a simple life, and on the other the worldly experience and arguments of his mother. To persuade him, she lays bare her own life in one of the most masterly realistic scenes of Augier's drama. The passage is too long to quote entire, but its quality can be judged from a few speeches, chosen from Mme Huguet's recital of her early romance, their struggles with poverty, and the loss of illusions and idealism.

MME HUGUET. " Motherhood came soon. . . . What shall I say to you? The rich have truly a noble privilege, for which they should be envied by intelligent people, and which justifies the pride of money. It is the power to keep at a distance the degrading facts of common existence, and not to allow

their contact to lessen the higher things life may offer to man.
With them a mother is still a woman, whose motherhood only
enlarges the soul, and takes from it nothing of former joy,
but doubles it by doubling her heart. For she still has the
leisure to be a wife; she remains charming and eager to please.
The maternal duty which she has reserved is to cherish the
child, bathed by other hands. With us she is a slave; per-
force she gives up the care of her mind and that of her person,
so that charm disappears from her and her house, and love
follows charm, and love is right."

And as to the effect of this life on mind and character,
she adds:

" Inevitably one changes character; of parsimony one makes
constant study; the petty interests that he once despised
absorb him gradually, increased by need, and the noble im-
pulses, the sublime fancies which have brought us to these
bitter hours find themselves replaced in a disillusioned heart
by the bitter regret for what they have cost. One day your
father — "

PHILIP. " Enough, enough! — One day my father? "

MME HUGUET. " Your father returned one day more serious, and considering closely my dress: ' Take care,' he said,
' you are getting old.' He had just seen rich, happy, and
elegant, the woman whom he had formerly rejected! "

PHILIP. " It is not true! You mean — you still loved each
other! You wish to discourage me by these somber words.
But against your story my whole being protests. My Cyprienne! An angel! A daughter of heaven. No, no! She
was created for my happiness. . . ."

MME HUGUET. " I also was an angel when your father
married me, and I have become, under the breath of poverty,
a creature as practical as a business man. What this poor
child would become, you can see! " [2]

[2] Act IV, scene V.

A more vivid evocation of all that is hardening for a woman in this struggle with poverty and for petty economy would be difficult to find, as would a more perfect product of such life than Mme Huguet. She is so convincing, indeed, that the author must seriously wrench the logic of events, to give the victory in the end, as he does, to youth, love and idealism. No doubt the questions at stake can not be as poignant to us as to the French, who have no such abundant opportunity to acquire wealth as is found in this country, but our youth also will find, in this play, problems of gripping intensity.

The salient features of Augier's drama have been characterized, but a brief consideration is peculiarly inadequate to give an idea of his full worth. A summary treatment may well suffice with a dramatist whose power lies in some master quality, but in this case the supreme merit is precisely one of ensemble, including numerous factors. It is this broad appeal that offers his greatest excellence and promise of durable worth. A strikingly popular success may be had by a play that exploits a single dramatic virtue; exciting action in *La Tour de Nesle;* or passionate emotion in *La Dame aux Camélias.* But such plays do not entirely satisfy. The spiritual nature has its center of gravity, its mental and moral poise, quite as much as the physical body, and whatever tends to throw it violently off its balance is disconcerting and is sure to result in quick reaction. A play strikingly exciting in this way brings immediate revulsion, and we leave the theatre after such an experience depressed, perhaps saddened or disgusted, rather than satisfied or inspired. Furthermore, a single dramatic appeal, be it action, passion or any other, is too narrow a foundation for the support of a dramatic system. It is too quickly covered; a broader field is required. This suggests the solid worth of Augier. He appeals to the whole man. With his liberal observation and impartial judgment, his honest and instructive morality and belief in the good, he has given us the most balanced dramatic expression in his century of bourgeois society, and, in fact, one of the most important in French literature. His limitations are those implied in the word bourgeois, taken in its widest acceptation, and of optimist, used in its best sense. But the bourgeois, or great middle class, is the heart of France, and optimism is the philosophy on which the hope and progress of the world are built.

CHAPTER IX

OTHER DRAMATISTS OF THE REALISTIC THEATRE

LABICHE, PAILLERON, SARDOU

To place in a single chapter authors so diverse in qualities and genres as Labiche, Pailleron and Sardou, would seem equivalent to making a pigeonhole for the miscellaneous, for those who are not important enough to have each an individual label. This is in part the case but there are additional and more logical reasons for grouping them. What distinguishes dramatists such as Augier and Dumas is the serious character of their work, its durable worth, or at least its important influence in the history of the theatre. On the contrary, the chief aim of the three writers above has obviously been to amuse or entertain for the moment; the interest of most of their plays has been brief and their influence on the drama has rarely gone beyond drawing crowds to the theatre. However, each of these authors might properly be called a master in certain respects, and this is a distinction sufficiently great to warrant their treatment here, in preference to a number of other popular playwrights of this period.

EUGÈNE LABICHE (1815–1888)

Eugène Labiche was the greatest French humorist of the nineteenth century stage. He was not thinking of

171

literary merit in writing his plays and he intended them merely to amuse, but in spite of this, he has produced, along with many farces and vaudevilles, some worthwhile comedy.

Labiche was a Parisian, virile, with an unusual fund of common sense and without the slightest pretensions. He wrote for the minor theatres and those specializing in the comic genres, and the popularity of his hundred fifty-odd plays, produced mostly between 1845 and 1875, brought him a fortune.

He had attracted little attention from the serious followers of the theatre and had already retired from active writing, when he was induced by his friend Augier to collect and publish about a third of his plays. These collected works brought a chorus of praise; the critics discovered in him a real master of the humorous or comic genre, and the approval was so general that he was elected to the French Academy in 1880. In this decided reaction in his favor he was probably exalted into a greater author than he was in fact; he laughed over his candidacy for the Academy and said that if he were an Academician he would not vote for himself. With all that, the passage of time seems to confirm the absolute value of a certain part of his work.

Labiche's plays may be put in two groups. By far the greater number are pure farce comedies, such as *Le Chapeau de Paille d'Italie* and *La Cagnotte*, intended only to amuse, and without serious thought or application to life. There are, however, a few, of which *Le Voyage de M. Perrichon*, *La Poudre aux Yeux* and *Le Misanthrope et l'Auvergnat* are perhaps the best known, that have in addition a vein of philosophy which gives them greater import and higher rank. It is in these latter that his more durable merit and his interest for the reader are found, although the first class had an equal share in his stage success. What the two classes have in common is their system of the comic and the fact that they are practically all caricatures of petty bourgeois vices: narrowness, egotism and stupidity. Labiche's comic system and the force of this ridicule form the chief interest of his theatre.

All of Labiche's plays have as their main object to create laughter by any means possible, and usually by processes that are quite mechanical. The most frequent of all of these methods is the *qui pro quo,* the mistaking of one person or thing for another: a janitor for a senator, a butler for a prime minister, or some one who wears the wrong coat for its owner.

Obviously such means are a large resource of farce comedy everywhere and are worn threadbare — although they still serve wonderfully to excite laughter — but Labiche has built them into a system of the comic which has the merit of recalling the farcical side of Molière. Also, like Molière's comedy, Labiche's plays show a large strain of Gallic genius and go back to the medieval farce for their source.

Perhaps there is no author who illustrates more perfectly than Labiche Bergson's essay on the philosophy of laughter, and it is interesting to see how long it has taken a serious subject like philosophy to find names and a theory for a secret known by comic writers since *Pathelin,* and before. If Labiche had been living in

1900, when this essay appeared, he would probably have been as astonished over his philosophic system as M. Jourdain was to learn that he had always been speaking prose.

Bergson has called attention to the fact that the comic regularly has in it something of the mechanical stiffness of the automaton. We laugh at the stiff wooden figures that represent human beings, the eternal comic of the puppet show, or at human beings who imitate wooden figures. We are amused at a person who is so awkward as to fall, or to involve himself in some other mishap. Further, it is only the *human* that amuses; an object of nature, a landscape, a tree, or even an animal is not amusing unless it, in some way, has human attributes or suggests a human being. Also the comic appeal is greatest when it is not accompanied with emotion, deep feeling or sentiment; heartless laughter is frequent but soulful laughter is rare. From these characteristics Bergson deduces a definition of laughter, or, more exactly, he indicates its function by stating that "this mechanical stiffness of the automaton is the principle of the comic and that laughter is society's defence against this automatic ineptness, that laughter is, so to speak, the punishment of stupidity."

Labiche's farces illustrate perfectly the above principles. His characters resemble strikingly automatons in their senseless actions and stiff repetitions of the same movement or word. In *Le Chapeau de Paille*, Nonancourt carries about his pot of myrtle for a whole day, and each time he encounters his future son-in-law cries "*Tout est rompu.*" Colladan, in *La Cagnotte*, takes his pick-axe through all the boulevards, shops and parlors of Paris. In order to give this stupid character to his comic figures, Labiche has removed their brains, leaving only enough of the spinal cord and nerve centers to govern the ordinary, reflex motions of life. His characters respond in a life-like way to an excitation of any sort, but it is only reflex, mechanical action. If you tickle their toes they kick, but in an unseeing manner, without intelligent aim. They are stupid automatons imitating human actions.

Furthermore, they are practically without sentiment, certainly without great emotion, and consequently they do not inspire any. Labiche's slight use of women in his chief rôles has often been cited. He himself said that women were not funny. He has no use for the sentiment and emotion usually associated with their rôles.

We find, then, that Labiche's characters are perfectly constructed in order to inspire laughter, and furthermore that they are substantially caricatures ridiculing the little French bourgeois, whose class they usually represent. If, as Bergson says, laughter is society's punishment of automatic ineptitude, Labiche may well be considered as society's champion flagellator of French bourgeois stupidity.

The more genuine comedies of Labiche are generally built up on some philosophic observation of life, which illustrates the keen insight of the author. They are not thesis plays — Labiche is never so rigid as that — nor is the action of his characters in such plays all motivated by this central theme, for he cared little for logical plot; but a series of comic scenes are made to illustrate this philosophic maxim which he takes as the basis of his play and which gives it force and unity.

The lesson of *Le Voyage de M. Perrichon* is that we are less inclined to like our benefactors than we are those for whom we have done favors; the latter flatter our vanity. The Misanthrope loves brutal truth on all occasions. He finds in the Auvergnat a servant after his own heart, and only half the unity of time is needed to destroy his philosophy — and get rid of his servant. *La Poudre aux Yeux* is a highly amusing duel of mutual pretensions, which leaves us face to face with the thought that a good deal of the struggle and distress of modern society is due to mutual deception, through each one wishing to appear richer or more important than he really is.

But Labiche was not a great philosopher. He made no claims to being a thinker. Even his social satire was good-humored, and he had little of the usual keen wit of the French. His was rather the broad Gallic jest. But he was fundamentally comic, and that is no small merit. No doubt such a theatre is restricted and hardly rises to the highest possibility of drama — that of being an intellectual amusement. None the less, among the restricted purposes of the dramatic genre this power to excite hearty laughter is one of the sanest and most hygienic. It appeals to one of man's distinctive traits, his function as a laughing animal.

Because of the special character of Labiche's comedy, he was little affected by the Realistic Social drama of his day. His plays are not serious enough to concern themselves with social problems, and his gay, improbable plots have little in common with the *pièce bien faite*.

The same is also true with regard to conventional realism; there is little chance for that in a farce of which the action and characters are both often fantastic to the point of the absurd. It is a theatre apart, then, from the prevailing dramatic form, but it is none the less thoroughly French, belonging to a genre so vigorously national that it has flourished almost unchanged since its earliest appearance in the fifteenth century. It is the farce of the *Cuvier* and of *Pathelin*. It is the comic element of Molière, of Regnard, of Beaumarchais, and of how many other lesser masters. It is the glory of Labiche to belong to this line, although he was not one of the greatest of these, and his comedies are a proof of the vitality of the comic genre, coming as they do at a time when the accepted theory would combine the serious and the comic in the same play.

EDOUARD PAILLERON (1834–1899)

Pailleron is a dramatist of a single play, and as such his claim might be questioned to a place in a book dealing with the main currents of drama and confined to significant authors. However, the one play in question, without being an absolute masterpiece of literature, illustrates so perfectly the high excellence of the French in a legitimate kind of comedy, that it deserves to be included as a representative of the many others that must be omitted in a brief treatment.

Pailleron was born in Paris, received a good education and early showed a taste for letters. As a student of law, which has been the usual finishing course for well-to-do young Frenchmen, he was more devoted to poetry than to study for the bar; and after graduation, and a brief period in a law office, he turned to literature and began his dramatic career in 1860, with *La Parasite* at the Odéon. He was a man of culture, equally at home in verse or prose and notable especially for a brilliant wit, pointed regularly with a bit of satire. At his best he suggests Marivaux in his refinement, Musset in his airy gracefulness and even Molière in the spirit and manner of his social ridicule. He is as inexhaustibly clever and witty in his dialogue as Labiche is humorous.

Pailleron was the author of several plays, both in verse and prose, for the most part brief comedies, and he had considerable success in the theatre with more than one of these, such as *L'Age ingrat*, *L'Étincelle* and *La Souris*. His best work, however, is *Le Monde où l'on s'ennuie*, performed at the *Comédie* in 1881. This delightful three-act comedy was not only one of the greatest stage successes of its day, but after a full generation, it has retained all of its favor and freshness.

In composition it is a pure comedy of intrigue, and in fact a quite complicated one, abounding in amusing situations. As an imbroglio, it would do honor to Scribe or Sardou, but it surpasses them both in the originality and cleverness of its wit and social satire, and in the effectiveness of its character sketches or caricatures. These latter have been regularly identified with certain personages of Pailleron's day, but the importance of this assertion is slight; they are at least vividly sketched from life.

The theme of the play, its importance, and the way it

is treated, all show the merits and limitations of the author. In general it is a lively fusillade directed against affectation, pedantry and self-seeking, with random shots at any of the other allied foibles or pleasant vices that happen to stray in range of the writer's guns, more remarkable for rapid fire than for penetrating power. The dramatist himself has well defined the theme of his play and the aim of his satire in the speeches of Paul in the beginning, where he instructs his wife concerning the character of this circle in which they are to spend a week end.

" PAUL. This society, my child, is a Hôtel de Rambouillet in 1881: a society where one proses and poses, where pedantry takes the place of learning, sentimentality of feeling, and preciosity of delicacy; where one never says what he thinks and where one never believes what he says; where perseverance is statecraft, friendship a plan and even gallantry a method . . . in short, society that is serious!

JEANNE. But that is society where one is bored.

PAUL. Exactly.

JEANNE. But if one is bored by it, what influence can it have?

PAUL. Influence! What simplicity! The influence of boredom with us! Why, it is most considerable; it is enormous! The Frenchman, you understand, has for boredom a horror carried to the point of worship. For him, boredom is a terrible God whose religion is good deportment. He understands the serious only in that form. I don't say that he practices this religion — far from it! but he believes in it only the more firmly; preferring to believe rather than to go and see. Yes, this gay people despises itself at heart for being gay; it has lost faith in the good sense of its former laughter; this skeptical and talkative people believes in those who keep silent; this amiable and expansive people allows itself to be impressed by the pedantic display and pompous stupidity of the pontiffs of the white cravat; in politics, in learning, in art, in literature, in everything! It mocks them, it hates them, it flees them like the plague, but they alone have its secret admiration and its complete confidence! The influence of boredom? Why, my dear child, there are only two kinds of people in the world: those who don't know how to be bored and are nothing, and those who know how to be bored and who are everything — next to those who know how to bore others! " [1]

This amusingly paradoxical passage indicates what there is of a serious element in the play, and it is obvious that this is rather slight — just enough truth to make it plausible. But it is obvious also that ridicule of the qualities mentioned is sure to delight an audience. French critics have thought to see in this popular applause of satire aimed at pedantry, seriousness and learning a particular manifestation of the Gallic spirit. In restricting it to France, they are mistaken; these subjects have constantly offered shining marks for ridicule in other countries, and no doubt will always do so. Since the time of Molière at least, the effectiveness on the stage of satire aimed at affectation in the learned professions has been fully recognized. No doubt such attacks are often justified. In this play, however, it is difficult to discover much ground for righteous indignation and still more difficult to find characters who can safely throw stones. But these considerations will hardly affect the public's applause of such satire. Its approval, whether justifiable or not, is a manifestation of popular psychology similar to that of popular imagination noted in the elder Dumas's

[1] Act I, scene II.

plays. Nothing is more popular than to take flings at the stupidity of the scholar, the baseness of the great and the wickedness of the rich — probably because nine-tenths of humanity are neither scholars, nor great, nor rich.

With all that, much of this applause is merited by the cleverness of the performance. Its burlesques of the society professor, the heroic poet and the English " blue stocking " are among the best in dramatic literature, and there are numerous scenes which convulse with laughter without descending in tone or language from the highest plane of good taste and polite society. Its style and dialogue are among the best examples of the high art of Parisian conversation.

In short, *Le Monde où l'on s'ennuie* is written chiefly for entertainment, but it is entertaining in a wholly commendable way. It is highly amusing, but also re-fined; it offers a momentary intellectual stimulus even if it is not really thoughtful. It can hardly be called an absolute masterpiece, but it is a thoroughly good pace-maker, and any play that really surpasses it should be put in the first rank.

Above all is the fact that this play is characteristically French. Its sparkling wit, its pointed satire, its ar-tistic dialogue and its clever character improvisation are the distinctive qualities of light and refined comedy. Anyone who reads it with this thought can understand why the French are supreme in this particular genre. Moreover, any theatre is fortunate which is rich in such comedies as this. It reaches a general audience and at the same time tends to cultivate a taste for high standards in a kind of comedy that is only too often tempted toward vulgarity, coarseness and mere horseplay.

Victorien Sardou (1831–1908)

So much thoughtless handclapping and hasty ink have been wasted on Sardou's plays, even in America, that one is tempted to believe that the soundest evaluation of the author, in a book devoted to the chief dramatic influences, would be to omit him. Perhaps this will be a possible solution after another generation, but it is difficult to ignore recent events that bulk large at the time, whatever may be the verdict of posterity. Besides, if one may question Sardou's serious influence on the French drama, there is no denying that his near three score plays, beginning with *La Taverne des Étudiants* in 1854, and ending with *L'Affaire des Poisons* in 1907, offer an unusual barometer of the state of the French theatre for some fifty years; its chief conditions and variations, even some of its briefest moods are recorded in them with remarkable fidelity.

Sardou is often characterized as a disciple of Scribe. This he undoubtedly is, so far as point of view and attention to technique go. But in substance he was no more a disciple of Scribe than of many others; in fact his most notable characteristic is that he took from all his predecessors and contemporaries whatever he could use that was dramatically effective. His talent is broader than that of Scribe, without being superior, however, and he is thoroughly characteristic of certain very constant French dramatic qualities, as well as deficient in some others.

Sardou was of southern Latin stock, but was born at Paris, where his father had come to follow divers occupations and eventually that of teacher. He was early devoted to books and received a fair education. When he was seventeen years of age his father's school was closed by the Revolution and Victorien, then a medical student, was left in Paris without means. The next few years were full of bitter struggle and privation. He turned from medicine to history, did hack-writing and tutoring — anything to earn a wretched living. Especially he endeavored to succeed in the theatre, and for a long time wholly in vain. His failures, either to secure acceptance of his plays or to win popular favor when accepted, were so continuous that he very nearly became famous as an unsuccessful playwright before he did so as a successful one. It is curious, then, to see how popular he became in the end, as attested by the enormous runs of some of his plays.

Sardou's dramatic activity is among the longest in history, and is marked by many notable successes. His plays brought him an immense fortune. Some were represented in Paris many hundreds of times and played in numerous other countries. No less than half a dozen English adaptations of more than one of these have been made in England and America.

A full account of the author's career in the theatre, with its failures and successes, with the accusations of plagiarism, and with its lawsuits and triumphs would fill a book — and has filled several — but reduced, today, nearer to its absolute proportion of importance, this career can be briefly indicated by mentioning a few

titles. His first play, *La Taverne des Étudiants* was a
disastrous failure and it was not until 1860 that he had
a success with *Les Pattes de Mouche,* a Scribesque intrigue, not at all deserving the serious attention it has
had.   In fact, of the first score of plays written, the
only one that might still deserve such attention today
is *La Famille Benoîton* in 1865, and this is interesting
more as a great stage success, and as a reflection, in the
form of a comedy of social satire, of the mania of speculation, money-making and luxury, then at their height, than
as an artistic or durable work.

La Patrie, an elaborate historical drama, in 1869, is
possibly Sardou's best piece, and will receive special attention, as it displays most of his qualities.   *Rabagas,*
in 1872, is an example of his opportunism in dramatiz-
ing some of the prominent figures of the war period, and
Dora, in 1877, is a skillful exploitation of the spy mania
that followed it.   This latter play, in various adaptations,
has had many successes in English-speaking countries.
Sardou wrote much more worthy dramas than *Dora,*
but Anglo-Saxon audiences seem to have liked none of
his plays better than this, unless it be *Divorçons,* in
1880, which is less worthy still.   *Divorçons,* a comedy
bordering on farce, is highly amusing, but is unnecessarily
suggestive, if not indecent at times, and makes the flimsi-
est possible use of the divorce law then being discussed.

Daniel Rochat, in 1880, might be mentioned to show
Sardou's qualities, and essential failure, in attempting
serious Social drama, such as that of Dumas and Augier.
Fédora, in 1882, is a good representative of the numerous
plays which Sardou wrote to furnish a rôle for well-known

Setting for 7th scene of *Patrie*

actresses, and particularly, as in this instance, for Sarah
Bernhardt. This is a vice — for as the main inspiration of a drama it can hardly be less than a vice — with
which we are quite familiar in this country.

Théodora, in 1884, is the summit, in the magnificent
staging and scenic effects of historical drama, of that
notable career of Sardou of which *La Patrie* is a fine
early example. In such plays, the particular talent of
Sardou had its fullest scope. He can visualize and manip-
ulate perfectly every factor or figure of a vast panorama.
In doing so he is realistic, picturesque, exact, and always dramatically effective. He is one of the first in
France to make the crowd, the *figurants,* a really active
or vital part of such plays.

La Tosca, in 1887, is one of the most intense in feeling of Sardou's dramas, and since it has come to be
widely known as an opera, deserves to be mentioned as
representative of several of Sardou's plays which have
been made into opera libretti, or are partly operas in
their original form; for a number have used music as
an auxiliary.

Sardou did not confine himself to any single form of
drama; he has written farces, comedies, dramas, opera
libretti, and, what is much more significant, nearly all
the possible combinations and permutations of these
forms in the same work; for he would not keep any
class of theatre-goers away from a performance because
they do not care for a particular genre. This mixture
of the different kinds and appeals of drama in the same
play is the author's most striking characteristic.

A good example of this is *La Patrie,* which is probably

his strongest play and the one where this composite character is least evident. First, it is fine spectacle, magnificently staged, realistic in the scene at the Butcher's market and elsewhere, and strikingly picturesque in the action about the walls of the city, and in its processions of soldiers. Second, there are constant features of melodrama to give thrills, such as the slaying of the sentinels or the shooting of the bell ringer. Third, this melodrama is relieved a little — in this play much less than usual — by touches of comedy such as that of Jonas and the bugler. Fourth, one half the plot, the triangle of Rysoor, Karloo and Dolores, is a drama of guilty passion squeezed to its last bitter drop of emotion. Fifth, for those blasé to immoral love there is the pathos of Rafaële; and who can resist the tenderness of filial and parental affection and suffering? Sixth, there is the aid of harmony and music, the rolling of the drums and the effective dirge of the priests in the death procession. Seventh, the second half of the plot is a heroic tragedy of patriotism, offering the strongest contrast to the sordid drama of passion. Finally, any who may have been able to stand on their feet against the single force of these appeals are swept away in a last highly-keyed tragic scene of death on the funeral pyre, of conscience-wringing remorse, of panting, almost inarticulate cries of passion, love, hate and vengeance and of final stabbings and suicide.

The appeals of this play illustrate the author's aims and methods. Evidently, instead of having observed life and humanity, the heart and character of the individual, Sardou has devoted himself to the study of the theatregoer: his wishes, whims and weaknesses. The audience is served then by a marvelous chef, with a dish that appeals as much as one dish can to the combined tastes of the average audience. It is a little like the famous dish of Alice in Wonderland which tasted of ice cream, hot toast, pickles, cake and so forth — except that Sardou includes stronger flavors to suit an older and more varied audience. No doubt each one gets his particular delicacy, which aids him to swallow the rest, but a durable work of art is impossible with such methods.

Especially do his works lack worthy aim and the unity of effect inspired by an inner conception. If a committee could write a play, Sardou's might have been written by a playwright, a stage manager and an actor, combined with a historian, or an archeologist, or a journalist — the fourth member would vary in different plays but the first three are constant.

Wit, dramatic style, and even passion, Sardou had at command, and he could apparently create strong characters if he would give them autonomy. What he failed to have is any adequate personal conception of the life and society of his times, and he has given us no original picture of its vices and faults, nor any real reflection of its meaning and philosophy. We find preëminent a perfect knowledge of dramatic art and a cleverness and versatility without equal, but he reflects only the tastes and fashions of the stage.

Labiche, Pailleron and Sardou, then, do not belong to the class of the most significant authors who furnish food for thought and who have had a certain influence on the development of French drama. Nevertheless, they do all offer examples of some of the most racial qualities of French dramatic genius: wit, cleverness, social satire and skillful technique in writing actable plays. Further, their work is, as a rule, morally wholesome in tendency, and at the same time highly popular. The importance of such writers for the stage is perhaps not realized. To be healthy and live, the drama must be popular in a broad sense, and it can not be so on masterpieces alone. It takes many plays of second rank to produce one of outstanding merit.

CHAPTER X

HENRI BECQUE AND THE THÉÂTRE LIBRE

THE significant work of Dumas and Augier was done by 1880, and with the weakening of their master hands, the chief faults of the form of drama they represented became apparent. The most fundamental of these was the artificial duality caused by combining the well-made play of Scribe, a comedy of intrigue complete in itself, with a social study, a character analysis, or the demonstration of a thesis. This inherent lack of singleness of purpose, difficult to conceal except for a master of dramatic art, and the further mingling in the same play of all forms of the serious and of the comic theatre, best exemplified in Sardou's pieces, were sure to bring about a strong reaction from the French, whose conception of art and of beauty lies so much in unity of aim and harmony of tone.

The inevitable revolt against these and other minor faults is perhaps coincident with the positive attempt of Naturalism to capture the stage, more than it is a result of this endeavor, but the two movements are inseparably united. They did not lead to the formation of a new school or genre — in fact, the attempt of the Naturalists to establish a school of drama failed quickly and decidedly — but they modified sufficiently the course of the theatre to make this an important date. The result was

189

not only to overthrow the tyranny of the well-made play
and simplify the genres, as well as to abolish minor conventions, but especially to win greater freedom in general;
recent and contemporary drama has been free to follow
various channels, and has been little hampered by any
rules except those inherent in the theatre.

The three chief agencies in this attempt to modify the
Social drama of Dumas and Augier are Henri Becque,
the Naturalistic school of the novel headed by Zola, and
the Théâtre Libre, founded by Antoine. The coöperation
of all three might be thought of as the effort of extreme
realism, or Naturalism, to establish itself on the stage.

Literary realism is a relative term, varying with the
epoch; there is the realism of Molière, of Dumas fils, and
of Becque or Zola. Moreover, it can not be taken simply
as a truthful picture of life at any time, although that
may be its professed ambition; there is frequently much
in it that is quite conventional, perhaps even unrepresentative of life as a whole. The extreme realism of
1880 had as dominant characteristics its interest in the
physical, sordid and ignoble sides of life, or at least
in common, everyday life, and a pessimistic philosophy
or point of view. Its methods professed to be inductive,
and it secured its effects largely by an accumulation of
detail, in the manner of the scientist who arrives at general laws through experiments and the collection of phenomena.

The general causes underlying Naturalism are for the
most part those mentioned as explaining the realism of
1850, but some of them have been intensified and others
can be added.

The pessimistic point of view of Naturalistic literature is the result of various influences. It is true that a strain of pessimism can always be found in the French drama, and, at times, it is quite marked with the writers of the Romantic school, who preceded the realists. But with the Romanticists it is more frequently a matter of mood and not a permanent point of view. With the realists, and particularly the Naturalists, it is erected into a philosophic system; indeed, it takes philosophy as its basis.

The current philosophy of this period, positivism and determinism, the philosophy of Comte, Taine and Renan, was frankly skeptical. If it did not entirely eliminate God, it largely took away the faith and consolation of the church and religion. We are not concerned here with the truth or falsity of such philosophy; the only question is that of its immediate effect, and it is certain that such skepticism, if it attacks seriously faith and religion, the hope, consolation and idealism which these give, makes for pessimism. However, a reasoned philosophy is more a matter for the educated few than for the masses, and there were other more general causes of pessimism.

Not the least of these general influences was the condition of French national or political life just at this time. It was the discouraging period following the French defeats of 1870, in the midst of the difficult struggle to reëstablish stable government. The generation writing from 1880 to 1890 had passed through this troubled epoch at its most impressionable age, and even the older generation was profoundly affected by it. We have seen the echoes in the theatre of Dumas and Augier. A more

striking example could be found in Taine's comparison
of the English and the French governments, often so
pessimistic with regard to the latter.

The influence of science, democracy and commercialism
has been mentioned in the chapter on the Realistic theatre,
but it had become intensified in 1880. The materialism
is especially to be noted. Old standards had fallen. The
nobility, with its code of honor, *noblesse oblige,* had
largely passed, and the clergy had lost much of its power
and influence. Money was a greater force than ever
before in French society, and in many ways a corrupting one. It was not surprising, then, that the moralist —
and the French dramatist is frequently a moralist —
should judge such society pessimistically.

But after all, realism, Naturalism, and pessimism were
the natural stages in the inexorable progress of the logical French mind, starting with the Romantic principle
that art should imitate nature and that all life is the
proper field of drama. The Romanticists and the early
realists combined the elevated and the common sides of
life, but it was certain that the French artistic sense
and love of unity would in the end revolt and tend, in
a single play, to devote itself to the one or the other.
With a number of converging influences to aid, and above
all through the attraction of a largely unworked vein,
this meant for the prevailing Realistic School the field
of common or sordid life, and in the end the exploitation
of the ignoble character.

The process is gradual and is marked by the restriction
of the sympathetic figures, to the point finally of substantial elimination. This in itself means pessimism, and

its ultimate goal is the *comédie rosse*, where all the characters are too contemptible to merit the interest of a respectable audience. Such a play, whatever be its technique or ending, if it is taken seriously, is pessimistic.

These were the chief influences which before 1880 had already established Naturalism in the novel, where much more easily than in the theatre this mode of expression finds its place. Zola was at this time the high priest of the Naturalistic novel, and, as we know, he gave more than his blessing to this attempt to capture the stage. He himself wrote plays and dramatized some of his novels, as a rule quite unsuccessfully, and especially he proclaimed much of the theory in numerous articles on the stage. Other writers, such as Curel and Hervieu, also began with the novel.

It is particularly interesting to note in the articles of Zola that he is not aware that there are any inherent differences between the novel and the theatre — and this attitude is most frequent in attacks at this time on the various conventions of the stage. It is not surprising, then, that Zola, and other novelists who were unable to comprehend the stage, should fail in their attempts to give a new dramatic formula. They might supply the theatre with an atmosphere of extreme Naturalism and offer the stimulation of success in another field, but the examples of this new comedy must come from some one with dramatic talent. This was the work of Henri Becque.

Henri Becque (1837–1899)

Becque's dramas can hardly be called the models of the Naturalistic theatre, since he was so rare a combination of certain very decided qualities — with others wholly absent — that he is really inimitable; but he first successfully overthrew the chief barriers that the Naturalists were attacking and led them on the stage, where each comported himself according to his principles and particular character — in most cases very badly. When the most extreme were driven off by outraged taste and decency, the really worthy were able to carry forward French drama in a new atmosphere of freedom, but their work is decidedly different from that of Becque, and they hardly owe him more than the liberty to follow each his bent.

Henri Becque, who was born and lived at Paris, led a life of poverty and controversy. The latter, at least, would seem largely his own fault. He was a misanthrope to the point of abnormality, and rejoiced in the most cruel attacks on his colleagues and on humanity in general. His failure to succeed as a playwright, in any broad or popular sense, he attributed to the ill will, or persecution of theatrical managers, and to the stupidity of the public. He went so far as to bring suit against one manager for refusing a play, and he takes vengeance on the public in all of his pieces.

His dramatic output is small, consisting of only seven or eight plays, and of these only two are really important, *Les Corbeaux* in 1882 and *La Parisienne* in 1885.

The subject of *Les Corbeaux* is the despoiling of the Vigneron family. The mother, three daughters and a good-for-nothing son, on the sudden death of M. Vigneron, a well-to-do manufacturer, are left in the clutches of a dishonest partner and an unprincipled notary, as well as of a horde of other *corbeaux*, and are plucked of all their heritage. One of the daughters is finally forced to marry this partner, a sixty-year old Harpagon, to save the helpless family from abject poverty.

The action of the play is hardly more exciting than the *résumé* just given. Its style and composition are absolute in their simplicity and hard realism. There is not a sign of color, not a tirade, not a single theatrical *coup*, nothing but bitter irony to give life or flavor. There is no plot beyond that indicated, the inexorable closing in of the vultures about their helpless prey, and these victims are too weak to do more than flutter in an aimless way. It is in plot and technique the Naturalist's famous " bleeding slice of life."

Human nature is seen at its worst. The victims do not count; they are only food for the vultures. It is in the circling, the croaking and the satisfaction of these latter that we find whatever drama there is; and of them all, the partner, the notary, the music teacher, the architect, the furnisher, the fiancé and his mother, not one shows a spark of honesty or honor, nor a moment's impulse of compassion. One would expect them to appear inhuman monsters, therefore, and yet that is exactly what they resemble least, and it is here that we find the supreme art of the author. Their villainy is so natural and so unconscious that it seems proper, and, in listening to them, we have only one doubt: are they honest like ourselves or are we dishonest like them?

The picture is complete in its realism both of language and detail, and perfect in its observation. However, its value may be questioned. It has no conclusion except its unrelieved pessimism, and, natural as this seems, it is certainly a most narrow and one-sided view of life. A family without a member or a friend sufficiently strong to defend its rights, in business contact with none but rascals, may be possible, but it is certainly rare. The author does not juggle the cards during the game in the way the Naturalists accused Dumas and Augier of doing, but he picks all the aces and kings before he begins. And the interest of this play, in any broad way, at least, is as questionable as its value as a picture of life. It is keen and strong, but somber and unentertaining; and the only serious reflection it invites is that we are all fundamentally dishonorable and egoistic — which is either an absurd bit of irony or a philosophic truth too remote to affect practical life.

La Parisienne is an even narrower " slice of life," the traditional little triangle, no broader or thicker than a tea sandwich. Clotilde is a perfect wife and a model mistress. As a lesson to her lover, and to secure an advantage to her husband, she dismisses this first lover and turns to another, but her sense of order and love of a serious, settled existence quickly reassert themselves and she returns to the first, and the perfect triangle is reëstablished. The plot ends exactly where it began.

Its artistry is of the same sort as that of *Les Corbeaux*

but even more flawless. The simple beauty of Clotilde's unconscious perversity would be almost touching if the author had not so rigidly excluded all sentiment from actions so natural and dignified. In fact, Becque has in this play arrived at such a perfect mastery of this genre that he occasionally allows his characters to give little moral lectures, without their seeming out of place. Take, for example, the one uttered by Clotilde's lover when he learns that she is on friendly terms with a frivolous and somewhat ultra-modern society lady.

" Think of me, Clotilde, and think of yourself. Consider that an imprudent act is quickly committed and can never be repaired. Don't let yourself yield to this inclination for risky adventures, which today makes so many victims. Resist, Clotilde, resist! In remaining faithful to me you remain worthy and honorable." [2]

But one should not infer from the above passage that Clotilde's virtue was really in danger. This is nothing but Lafont's jealousy. How strongly anchored her principles were in all matters we see throughout the play, and she even acknowledges that they are somewhat old-fashioned:

" You mean that I am old-fashioned! I haven't changed. Oh, as for that, yes, you are right; I am downright conservative. I love order, tranquillity and sound principles. I want to have the churches open when I care to go to them. . . . You are a free-thinker! I believe you would even get along with a mistress who had no religion. How horrible to think of it! " [3]

[2] Act I, scene I.   [3] Act I, scene III.

And all this appears entirely sincere and unconscious
on Clotilde's part. As was said, she is a model wife and
mistress. Her devotion to her husband and concern for
his interests are unfaltering. Also, she wishes the best
of relations and good feeling between the members of
her *ménage à trois*. She even goes so far as to accuse
Lafont of not caring enough for her husband — quite un-
justly, for the two men are the best of friends:

"CLOTILDE.   You don't like my husband!
LAFONT.   Why, yes, I do, I assure you.
CLOTILDE.   No, I warrant you that you don't. You don't
care for Adolphe, I can see it in many ways. Perhaps it is
because your characters don't agree, or possibly it is the situation that is responsible for it." [4]

The peculiar merit, then, of Becque is that he puts on
the stage characters capable of any baseness and without the slightest moral consciousness, but who preserve
the language, sentiments and outward appearances of the
most honorable of people. This is the *comédie rosse*. *La
Parisienne* is the first perfect example, perhaps, and certainly it is one of the most artistic. It is because of its
artistic qualities that the French, even the serious critics,
have so frequently admired the play. Except for this
artistry, and for its constant irony, it is difficult to find
anything of value in it. One can hardly accuse the author
of confusing vice and virtue in his characters, since virtue
is absent, but one can not help thinking how difficult
it has been made for virtue to secure a certificate of
good moral character when she does return. In any

[4] Act III, scene VI.

case, such pictures of life are almost discouraging to the maintenance of respectability, and if the author's point of view were general, one might hesitate to practice any virtues, in order to avoid the accusation of hypocrisy.

Becque has discarded the technique of the *pièce bien faite*. His plays do not come to an end. The curtain falls when the author has got all he can out of his situations and characters. The conclusion is left to the audience. The Naturalists' argument was that life does not begin or end, and all one can do is to give a cross-section of it. If this cross-section means something, all the better, but in any case they held that one must give it as it is, without intervention on the part of the author, and even without attempting to apply or explain it. They abolished the *raisonneur* and made the theatre purely objective. Especially, one should not touch up his pictures to make them more beautiful or agreeable. The public must learn to look life squarely in the face, however disagreeable that face may be.

This latter principle would have been more reasonable if the Naturalists had not chosen so regularly to visit life in her ugly moods. They objected to colored photography, but their own pictures were too constantly confined to the Rogue's Gallery. Human nature is seen only at its worst, and there is no relief of comedy, none of spirituality, nor of imagination, while the bitter irony practically destroys the possibility of sentiment. The tone is single and simple throughout, but it is also frequently somber and monotonous.

The chief merits of this theatre are its reliance on

observation, and its power of character analysis, in which it places the main interest. These qualities, with the further freedom that had been won from the too narrow restraint of plot, form the new starting point of the modern theatre, the one from which most of contemporary French drama proceeds.

The immediate effect, however, of Becque's philosophy and characters was something very different. Unfortunately, his cynical views of life accorded too perfectly with the wave of pessimism that existed among the young writers of France in the last two decades of the nineteenth century, and for a time baseness became the theatrical fashion. While Becque should not be held responsible for all the excesses of his followers, there is no doubt that he first, in his *comédie rosse,* took away all virtue from comedy and gave it the taste of vice that started it on its famous Naturalistic orgy in the days of the Théâtre Libre, an orgy ended only when *delirium tremens* forced it to become sober.

THE THÉÂTRE LIBRE OF ANTOINE (1887–1894)

The Théâtre Libre, founded and controlled by Antoine from 1887 to 1894, is generally considered as the practical manifestation on the stage of the extreme realistic reforms typified by Zola and the Naturalistic novel and exemplified in the plays of Becque. Since it coincided with other influences and came at a period of natural reaction against certain features of the drama in vogue, it is not sure that it had all the importance in the development of the French theatre that is sometimes given to it. But whether it be simply the gnat buzzing on the yoke or really one of the oxen pulling the load up the hill, it offers in any case a suitable peg on which to hang the date of a partial reform in the modern French drama, and it illustrates in itself the limitations and failure of extreme realism, or Naturalism, on the stage.

André Antoine was a humble clerk in the Gas Company at Paris. He had had but slight education and little experience as an amateur actor when he founded the Théâtre Libre, but he was irresistibly attracted to the stage, and he soon developed remarkable qualities as an actor. In later years, through the originality and sheer force of his native genius, he became the outstanding theatrical manager of France.

He organized his theatre with the coöperation of a few amateur actors. They were absolutely without funds, and only on his monthly pay day was Antoine able to furnish the rent for the small hall they had hired; he even carried his letters of advertisement himself, to save postage. His first performance, in 1887, was a very doubtful success, and it required still greater courage and efforts to undertake another. However, this second performance brought valuable public notice, and he was encouraged to resign from the gas office and devote himself entirely to the project. The theatre flourished for four or five years and then declined, and Antoine resigned from it in 1894. Later he became a well-known actor, organized another theatre, and was for some years director of the National Theatre of the Odéon.

The avowed aim of the Théâtre Libre was to give opportunity to unknown authors, especially to those representing the Naturalistic ideas, and one of its greatest glories has been to bring before the public a number of new names which have since become famous in the French drama. Brieux and Curel are among those who were discovered by Antoine. Also the Théâtre Libre was one of the first theatres at Paris to represent any considerable number of foreign plays. Ibsen, Tolstoy, Hauptmann, and various other foreign dramatists found place on its programs, and along with the organization of the *Oeuvre* theatre, which has devoted itself particularly to this field, it inaugurated a much to be desired practice in France. The French have been exceptional, and on the whole quite unjustified, in the slight attention they have given to foreign plays, and notable progress has been made in correcting this attitude during the past thirty years.

It is probable, however, that the greatest service of the Théâtre Libre is to be found in its attack on French theatrical conventions, particularly on the style of acting and staging. The French have been unique in this respect. Conservative, and even given to routine by nature, and with all their drama first produced at Paris, in theatres subsidized in part by the government and aided by the National Conservatory, they have kept their theatrical traditions most intact.

No doubt, many of these are admirable, but they were largely formed in the Classic or, at latest, Romantic schools, in the elevated, heroic genres, and were strikingly out of keeping with the spirit of the realistic drama in the second half of the nineteenth century. Moreover, this incongruity is heightened by the natural French love of fine rhetoric, which is so foreign to Anglo-Saxons. The dramatic tirade, which by its oratory lifts a Frenchman out of his seat and makes an American wish to crawl under his, still persisted in the realistic prose drama at this time, where it was clearly not at home; it was perhaps even an anachronism in the temper of modern society.

Antoine attacked all these conventions and succeeded in transforming some of them. As in other things, his actors often went too far. They talked into the fire and turned their backs too much to the audience, and sometimes did not make themselves understood, but in general their influence in changing theatrical conventions was salutary. It is only to be regretted that the strength of French tradition has prevented it from extending further. Antoine was one of the first in France, following the initiative of Sardou, to utilize fully the crowd on the stage, and his reforms in regard to realism and simplicity in staging were excellent.

If there were more revolutionists such as he to attack the abuses that still exist in the Paris theatres, due to routine and tradition, the really remarkable merit of the French theatre today would be more immediately apparent, at least to foreigners. It is true that many of these abuses are minor, relating to ticket-selling, seating, scenery and declamation, and the French may well point out that " the play's the thing," but this can hardly justify eighteenth century conditions in the theatre. In fact such conditions seem all the more regrettable, when they tend to mar the enjoyment of the perfect diction and admirable art of the actors to be found in the well-balanced performances given by the national, and by the other good theatres at Paris.

The Théâtre Libre was a subscription theatre. It was able thus to escape the censor, and to present plays that were forbidden on the other stages, but it also had the disadvantage of being confined to a restricted public. This was one of the causes of its decline. Encouraged by the applause of the partisans of Naturalism, and yielding also to his own preferences, Antoine, who had at first welcomed plays widely different in form and spirit, soon turned almost exclusively to the Naturalistic form, and even to a special type of it written for his theatre.

This type may be best comprehended as a deformation of Becque's *comédie rosse*. Becque's dramatic characters are despicable at heart but impeccable in manner and speech; in fact the essence of his art is in this contrast between their real character and their assumption of the complete guise of honorable people. The characters created by the extremists of the Théâtre Libre are not only despicable but delight in being so. They are base, ignoble creatures who rejoice in covering themselves with mud. The chief effort of these young authors seems to have been to scandalize the bourgeois — except when they delighted in puzzling him with disconnected scenes and plays without beginning or end.

In short, there are to be found all the disagreeable features of Naturalism: pessimism, coarseness and ugliness; and all of the anarchy in technique that was a protest against the well-made play. The public was soon disgusted. Extreme realism, such as is found in some of the novels of the Zola school, was clearly proven to be

impossible on the stage.   The Théâtre Libre failed as a
purely Naturalistic genre.

Possibly the success of French Naturalism dealing
with common and vulgar characters would have been
greater on the stage, if it had been less cynical and con-
temptuous toward the life it so largely treats.   In this
respect, French realism seems to distinguish itself, in
degree at least, from the realism of other countries.
There is in Russian Naturalism, for example, a certain
mysticism, doubtless a product of faith and religion,
which gives it hope and some spirituality; and in English
realism one finds a sentimental sympathy for the common
characters, often even for those most ugly and sordid,
which again keeps such literature from being so entirely
cynical and depressing as that characteristically written
by the French.

A complete explanation of the causes for the attitude
of the French is perhaps difficult and too complex to be
attempted here.   However, one of the chief reasons is to
be found in their conception of the artistic and beautiful,
in their fondness for the perfect in line and form, and in
their consequent contempt for the coarse and common
clay with which they must work in this genre.   In any
case, the French rarely show the hearty enjoyment often
found by the English in the common and vulgar scenes
of life, and in the drama especially, where good humor,
sympathy and emotion are such necessary appeals, the
scientific hardness of French realism is a serious handicap.

The shortcomings and failures of the Naturalistic reforms treated here are obvious, but there are also important gains from this attempted revolution.   No en-

tirely new and important genres were set up. Authors
continued to write plays of the same general character as
before, often even the outright Social dramas of Dumas
and Augier, but usually with modified forms and emphasis. Above all, the tyranny of the well-made play was
overthrown and plot became less rigid and less important.
Action was made dependent on the characters instead of
having the characters controlled by the action, as was
often the case before; and with this tyranny of plot
broken down, both life and characters can be presented
more fairly.

Most important of all, there has been a decided tendency away from drama dealing with specific problems
and social questions, toward an analysis of character;
there is less social and political science, and more psychology, philosophy and humanity.

This seems a decided gain. The only dramatic subject
of perennial and universal interest is human nature,
mankind. It is entirely proper, and perhaps even necessary, to study human nature in connection with its external manifestations, its reactions toward the life and
problems of the day, but this study should emphasize
man and not simply his actions. The French theatre,
then, has returned far toward Molière. He too was a
realist, a satirist and a philosopher, and he also was a
writer of social drama, if the emphasis is placed on character as was just stated.

Furthermore, we find a complete restoration of the
theatre of observation — with imagination again under
restraint. It will be noted that this faculty of the mind
is entirely absent in Becque. This subordination of

imagination is the usual French tradition. And finally there is again, as in the Classic period, a decided tendency toward unity and harmony of tone, toward a separation of the kinds, or at least against such mingling as was found in the plays of Sardou. The separation of the genres is so much in conformance with the French ideas of order and beauty that it seems likely to reëstablish itself, largely without any specific effort to this effect. All these tendencies will be noted in the contemporary authors who inherited from this reform.

CHAPTER XI

EUGÈNE BRIEUX AND THE USEFUL PLAY

EUGÈNE BRIEUX (1858–   )

BRIEUX is one of the most highly respected living playwrights in France, and in England and America he has been recently the French dramatic writer, except possibly Rostand, the most widely discussed. Many of his plays have been translated into English, and a brief search through English and American magazines reveals more than one hundred articles dealing with his work. Probably no such attention has been given to any other living French dramatist in Anglo-Saxon countries.

However, Brieux has been, in France, the object of considerable criticism, of which some is doubtless valid, and the discussions in England and in this country have too often been without the background of French dramatic history necessary to insure a just evaluation of his plays. He would seem, then, the French contemporary dramatist whose works could best be studied, not only to throw light on the French stage, but also to indicate the recent trend of dramatic taste and appreciation in Anglo-Saxon countries. Obviously he is either an author of outstanding merit or there is something in his work that is in especial accord with the tone and temper of modern society.

The problems connected with Brieux are several and some are difficult to solve. For example, the critics have not agreed in finding in his plays a philosophy that explains consistently all his ideas. Again, his apprenticeship in the Théâtre Libre has led to an interpretation of his work which is in part at least false, so that similar reformers in England and America have put him forward as a champion with his dullest weapon; to many he is known as the author of *Damaged Goods,* perhaps his poorest play. Likewise, he is often called the creator of the Useful Play, of which he is in France only a belated exponent. Finally, the interest in Brieux, in this country especially, has not been fully explained.

Eugène Brieux was born in 1858 in Paris. His father was a carpenter. Thus he comes from the common people, knows their life and has never disavowed them. His regular education did not extend beyond the common schools. He was left an orphan in his early youth and at fifteen was earning his living as a clerk. However, he had a passion for reading to which he devoted all he could afford both of time and money. He even managed to acquire a fair knowledge of Latin. Quite early in life he had literary ambitions. In his address on his reception into the French Academy, he tells us that he had vowed at fifteen to become an Academician.

He began to write plays while young, and one of them, *Bernard Palissy,* written when he was twenty, in collaboration with Gaston Salandri, was played at the Cluny theatre. It had only one performance and did not deserve more. He now entered journalism and spent several years in newspaper work in cities outside of Paris, and particularly in Rouen. Meanwhile he continued to write plays, but none of these early pieces was fortunate enough, or good enough, to secure a performance.

Brieux won his first real recognition, as did a number of other young dramatists of the times, at the Théâtre Libre. His *Ménages d'Artistes* was played there in 1890, although his earliest important success was *Blanchette*, in 1892. He pays warm tribute to Antoine, the founder of the Théâtre Libre, in the preface to the French edition of this latter piece, and mentions that during the preceding ten years his plays had been rejected by all the theatre managers of Paris. However, an examination of these early efforts tends to confirm rather than to discredit the judgment of these managers.

Brieux is often spoken of as a product of the Théâtre Libre in its effort to establish extreme realism on the stage, and the influence of this movement is in fact evident in several of his plays. But *Blanchette* is not a characteristic play of Antoine's school; it deserved, and doubtless would soon have secured, representation in the well established theatres; and it would be a mistake to judge Brieux simply as a disciple of the Théâtre Libre.

Since it is a prevailing practice, more than any inherent reason, which has determined that modern realism, and especially Naturalism, is to deal largely with the vulgar and sordid in life, or, at least, with common, everyday life, and with its physical rather than its spiritual side, we must, on the whole, classify Brieux as an outright realist, like the others in the Théâtre Libre movement. Many of his dramas present slices of life that are not beautiful.

But the Naturalism of Brieux is more incidental than it is a fixed attitude toward life. Although the manners and pretensions of the front parlor can sometimes be better judged by entering it through the backyard and kitchen, as the Naturalists did, there is no indication that Brieux has any morbid fondness for exploring backyards. For the most part he sees these only because his dramatic characters have no front yards. His interest is after all in the living room — which is often the only room for the classes he treats. Only occasionally was he a writer of the *comédie rosse*. In fact, he is neither morbid nor a pessimist, and his technique, where it resembles the slice of life of the Théâtre Libre, is probably more often due to lack of dramatic skill than to *parti pris*.

With the success of *Blanchette*, which has remained one of the best and most popular of his plays, Brieux had returned to Paris, and, although he continued for a few years to write as a journalist, he finally gave himself up entirely to the stage. For the past thirty years, Brieux has produced on the average a play a year, except during the Great War, when he threw all his energies and resources into relief work. In 1910, he was elected a member of the French Academy. He has shunned publicity and his private life is little known.

In addition to *Blanchette*, five or six other plays of Brieux stand out as significant. Among these is *Les Trois Filles de M. Dupont*, appearing in 1897. Although its theme is not so generous as many of Brieux's, and its tone and realism are those of the Théâtre Libre, it offers some of his strongest character drawing, perhaps because in it, as in *Blanchette,* the author is not obsessed by his thesis to the point of neglecting his characters.

In 1900 appeared *La Robe Rouge,* an attack on the abuses of justice, and often called his strongest play. Its dramatic action is firmer than that of *Blanchette,* but it is doubtful if it, or any other play of Brieux, is better or more enduring than his first success.

In 1901 were given two of his most significant pieces, *Les Remplaçantes,* a very effective Thesis Play aimed at the evils of wet-nursing, and offering excellent characterizations of peasant life, and *Les Avariés* (Damaged Goods). This latter play, widely discussed and translated, is a plea for reform in combating the social diseases. It marks the farthest point in the development of the Thesis Play, and is, in fact, hardly more than an illustrated dramatic lecture. Perhaps two of the most important plays since 1901 are *Maternité,* in 1903, a Thesis Play of the same violent and reformatory character as *Les Avariés,* and *La Femme seule,* in 1913, a plea for the economic emancipation of woman. Of considerable interest to Americans, although not one of his strongest plays, is *Les Américains chez nous,* appearing in 1919.

Three plays of Brieux, *Blanchette, La Robe Rouge* and *Les Avariés,* deserve special consideration in order to mark the range of his most significant work, and particularly to show the evolution of the dramatist impelled by his moralistic mission. It will be seen that this development is very similar to that of Dumas fils.

Brieux has done nothing finer than *Blanchette.* He has occasionally shown better technique, has several times invented a more interesting plot and has often attacked more striking themes, but not once has he written better and more enduring drama. In no other play is life more perfectly represented by real characters in situations that are fundamentally, even if not stressfully dramatic.

One reason for this is that of the dramatist, moralist and reformer, who are found united — perhaps sometimes, divided — in Brieux, this play is the work of the dramatist. At the very most, the other two are present to judge and applaud. As a rule they take a larger part in the representation, with the result that, although we may often find more intense creations or characters, who kindle more quickly our pity or indignation, we soon discover that their warmth is largely the reflected heat of the reformer or moralist and is not from their own hearts. And we grow a little cold over the deception. Also, there is here no *raisonneur* in the foreground, to shut out our light.

There are two good dramatic themes, closely united, in this piece: the futility of Blanchette's education and her estrangement from her family and class. The second of these themes is of universal application wherever children are educated above their parents, or even long separated from them, and to the parents this is, no doubt, always tragic, owing to the general law of life that parents live largely for and in their children, while the younger generation goes light-heartedly forward to meet life, with little thought of those who are left behind.

It is true that Brieux calls only slight attention to this general situation, but it is there, in the background. He prefers to get his main effect from Blanchette's hu-

miliation before her friends, and from her parents'
inability to understand her higher aspirations.

The implied plea against educating the masses above
their station and opportunities has been pointed out by
all the critics. However, Brieux himself specifically disclaims any intention of criticizing universal education
in this play.[1] He wished simply that education should be
practical and that opportunity should keep pace with it.
This is in line with Brieux's usual attitude. But as
long as there exists in France the present widespread ambition to enter public service, the problem of *Blanchette*
will remain unsolved.[2] The fact that Brieux did not write
his play to support a definite thesis only makes more
effective a conclusion that derives naturally from the
situation.

The best of *Blanchette* is in the life and characters
depicted. This life Brieux knew and interpreted from
the inside. From this standpoint the play is one of the
best pieces of modern realism on the stage. Its realistic
characterizations stand as Brieux's most substantial contribution to the modern drama. Père Rousset is strongly
drawn — as perfect, within the narrower frame of course,
as a Père Goriot of Balzac. Look at him from all sides,
parental vanity, peasant cupidity, paternal tyranny —
not a stroke of the brush has faltered.

One should note, also, how Mme Rousset, who is usu-

[1] The authority for this is Brieux's own statement, made to the
author in 1922.

[2] In the Department of the Seine, there were 7139 female applicants
for 54 vacant positions in 1890 — *Journal des Débats*. It will be noted
that *Blanchette* appeared in 1892. Moreover, the lesson of *Blanchette*
applies not only to public instruction but to many other lines of public
service.

ally kept so well within her patient rôle of the peasant's wife, is suddenly made to stand out as the furious *femme du peuple,* in the scene of her red rage at Blanchette's rebellion. Hervieu could not have revealed more strikingly the primitive savage in human nature breaking through its veneer. Even minor characters are perfectly done. Weeks after you have seen the play, you recall perfectly every feature of the roadmaker, Bonenfant, except you can not remember whether you saw him in the play or on the road.

Blanchette herself is the only one about whose characterization a question can be raised. She is obviously a mixture of good and of less sympathetic qualities, and some of the latter are in part responsible for the tragedy of family estrangement. But would she be truer to life if she were more perfect? And after all we should not exaggerate. She is not devoid either of character or of color, and is, perhaps, average or natural in both respects. It is difficult to make such a character highly interesting, since strong relief is demanded by the drama, but she is conceived with the realistic idea of avoiding any over-emphasis.

In short, *Blanchette* is an excellent example both of Brieux's work and of the Naturalistic drama; both are here at their best, in a fortunate state of balance and sobriety, which is much rarer perhaps with such drama than it is with Brieux. Particularly, it is to be noted that *Blanchette* is a product of the dramatic realist. It is based directly on observation. It is Brieux's *Dame aux Camélias,* and like Dumas's first play, it will perhaps live longest of his work.

La Robe Rouge is a Social drama, based also largely

on observation, no doubt, but in which the author is more concerned with his problem and with social satire than he is with giving original characters or a realistic picture of life. He is here at his best in experience and in command of his dramatic technique and has given one of his most strongly constructed plays. The theme appealed especially to his strong pity for the weak and unfortunate. The law, made for the protection of society, is necessarily cruel to the individual who is caught by it, and the cruelty is in this case heightened by injustice due to the ambition and self-seeking of the judges. We have, then, a drama of high emotional intensity, higher and more sustained than *Blanchette*.

With all this, *La Robe Rouge* has much of the transitory character and interest of the social problem play. While the author has perhaps suggested no feasible reform by this play — at least it is not a narrow Thesis Play — we can well understand how some change in the judicial system would take away the chief interest of this theme; for the main interest is in the theme, the situations and the satire on these, and not in the characters, nor in a realistic picture of life, as it is in *Blanchette*. *La Robe Rouge* is a product of the dramatic moralist, and is representative of a large part of Brieux's work. In such plays, he is perhaps more consciously a moralist than he is a dramatist.

Les Avariés has been one of the most widely known examples of what is sometimes called the Useful Play. Properly speaking it is not a play but an illustrated lecture by our old friend, the *raisonneur* of Dumas. There is no action, no clash of characters, no struggle in any proper dramatic sense. The dramatic figures are not real characters; they are only exhibits A, B and C from the Doctor's skeleton closet.

Doubtless the appearance of such sensational exhibits on the stage accounts for a part of the public's curiosity and interest, but it would be unfair to deny that there is emotion of a certain sort in this piece. Brieux, the social reformer, has felt deeply on this subject, and he succeeds in communicating some of his indignation to us, although we have been lured to a lecture for the good of our soul — and body — when we thought we were taking an evening off for diversion. But this piece is not fully within the province of the theatre — not even if its partisans define as in the province of the theatre anything an audience will pay two dollars to see. The interest is not dramatic interest. *Les Avariés,* then, is the product of the moralist and reformer. Impelled by these qualities, Brieux has gone to extremes, exactly as Dumas did in *La Femme de Claude.* A considerable portion of his work is of this character, although he has usually preserved a better dramatic form than he has in this play.

In France, Brieux has been much criticized as a dramatic artist. This is natural in a country where form and style are national virtues, and where the art of writing plays has been brought to a point hardly short of perfection. Nevertheless, measured by less exalted standards, there is justification for this criticism. Brieux's insufficient training and lack of familiarity with the classics are reflected in his language and style, although his somewhat inelegant style is in part due to his frequent treatment of the uneducated classes. His peasant speech is taken from life and is effective.

His construction and dramatic technique often leave much to be desired. Here, it is true, opinions differ in proportion as the critic is a supporter of the well-made play of Scribe and Dumas, or a partisan of the slice of life theory of the extreme realists of the Théâtre Libre. In England, and in America especially, Brieux has been claimed by the latter group and highly praised for his supposed reaction against the too logically constructed plot. However, to attempt to make of Brieux a leader or reformer in dramatic technique is entirely unwarranted, and it is much to be regretted that his presentation to English readers has been so injudicious and so imperfect.

As a matter of fact, the majority of Brieux's dramas adhere no more to the slice of life theory than they do to that of the well-made play. A few only are strongly constructed, and some are very poorly constructed, but it is difficult to see in any case that this is due to realism and fidelity to life as opposed to an artificial logic. Few authors have revised their plays more often, as the result of advice or criticism, and these revisions have usually been along the lines of better construction. The evidence is that Brieux has regularly constructed his plays as well as he could, without any conscious adherence to the theories of the Naturalistic school. That he does not have exceptional skill in this respect is certain. In fact, he hardly has the minimum — which to us may seem a maximum — that appears to be the birthright of every French dramatist. Evidence of this is abundant, but when we see Brieux simply take the scissors and cut *L'École des*

Belles-mères from *La Couvée* — that is, a surprisingly good one-act comedy from a very poor three-act one; or when he takes a strong novel such as Hervieu's *L'Armature* and makes from it an insufferably dull and heavy play, it is clear that his chief merit is not his skill as a playwright.

One must add to this that Brieux lacks notably the usual French wit. At the most he has, and that somewhat rarely, a certain comic vein, which is not light or gay enough to relieve greatly his tragic or painful scenes. His plays are often, it must be confessed, somewhat heavy and depressing. In short, Brieux is certainly not a dramatic artist — a fact which he himself readily admits.

Since it is not the dramatic artist that we find in Brieux, nor the ability to entertain by wit or amuse with the comic, we must look elsewhere for an explanation of his dramatic power. Obviously much of this lies in his themes. He is important for these especially, and not at all as a creator of any new forms of drama, as certain English and American critics, forgetting the plays of his predecessors, have been prone to assert. Of the Theatre of Ideas, of Social drama, of the Thesis Play, of the Useful Play, not once is he really a creator. These were all invented, popularized and exploited long before by Dumas fils and Augier.

However, he has widened the scope and interest of more than one of these forms. We all know that Dumas, great as were his originality and dramatic power, dealt with a very small fraction of Parisian gay society, and his one subject is immoral love. Augier, it is true, was more

representative and gives an excellent picture of the comfortable *bourgeoisie,* with an interest centering largely
on money and marriage. However, both of these classes
are toward the peak in the pyramid made up by the
social strata of the French people. Brieux's slice of life
is cut from the base of this pyramid, from the stratum of
the common people, and is immensely broader. Here
is one of the great secrets of his power and of the wide
interest he has attracted, not only in France but elsewhere. The base of society is of equal concern to all;
if the foundation is shaken, the whole pyramid falls.
Moreover this foundation, the common people, is in its
psychology and problems much the same in all countries.

One needs to make but the hastiest survey of Brieux's
plays to see the large number of themes of broad or of universal interest: education of the masses (*Blanchette*), political corruption (*Engrenage*), organized charity and pau-
perism (*Bienfaiteurs*), gambling (*Résultat des Courses*),
rearing of children (*Blanchette, Couvée*), the courts
of justice (*Robe Rouge, Avocat*), social diseases (*Avariés*), illegitimacy and birth control (*Maternité*), superstition and religion (*La Foi*), economic independence of
women (*Femme seule*), and so forth. Obviously he has
greatly extended, beyond that of Dumas and Augier, the
scope of Social drama, and especially marked is his superiority in this respect over so many of his contemporaries,
who have tended too often to choose some ingenious paradox on society for the subject of their plays.

It is at this point, it would seem, that might be decided,
in part at least, one of the questions raised in the beginning of this chapter. Whatever may be his final merits

as a dramatist, Brieux's choice of themes, and the classes he treats, bring him strikingly in accord with his generation. He is writing for a democracy, where everyone reads and goes to the theatre. There is no longer a cultured class, even in France, which dominates literature.

In the seventeenth century the drama could be as subtle, as artistic and as intellectual as it pleased — in fact, it must be so *to please* — and even as late as Dumas and Augier, good language, good breeding and wit were natural and traditional, if not necessary qualities for the dramatist to secure an *entrée* into the still fairly polite society of the theatre. But today society in France, as elsewhere, has been leveled, perhaps much of it *up* considerably, but certainly some of it *down*, also. This public, taken at its level, is, as compared with that of the past, immeasurably vast. Brieux, the child of the common people, and the journalist, has quite naturally found that level, not only in his themes and the classes treated, but in his adoption of the prevalent realism of his day — for surely there is inherent connection between democracy and nineteenth century realism.

The interest of Brieux's themes is evident, but these do not offer, after all, the final criterion in judging a dramatist. It is not sufficient to be simply an observer and reproducer of life, however important that may be. Drama is not a snapshot of life but a moving picture, and the director has more to do than to set the camera, close his eyes and turn the crank. He must select and combine to make the picture a harmonious whole, and if this picture is to mean anything in an artistic way, the dramatist must have a point of view of his own. In other words, he must have a philosophy of life. No better definition of modern drama has been suggested than that it is a judgment on life, if one will accept this characterization in its most liberal meaning, as being the author's genuine reaction, conscious or unconscious, toward the life he portrays.

The most significant French dramatists do have, regularly, a point of view or a philosophy; for example, the greatest of all, Molière, is the philosopher of good sense and measure. Dumas fils also had a philosophy of his own, paradoxical as it was, and Augier was always the intuitive champion of the sacredness of the family, and the defender of stable society. Hervieu, who was one of Brieux's greatest contemporaries, saw life controlled ever by a few primary instincts, such as egoism, which were constantly breaking through the veneer of civilization. What is the point of view or the philosophy of Brieux?

It must be confessed that the answer to this problem is most difficult. As a rule, Brieux's Anglo-Saxon critics have either ignored the importance of the question or have ascribed to Brieux a multitude of aims, which in no way can be combined and harmonized into a basic philosophy, while the French criticism, which is keener, has tended to deny to Brieux a consistent personal guide to life. The French critics are probably right if Brieux is judged by usual French standards, according to which a philosophy should be, first of all, an intellectual guide to life, one capable of rational justification. It is doubtful if any such key can be found to the work of Brieux.

Nevertheless, a careful survey of Brieux's significant dramas shows a common motive in their conception, and one which quite regularly explains his conclusions in the numerous problems of life which he has raised. This philosophy of Brieux, if philosophy it can be called, is that of *social pity*. It is Christian charity based on sentiment and is dependent entirely on feeling, the feeling of a kind, honest and sincere man, and is thus purely a philosophy of the heart. Its consistency is certainly not that of the intellect. This explains why Brieux so regularly may arouse our feelings of pity, sympathy, or indignation, but so rarely offers a well reasoned solution — if he offers a solution at all.

One can note how this feeling of pity dominates in nearly all of his plays.[3] In *Blanchette,* we are moved both by the tragedy of family estrangement and by that of Blanchette's economic helplessness. But the first is the inevitable price of progress, and, as for the second, no solution is offered. In *L'Engrenage,* we are indignant at the political corruption and sympathize with the weak but honest man who succumbs, but what does Brieux propose to remedy this? In *Les Bienfaiteurs,* he finally disclaims intelligent charity, but would give at random, for the sake of the giver's soul, whatever be the social consequences. Our hearts are grieved over the sad fate of the three daughters of M. Dupont, but what shall we do about it? We pity the unfortunates in *Résultat des Courses,* but the dénouement is not a solution, nor even a judgment; it is only a sentimental family reunion. In *La Robe Rouge,* Brieux's pity and indignation are so great

[3] In his address before the American Academy of Arts, he has clearly stated this dominating motive: " It has been my desire that the amount of suffering in the world might be diminished a little because I have lived."

that the chief victim is made to assassinate the chief author of the injustice — in reality a passional crime. *Les Remplaçantes* is a moving plea, filled with pity and indignation, for the child, and *La petite Amie* and *Maternité* are similar pleas for the girl-mother. Even *Les Avariés*, Thesis Play as it is, is infinitely more an appeal to our feelings and to our indignation than it is a rational treatment or proposal of reform.

In *Le Berceau*, Brieux's pity for the child and parents, tortured in their filial and parental love, finds no real solution. It is against divorce, yes, but logically it would call for a second divorce. In *La Déserteuse*, his sympathy for the child would dismiss the unworthy mother and give another her place, despite mother-love, but in *Suzette*, he would, on the contrary, pardon and take the guilty woman back because of his sympathy for this mother-love, and at last, in *Simone*, he shows how love and Christian charity revolt at Dumas's advice to kill the unfaithful wife and mother. Finally, in *La Foi*, while denying the gods and religion, Brieux has so much pity for the wretched and ignorant that he would give them back a god and master to pray to, even if it is the cruel god Stork, rather than the harmless god Log.

In all these, and in other plays, we see that Brieux is regularly on the side of the weak and defenceless, usually the child or the woman,[4] and his motive is pity and

[4] In at least ten of his plays, pity and sympathy for the child, or the children, form the dominating motive. This making the child a center for his plays, and also his corresponding criticism of parents who spoil or who meddle with the lives of their children are practically *idées fixes* in Brieux. He is not at all a consistent defender of the sanctity of marriage. In fact, in the problems of marriage and divorce, the child seems to be his only real concern.

sentiment rather than reasoned justice. Perhaps this is not a philosophy, but is quite strikingly the doctrine of Christian charity. One might note again that this doctrine of Social Pity comes at a time when it might be expected to receive the most sympathetic response from the French, a people usually too much ruled by rationalism to be greatly influenced by a purely emotional philosophy. Brieux's was the generation that had been brought up on the humanitarian sentimentalism of Hugo's *Les Misérables,* where the sufferings and crimes of the individual call for the indictment of society as a whole.

Brieux is certainly not an intellectual socialist. He pities the lower classes, but he does not justify them. His socialistic utterances are too scrappy and inconsistent to form a theory. In fact, it may as well be said that Brieux is not primarily a thinker, much less a scientific one. Only a critic as uniquely original as Shaw could call him both. However, although his philosophy is one of sentiment, it is not necessarily sentimental. He has too much good common sense for that. And finally, his tendency to follow the intuitions of a charitable and honest heart has saved him from the finely spun theories and artificially logical conclusions so often found in that other great dramatic moralist and reformer, Dumas fils.

Brieux did not invent the useful stage nor the Thesis Play. Dumas not only preceded him, but expounded even more forcibly than he the theory of such drama. However, Brieux, perhaps because he is less a dramatic artist than Dumas, owes more especially his success to this side of his drama, and his influence has been so great that one feels called on to examine anew these theories. Does art exist for art's sake, or must it have a utilitarian aim? Is the primary purpose of the theatre to amuse, or should it instruct and reform?

Probably it is true wisdom to avoid either extreme. The dilemma is, after all, an invention of logic. In actual life, nothing is rarer. So there is hardly need of being impaled on either horn. In a general way, all art may have as its aim human improvement; certainly it can if culture, or even civilization itself, is an improvement. But this does not mean an obvious moral. In dramatic art, there is probably no valid objection to the Thesis Play if the thesis is the honest working out of the author's philosophy in presenting the life and action of his characters, rather than the prepared plea of the lawyer. In this better sense, *Tartuffe* is perhaps a Thesis Play.

We can commend, then, such plays of Brieux as *Blanchette* and *La Robe Rouge,* where life, character and action are not sacrificed to a thesis. On the other hand, *Les Avariés* represents a doubtful tendency of the stage, and this not simply because it is didactic, or useful, or propaganda, but because it is not primarily dramatic. The partisans of such drama may, it is true, prophesy differently and appeal to the judgment of the future. None the less, there is hardly need to wait a hundred years to learn that it will be the interest in the dramatic rather than in the didactic which will prevail. We have the history of the past to guide us. French drama is a thousand years old, and in its beginnings in the Christian mass it was entirely didactic. We find, however, even before it changed its speech from Latin to French and escaped from the church, that the dramatic impulse and interest began to prevail at the expense of the didactic, and this process has continued ever since. For five hundred years after its birth in the church, it proclaimed its pious or moral aim, but its dominating tendency was always to interest and amuse. Dumas, Brieux, Shaw and others may proclaim, then, and proclaim seriously, the new era of the Useful Play, but judged by its history of a thousand years the theatre does not promise to rival seriously the church or the school as a moral agency.

It is sometimes claimed that Brieux is more popular in England and America than in France. An explanation of this should be interesting. We have seen that the forms of drama he has used were created forty years earlier, but he is their best exponent at a time when such forms have been attracting the most interest in Anglo-Saxon countries, so that, often, he has been mistakenly given credit for them. Furthermore, Brieux's limitations as an artist, his style and form, so much criticized in France, are hardly handicaps when he is translated and played in English.

However, it is especially his themes which have attracted. He has largely given up the too frequent triangle play and has treated themes of more general interest, not only in France but everywhere. Moreover, in America especially, the Useful Play, of which Brieux is the best present exponent, was bound to attract great interest, as the utilitarian always does in this country. Brieux not only carried it into fields in which we are interested, but he has been the champion of a number of ideas with which we, perhaps, sympathize more universally than the French, such as self-reliance of youth, economically and in marriage, economic and social independence of women, anti-gambling restrictions, protection from social menaces by laws, and, finally, reform through sentiment. In fact, it would seem exactly this basic philosophy of Brieux, mentioned above, which is one of sentiment and feeling rather than of intellect or reason, that makes him especially sympathetic and comprehensible to Anglo-Saxons. French literature has always been differentiated nationally from Anglo-Saxon through being constantly more rationalistic and intellectual, rather than emotional or sentimental. In Brieux, we have found a kindred spirit.

Despite the somewhat un-French balance in a few of Brieux's qualities, his national lineage in the drama is clear and legitimate. As a writer of social plays and a reformer, he is a continuer of Dumas, and as a realist and moralist he is in the best French tradition. In his notable deficiencies in the finer virtues and beauties of art and style, his journalistic attitude, and other qualities that bring him nearer the common people, he is only continuing — with a rather long stride — the process already noticed of democratizing the stage. There are obviously certain reasons why his work may be exceptional in these respects, but it may also be symptomatic.

CHAPTER XII

FRANÇOIS DE CUREL AND THE THEATRE OF IDEAS

FRANÇOIS DE CUREL (1854–)

FOR the qualities that make of the drama serious literature and not solely an evening's entertainment, no French
writer during the past thirty years has stood higher than
François de Curel. However, he has not been known in
France as one of the most popular playwrights, and in
Anglo-Saxon countries his excellence as a dramatic author
has rarely been recognized. In both intent and temperament he is too far removed from the commercial theatre,
and his few popular successes have been won with too
much difficulty, for foreign managers to risk importation
of his plays.

In spite of his failure to win wide success on the stage,
Curel is a dramatist whose work is highly salutary and
of a type perhaps none too frequent in France. His
dramas should be a powerful influence in widening, in the
most promising direction, the horizon of the modern
theatre in general. Moreover, his plays not only represent exceedingly well some of the great currents of
thought of his age, but they are also good examples of the
freedom won for the French theatre toward the end of
the nineteenth century. Less than any of the other im-

229

portant dramatists discovered by Antoine, perhaps, is Curel a Naturalist, yet none has profited more from the opportunities offered by the Théâtre Libre.

François de Curel was born at Metz in 1854. On his father's side he belonged to the oldest Lorraine nobility, and his mother was a de Wendel, a family established in the iron and steel business of Lorraine for over two hundred years and today among the most important steel owners in Europe. His connection with this latter family is of considerable importance, since, because of it, he received in part a technical training and came into contact with labor problems. However, on account of choosing French nationality, he was not allowed by the Germans to manage personally his factories in Alsace-Lorraine. Owing to this fact, perhaps, his early interest, equally divided between science and literature, turned in later years entirely to the second field.

Among the important influences explaining the character of his work are his aristocratic affiliations and sympathies, his enforced leisure, spent largely in reading and hunting in the forests of his estates, and finally his racial heritage from a province and people whose characteristics are sufficiently marked to deserve an independent history. Thoroughly French as he is in feeling and sympathy, Curel still seems to have something of the North; he is more meditative, more speculative, more individualistic, and less completely a social being than the usual Frenchman.

Like so many of the young dramatists of his day, Curel was discovered by Antoine of the Théâtre Libre. After trying his hand with no great success at the novel,

and after failing to secure representation in the established theatres, he submitted three of his plays, *L'Envers
d'une Sainte*, *Sauvé des Eaux*, and *La Figurante* to Antoine, and all were approved. The first was presented at
the Théâtre Libre in 1892, and, although not a great
popular success, it won the author unusual praise from
the critics. It is a keen and realistic study of character,
but unattractive in subject and little dramatic in its
scenes and language. *La Figurante* was revised and appeared at the Renaissance Theatre in 1896, where it was
well received, although it is not among the strongest
of Curel's plays. *Sauvé des Eaux* has had a most
checkered history. It was rewritten and played at the
Comédie in 1893, under the title *L'Amour brode*. It
failed absolutely. Curel again rewrote it under the name
of *La Danse devant le Miroir*, and presented it in 1914
with fair success. It is a play of exceptional characters
and of difficult psychology, more suitable perhaps for the
novel than for the stage.

While his first play was being rehearsed at the Théâtre
Libre, Curel wrote another, *Les Fossiles*, which appeared
at the same theatre in 1892. It is one of the few that
may have been somewhat influenced in its tone and character creations by the Théâtre Libre movement. While
its characters are too grandiose (they are really epic) to
be despicable like those of the *comédie rosse*, they are
atrocious, and in action and psychology the drama is
painful. But it is among the strongest and most significant of Curel's plays, the aristocratic spirit being one in
which he is most at home.

L'Invitée, in 1893, is the only other play that belongs

to the early period of Curel. It is quite similar in tone, intent and effect to *L'Envers d'une Sainte*.

Curel's next three plays, written from 1897 to 1902, are the high peaks of his drama; they tower above all the others in power and significance, with the somewhat doubtful exception of *Les Fossiles*.

The first of these, *Le Repas du Lion*, was presented in 1897 but was rewritten in 1920. It is a complex and somewhat puzzling drama, representing the clash of the aristocratic and the socialistic ideals. Perhaps its final value is less in the clash of these ideals than in the evolution of its leading character, an aristocrat who is drawn into all the strong social currents of modern society, trade-unionism, socialism, charity and religion, to emerge in the end, by an atavism which the author tries to rationalize, still the aristocrat and autocrat. Its character treatment and interest have suggested its comparison, not wholly undeserved, with *Hamlet*.

La nouvelle Idole, published in 1895 and played in 1899, is the most readily comprehensible and thoroughly dramatic of Curel's chief plays, and the one that comes nearest to being a masterpiece, an honor that one hesitates to accord to even the strongest of them, so imperfectly or so difficultly do they fit into the dramatic form.

La Fille sauvage, in 1902, is the author's most ambitious work, the one into which he has put the deepest philosophy. It is an attempt to give in a single play the whole spiritual history of humanity passing through the ages of superstition, religion, rationalistic doubt and moral decadence. It is highly symbolic throughout, and, although most imperfect as a play, is a drama of great spiritual and intellectual interest. In a number of his pieces Curel reminds one of Ibsen; in this case the resemblance is undoubted and striking.

In his remaining four plays, from 1906 to 1922, excluding *La Danse devant le Miroir*, Curel has hardly attained the height of the three just mentioned, although he has extended somewhat his range and interest and decidedly improved his dramatic art, a fact which is clearly reflected in greater popular success on the stage.

Le Coup d'Aile, in 1906, is one of the least exceptional of his dramas in its characters and psychology.

L'Âme en Folie, in 1919, is more notable and again deals with great problems. In this play we find Curel interesting as a Darwinist and as a student of natural science.

L'Ivresse du Sage, in 1921, strikes a new note for Curel, since it is largely comedy, almost gay throughout, although a serious vein is also to be found.

His last play, *La Terre inhumaine*, in 1922, is placed in Lorraine during the Great War, and has been hailed by critics as the finest of war dramas. It is a piece with clearly defined motives, with genuine action and with tense dramatic situations, certainly one of his best constructed plays for the stage, but it will probably not add as much as several others to the author's reputation in the Theatre of Ideas.

Curel's plays were not written for the sake of a theatrical career. They are genuine and spontaneous products of the man himself; hence they do not repeat themselves, and it is impossible to select one or two as entirely representative. Their highest interest is that they are spiritual records, taken at different times, of the intellectual progress through life of a soul thoroughly modern, yet with unusual strength of heredity and traditions, and all must be read to appreciate this. None the less, their strictly dramatic faults and merits, their obvious failings as stage plays and their worth in the Theatre of Ideas, and particularly the stimulating promise for the future of this latter quality, may be illustrated by two pieces, *Le Repas du Lion* and *La nouvelle Idole*. In the first of these the author enters the domain of social problems, and in the second that of modern science and philosophy, and these are the great fields most industriously cultivated by nineteenth century thought.

In *Le Repas du Lion,* a boy of fourteen, Jean de Miremont, in despair over the invasion of his beloved ancestral forests by a great steel company, floods one of its exploring shafts and causes the death of a drunken miner who had remained below. Moved by this unwitting murder, he swears to devote his life to the cause of the workers. He becomes an ardent champion of Christian charity, in which he believes he will find a solution of the conflict between labor and capital, and for a time he is a noted socialistic orator. But this is only an expiation, and he finally realizes that his real talent and mission are elsewhere. Moreover, he comes to believe that the surest field of service to the worker is neither in the church nor in socialism, but in industry, and that the greatest benefactor of labor and humanity is he who opens up undeveloped resources and new industrial projects. Consequently when his brother-in-law, the president of the steel company, is killed by riotous employees,

he becomes the head of this corporation and builds up
an immense industry.

It is easy to see that in the hands of another we should
have had an outright Social drama, perhaps with a thesis.
It is most significant that Curel gives us something else.
It is true that he discusses social problems, and these
discussions are competent, keen and often highly dramatic. Certain qualities of Curel's style are here seen
at their best, as, for example, in the various passages
in which he justifies the claims of the capitalist and great
industrialist as public benefactors:

" The great majority of men need to have their ideas and
actions suggested to them. A few persons, superiorly endowed,
plan and carry out before a crowd of imitators who copy their
slightest motions. . . . If I, as head of a great business,
organize an industrial center, where a whole population lives,
supports itself and multiplies, I am entitled to gratitude. . . .

Invent, be a creative force, and the prosperity of others
will flow from yours."

With regard to the accusation of egoism in this conception, he replies:

" Moreover, egoism has been slandered! Go to the bottom
of the most charitable hearts. . . . Some come to the aid
of the wretched because they are afraid of the deeds of violence
which exasperated poverty causes; others deprive themselves
of everything in order to increase their share of the joys of
eternity. All that is egoism and is often admirable! . . .

One has quite as many chances of being useful to humanity
by working for himself as by working for his neighbor. . . .

I have always noted this: all these benefactors prosper;
they all advance more rapidly and better than their fellow-

men. Once they have left the ranks, they rise above the heads of the others.

It is a general law, then, that it is impossible to aid one's fellow-man without surpassing him. From whence comes this conclusion, in appearance paradoxical, but in reality very logical: beneficence is one of the most intelligent forms of egoism." [1]

With the same line of reasoning he justifies, socially and philosophically, the desire and appetite for wealth and luxuries, as being the chief spur to progress and the means of elevating man above the savage, and for this reason he rejects collectivism or communism.

The passages above give an idea of the questions treated in this piece and their possible interest, and it is instructive to note that all the first and larger part of the drama is given to these. But it was neither in the intentions, nor perhaps in the power of Curel to write a purely social problem play, and, after having established his *milieu*, he suddenly drops this entire drama and turns to his real and usual subject, the psychological and philosophical evolution of a single character. This is his dramatic error, condemned both by the voice of some of his critics and by the bewilderment of the general public. Undoubtedly it is a plot which shows its loose ends. He simply puts aside the champions of the various doctrines of socialism, of unionism and of Christian charity, to whom he had given genuine rôles, life and interest.

Furthermore, the single character with which he carries the drama to the end decidedly lacks popular appeal or sympathy — and again this is often characteristic of

[1] Acts II and III.

Curel. Jean de Miremont as a leader and superman represents a restricted type, and not one whose opinions will flatter the general public. There is even in the conception of this character something which may possibly irritate the spectator, in the same way that Jean irritated the workers in comparing the great industrialist and his employees to the lion who kills and feasts on his prey, leaving the remains to the jackals. Finally, Jean, himself, is not only an aristocrat but he is too philosophic and too detached to appeal to popular imagination.

In fact, it is these latter qualities in nearly all of Curel's plays, and in Curel himself, obviously, that make against a decided success with the average audience. His thought here is of the highest quality and does him credit. He rejects all the specious and short-sighted solutions to the problems he raises. He does not believe that the struggles of life and its cruelty can be wiped out in a Utopia. He even sees in these struggles a means to progress, in which he does believe. He condemns none of the generous theories of life, but he puts his faith in none. In short, Curel has shown himself a genuine philosopher, highly endowed with reflective wisdom, but not a popular playwright. Dumas, with the sophistry of pure logic, or Brieux, from a mere impulse of pity, could take a less valid theme and write a much more stirring play. Curel does not have the strong emotional conviction inherent in an apostle; he is not an apostle.

La nouvelle Idole has been the most genuinely successful on the stage of all of Curel's plays, and in 1914 it was taken into the repertory of the *Comédie,* where it has been accepted as a classic. The chief conflicting motives of the drama are faith and science, the eternal struggle in the human mind between the intuitions and yearnings of the soul and the demonstrable facts of realistic experience. For it should be noted that, although faith and science are incorporated in separate characters, there is no clash between these two characters; the real drama, all that is truly poignant, is the agonizing struggle in the mind of Dr. Donnat. In this respect it is a drama in the truest French sense, measured by the standard set by Corneille and Racine and upheld by French genius ever since, a mental and moral crisis evolving intelligibly according to the principles of interior action.

The play is not only noteworthy in being one of the best written on a scientific subject, but it presents a problem of peculiar interest, the dramatic value and possibilities of a truly scientific character and philosophy on the stage, where effects are admittedly so largely emotional. To attempt the task set is to accept a wager against all the odds, and if Curel has succeeded, by sheer power of genius, the example does not encourage easy imitation. Dr. Donnat is too intellectual, too cold, to win easily an audience. The theatre warms largely by emotion. The fate of a Marguerite Gautier, unworthy though she be, will probably call for a hundred times more tears than the man who sacrifices himself for a scientific idea.

Curel seems to have felt this difficulty of making his intellectual martyr appealing, of inducing in his character the vital spark that will kindle the sympathy of his audience, and it is most interesting to see that when he fails to do this by intellectual argument he turns to emotional persuasion; when he despairs of science, he resorts to faith, although it is a faith harassed and even strangled by doubt. In the whole final act, though Dr. Donnat's science constantly destroys and denies God, his faith persists in re-creating Him and in appealing to Him, and this is the most moving act of the play.

As usual, Curel does not attempt in this play to decide finally as to the supremacy of the motives which he has placed in conflict. His aim and attitude are expressed in his own words in his preface: " I believe, in fact, that human nature, so heavily weighed down by inferior heredity, should neglect none of the means of rising that are offered it. To strive toward God through faith, toward truth through science, and toward beauty through love. . . . Such is the conclusion of *La nouvelle Idole*."

The play has a much greater value than that of a pure drama of science, interesting as that may be in this scientific age. It is one of the best examples of the Theatre of Ideas. As such it demonstrates how far one can go successfully in putting elevated and serious thought on the stage before a general public. Curel maintains here at its highest level his reputation as a serious thinker on the greatest problems of humanity, and at the same time has come nearest to, if he has not wholly succeeded in, incorporating these in good dramatic form of general interest. The attempt is ambitious and the success is sufficiently great for this play to stand as a challenge to every modern dramatist who believes in the high mission of his profession. Its example seems especially salutary at this time, when the easy appeal of realism, lowered to the level of a universal democracy, threatens the theatre seriously in those intellectual and artistic qualities which bring it into the realm of literature.

The one fact that stands out most clearly, in the study of Curel's plays and of his career in the theatre, is the difficulty he has in adapting himself to the dramatic form. Obviously this is due to two causes. In the first place, his constant preoccupation with ideas, often abstract and difficult, and his frequent choice of the great, eternal problems of humanity for his themes, would tax to the limit the most skillful of dramatists to produce a successful stage play. The way of the thinker on the popular stage is straight and narrow. However, it is also certain that Curel does not have some of the qualities that are most important for success with the public. His plays are frequently too argumentative, too oratorical, and written in a style too remote from ordinary speech. Furthermore, they not only contain unusual characters and situations, but often these characters arrive at decisions by mental short-cuts that baffle an audience and tax even the most thoughtful reader.

Finally, his construction in the larger sphere of scenes and acts is often awkward and faulty. The best proof of this is that most of his plays have been extensively revised, some entirely rewritten, as the result of criticism by managers and dramatic critics, and these revisions have in general been decided improvements. Undoubtedly, Curel, in his eager pursuit of ideas and in his development of characters, has paid little attention to what is effective theatrically. To an extent, this is a merit, but he often carries it too far. He is not a skillful playwright.

Nevertheless, he does have certain important dramatic virtues. His style is often most illuminating, as suddenly revealing as a lightning flash, and his characters, even when most exceptional or most symbolic, seem real persons and not mere abstractions. Above all they are not pawns or puppets. They are endowed with self-determination, free to work out their own fates, perhaps too free occasionally in following some secret inner urge, but, after all, with something of the imperfect and incomplete that makes us recognize real life.

Critics have attributed to no author more dissimilar characteristics than to Curel, both by comparing him with other writers and by ascribing to him unusual and sometimes contradictory qualities. The alembicated psychology and subtle dialogue of *La Danse devant le Miroir* suggest strikingly Marivaux and Musset; the monstrous egoists of *Les Fossiles* recall Corneille; Jean de Miremont in *Le Repas du Lion* justly reminds one of Shakespeare's Hamlet, and the author's undoubted kinship to Ibsen has been generally recognized in a number of his plays.

Some of Curel's qualities would seem to call for other forms than that of the theatre. Despite his lack of success in his novels, his subjects and highly developed psychology have often been pointed out by the critics as belonging more properly to that field. Also, his striking powers of imagination are everywhere apparent in a genre where imagination is most closely fettered. Moreover, although writing in a realistic period, and with Antoine, one of the founders of stage Naturalism, as his most frequent producer and constant mentor, Curel gives us many scenes that are highly poetic, and, in a number of instances, he has been characterized as epic. In fact, he deserves all these characterizations and others beside. This probably explains his comparative lack of success with popular audiences, which demand simplicity and easily comprehended emotion, just as it constitutes his greatest appeal to the *élite,* to the critic and to the student of the drama.

Curel is by character and temperament a thinker, and this quality of speculation and meditation has undoubtedly been encouraged by his somewhat solitary life, passed in great part in his Lorraine forests. Moreover, he is writing in a genre that tends toward definite conclusions and he deals with the great problems of humanity, such as the origin of the species, evolution, and other questions of science and religion. It would seem natural, then, to ask what are the author's own judgments or views on life.

However, the most certain conclusion from an investigation of the author's works is that he has, above all else, avoided dogmatic judgments. In such conflicting theories as religion and evolution, or faith and science, he has given to each a place, and a fine place, in the history and development of humanity, without deciding in the favor of any one.

That he is not an apostle either of faith or of fact is certain. Indeed, one might be tempted, seeing his uncertainty in his conclusions, to ascribe to him the philosophy of Montaigne, the *Que sais-je* of the doubter and skeptic. But he is not simply a skeptic, and still less is he a cynic; his doubts are not a system. They are not final. His philosophy would seem more appropriately characterized by the phrase *Que sais-je à présent?* He is too honest and open-minded to believe that he has captured the whole truth at the end of any of his great plays, but he shows no intention of giving up the pursuit, and above all, he invites us to take it up at the point where he stops.

He is as indefatigable in his pursuit of ideas through the maze of life as he was of the wild boar in his Lorraine forests. In the first case as in the second, darkness may end the chase, but it does not end his zest nor spell discouragement for the morrow. The follower of Curel will gain in interest in life and in healthful intellectual exercise; there is no blighting pessimism in his failures. In short, he is particularly the thinker, the man whom the great problems of life continually interest. For him, man is the thinking being, and perhaps we may say that this is his final philosophy, to be a man in this, the fullest, sense.

In the French drama he represents a rare and precious type. The thinker in the theatre is unusual enough in any country, but in France, despite the constant intellectual trend of French literature, the speculative thinker is especially rare. The French undoubtedly possess to a preëminent degree most of the dramatic virtues: taste, concision, logic, a superior gift of form and style, and, most valuable of all, a keen sense of social psychology, developed perhaps by their marked social instinct and favored by their unusual mass solidarity. These qualities have brought their dramatic art to a higher level of excellence, or even perfection, than can be found anywhere else.

Nevertheless, this very perfection of dramatic art and social psychology has often tended to stress unduly the rules, conventions and restrictions of the theatre, and to take the audience's approval and capacity for comprehension as the common denominator of all drama. In no other country have there been so many Scribes and Sardous.

Undoubtedly, rules and conventions are peculiarly necessary to the actable play, and the drama must be acted to exist. A measure of popular approval is indispensable. But in stressing this factor too much there is also danger of narrowing the stage. The temptation of a writer like Scribe is to create a dramatic mold, perfect in form but in which the content, the idea, may shrivel to nothing. The tendency of a Curel, occupied solely with the idea and with life, and negligent of technique and even of popular approval, is to break all molds and to give the heart of drama a chance to expand and to create a new life and art, in accord with the pulse of each new generation. A Curel, then, is as necessary as a Scribe to the health of the theatre, and, in fact, must appear from time to time if the drama is to have life and growth. The theatre, after all, is an *intellectual* amusement.

In the final evaluation of Curel's genius, one point should not be misunderstood. The meditative and speculative character of his thought may not seem entirely French, but this is true of his methods only and does not apply to the essential quality of his ideas. His speculation, or meditation, is primarily intellectual and very little emotional or sentimental. Moreover, it is not mystical, as it frequently is, for example, with Maeterlinck, nor darkly symbolical as it sometimes is with Ibsen. The symbolism of Curel is perfectly definite and, in fact, is, more properly speaking, allegory in the important cases where it is found, such as *La Fille sauvage*. Finally, his thought lacks the universal quality of Shakespeare's, which covers every mood and ranges through every class and situation of life. In short, it is purely intellectual speculation, confined to great, serious or rare questions, and as such it is completely and even peculiarly French.

CHAPTER XIII

PAUL HERVIEU AND FRENCH RATIONALISM

PAUL HERVIEU (1857–1915)

BRIEUX and CUREL, thoroughly French as they are in most respects, both have certain qualities that are not the most characteristic of French literature; for example, the philosophy of sentiment of the first, and the speculative and even symbolistic character of thought of the second. But it would seem impossible to find anything in the drama of Hervieu that is not completely national; in fact, all the work of this author is so entirely typical of the racial qualities that control French drama that it appears quite without individuality.

Hervieu not only illustrates perfectly the basic French traits, but he is, in many respects, strikingly representative of his generation. These assertions are fully confirmed by the universal esteem accorded him in France: by his favorable treatment at the *Comédie,* by the respect and praise of the critics, by his reception into the Academy and by his election to the presidency of the Society of French Men of Letters. For a period of some twenty years, from the decline of the Théâtre Libre to the outbreak of the Great War in 1914, the dramatic work of Hervieu might fairly be considered as representing the normal, or at least the most national trend of the French prose drama.

Paul Hervieu was born in Paris in 1857. His father, who had made a fortune in business, was from Normandy, and it is perhaps permissible to see in the son some of the robust, serious and positive qualities characteristic of the Norman stock. However, he was in his training, his associations, and his whole life and interests thoroughly Parisian. This latter fact is more important than is usually the case since it was the author's avowed principle, rarely violated, to draw his observations of life, the themes and figures of his plays, strictly from the society and class in which he himself was placed.

His education was completed by a law course and he had expected to plead at the bar, but, rather by accident, he was drawn into the diplomatic service. His ambition to write came comparatively late, and at first turned to journalism, and to the story and the novel. He was already well known as a novelist before attempting the theatre, and his first play of real merit and significance, *Les Tenailles,* did not appear until 1895.

In character Hervieu was reserved, serious and cold, at least in manner. He looked on life with the eyes of a moralist, and, on the whole, of a stern one, and had very little of the gaiety which often seasons this quality in the Frenchman. Except for this somewhat marked deficiency of wit and humor, Hervieu shows, in perfect balance, the influences of his generation: the seriousness and pessimism following the war of 1870, accompanied by the will and energy necessary to combat these, and the hard realism inherited from Henri Becque, without its cynicism and corrected by good taste and rationalism.

His first play, *Point de Lendemain,* is of no importance,

and the second, *Les Paroles restent,* performed in 1892, is much below his best work in significance. It is a piece of three acts, written to show the evils of gossip, and ends in a tragedy.

It was not until *Les Tenailles,* in 1895, that the dramatist is found in a characteristic theme and with full mastery of his form. In one aspect, this piece might be considered a feministic plea, similar to those so often found in Dumas fils. It portrays a woman who is desperate in her desire to escape from an incompatible marriage and who, when a separation is refused her by her husband as being without justification, deceives him. Later, to preserve a respectable name for her son, she refuses her husband the divorce for which she had formerly pleaded in vain. It is hardly, then, a thesis plea for divorce; it is rather the drama of two beings caught in the inexorable grip of a situation from which there is no escape, and who must suffer together.

La Loi de l'Homme, in 1897, is of very similar theme. However, here the wife is wholly blameless, and yet, through the peculiarity of the man-made laws, is unable to secure a divorce from the husband who has deceived her, and is only allowed by him a separation on very severe terms. Later, she is forced to return to him to permit a marriage that will insure the happiness of her daughter. Of all of Hervieu's plays this is the one which is most a thesis in the style of Dumas and directed against a specific social institution or abuse. It is a direct attack on the character of the divorce law of this period.

In *L'Énigme,* in 1901, the author turned definitely

away from the plays that attack a social institution or a law and took up a problem of human nature. The enigma is to know which one of two women is guilty, and a keen dramatic suspense is maintained until the last tragic moments of the play, by keeping the audience in the same doubt as the characters of the drama. The piece is also, in intent perhaps, although this is rather secondary in effect, a plea for mercy for the weak and guilty woman. Of more significance, especially in the light of later dramas of the author, are the many features of this play that resemble those of Classic tragedy. Its unity of action and its uniform tone and style, without a trivial or comic note, are in general characteristic of Hervieu. But in this case he has further conformed to the unities of time and place.

Hervieu's most widely known play, if not his masterpiece, is *La Course du Flambeau,* which appeared in 1901. It is also his most perfectly representative drama in every respect: tone, technique and philosophy. The theme of this piece is explained, in the first scenes, by the author's representative, Maravon. After describing the torch races of the Greeks where the sacred light was passed from one runner to another, and comparing these with the generations of mankind where life is handed down from parent to child, Maravon adds:

" Humanity racks her brains to persuade herself that she is not an ungrateful daughter, but she is such from birth, just as she is, from birth also, a good mother. Read again the commandments of Mount Sinai. There is not a word concerning duties toward children. Why? Because it was useless. Because all creatures had devoted themselves, by instinct, to the care of their young. But the duties toward parents are not passed over without mention, as a matter of course. 'Honor thy father and thy mother that thy days may be long on earth.' In this there is not only a command, but, for inducement, there is a reward to be realized in this world below. Believe me, filial gratitude is not spontaneous; it is an effort of civilization, a fragile attempt at virtue."

The aim of the play is to put filial ingratitude in contrast with maternal love, and especially to show how far, on occasion, the latter may go, and into what instinct it is to be resolved in a final analysis.

In pursuit of this purpose, the dramatist shows us Sabine Revel putting aside her own feelings and refusing a second marriage, in order not to prejudice the prospects and happiness of her daughter, Marie-Jeanne, who in the meantime has thought only of her own affairs and announces her engagement on the very day of her mother's sacrifice. Four years later, when her son-in-law is about to become a bankrupt, and Marie-Jeanne can think of nothing better than to have a nervous breakdown, which, in the eyes of the mother at least, threatens her reason and life itself, Sabine, unable to persuade her own mother to imperil their fortune in order to avoid this failure, steals her mother's bonds and attempts to secure the money on them. In other words, the author answers affirmatively the query whether an honest and honorable mother will steal to save her daughter's life and reason.

But even this sacrifice is not sufficient for the implacable logic and philosophy of the dramatist, and in the next act he places Sabine in the dilemma of either allowing her daughter to perish, or, in saving her, to imperil the weak heart of her own mother in the Alps; and the play ends by the tragedy of this second alternative, with the words of Sabine, over her mother's body: "She is dead! For my daughter I have killed my mother."

Naturally, a bare *résumé* of such a tragedy makes it seem more atrocious and less reasonable. However, such summary is less unfair in Hervieu's plays than is usually the case, since it departs so little from his own dramatic method. His plays, as built, are hardly more than skeletons, solidly joined but without the covering and color necessary to give the illusions of life. They have been compared to the steel framework of a building before it has been finished. Both these comparisons, although offering a picture that is extreme, contain much truth.

The chief element of this dramatic method is Hervieu's logic, which is even more rigid, and often less plausible, than that of Dumas; and in no play perhaps, is the danger of this peculiarly French quality better illustrated, especially when it is carried to an extreme as it is here, without the necessary correction of experience and observation. That a mother will sacrifice her own marriage for the sake of her daughter's is perhaps not remarkable enough to call for comment, whether it occurs often in life or not. But will an honest mother steal to save her daughter's life? In theory and logic perhaps, yes. But the actual facts are that hundreds and thousands of mothers everywhere, no more honest than Sabine is supposed to be, do allow their children to suffer, and even die, without breaking the lifelong rule of honesty; and the reason seems clear. In life, situations do not present themselves in the form of rigid dilemmas as they do in this drama. In cases similar to these, other alternatives, even though they be illusions, would offer themselves to the mind. In real life, how many mothers would actually ask themselves, " Shall I steal or allow my daughter to die? " or, especially, " Shall I kill my daughter or kill my mother " ?

Hervieu's strictly logical deductions, then, can hardly be maintained as true to actual life, but this does not wholly invalidate his work. The fault is in the rigidity of the development, and frequently also in the extremes to which it is carried, or the universality of its application, rather than in its general truth. This he usually establishes, and often impressively. This is true in the play in question, and particularly in the last analysis of Sabine's passion for sacrifice, which he reduces to a form of egoism. When her son-in-law is offered a chance to redeem his fortunes in America and her daughter decides to leave her behind, Sabine's violent opposition and bitterness enlighten us as to the true character of her sentiments. Her sacrifices, after all, were for the pleasure of living for and with her daughter. They were what she wished to do most, for her own sake.

Although this play does not conform to the unities of time and place, as did *L'Énigme*, it suggests none the less strikingly the Classic genre. This is seen especially in its simplicity and concentration of plot, its unity of tone and style, its logical evolution, and the constant analysis and intellectual justification by the characters of all their actions. It even approaches the traditional conception of *tragédie* in representing the individual, and the human will, seemingly so resolute, as helpless in times of great crises when in conflict with the primitive instincts, which rule our lives as arbitrarily as fate did those of the ancients. But most commendable in this piece are the questions and characters treated. It discards the eternal triangle play and deals with honest, sane and representative people. In this it departs fundamentally from the realism of Becque and many of his immediate successors.

Théroigne de Méricourt, in 1902, is a decided anomaly in Hervieu's work, and in his avowed theories of the drama. It is a historical play of the French Revolution, evoking on a grand scale some of its most stirring scenes, and was written for Sarah Bernhardt. With *Le Dédale*, in 1903, Hervieu returned to his proper field and offered another drama worthy to stand beside *La Course du Flambeau*. Although its theme of divorce and illicit love is a hackneyed one, this fault is fully redeemed by the dignity and originality of the author's treatment. It is not a thesis play, nor a play aimed primarily at the abuses of a law or at a social institution. It goes back of these to the great moral laws or instincts of humanity on which our statutes and social conventions are based, often so imperfectly.

In one important respect *Le Dédale* is probably Hervieu's best play; his characters here are the most individual, human and sympathetic to be found in any of his pieces. These characters are usually too nearly abstractions to be convincing, or too much the instruments of his deductions. They lack color, and they fail to evoke sympathy and interest in themselves, however much there may be in the problems in which they are involved. *Le Dédale* is one of the most human of Hervieu's plays.

L'Armature, a novel by Hervieu which Brieux dramatized, hardly calls for comment here. *Le Réveil*, in 1905, although it is built on the foundations of the traditional triangle play of guilty love, is immediately raised to a higher plane by the elevation of the motives that are brought into it. They are mother-love and conjugal respect and duty on the one side, and ambition and patriotism on the other. It is a good example of the unfailing worth and seriousness of the author in any situation.

Modestie, in 1909, is the briefest and slightest of comedies, and interesting only because it is not in the author's usual serious vein. *Connais-toi*, in 1909 also, which like *Le Réveil* is based on situations that might tempt an author to the easy success of a sensational or meretricious treatment, is a play of dignified purpose and, for the most part, worthy characters, and offers a serious lesson to all who may be inclined to criticize too hastily or harshly the conduct of others.

Bagatelle, in 1912, is a piece seemingly light in tone, motive and characters, but which ends most seriously. Its lesson is that one must not jest with love, with the morality of love and marriage. Historically it is very interesting as a sort of final word on one of the subjects which the author treated a number of times in his stories and novels, flirtation — especially the playing with temptation among the married women of the smart set, which

Hervieu so often treated. We see how thorough a moralist he is.

Le Destin est Maître, although not one of Hervieu's best plays, is strikingly significant as his last work. Certainly no other title could better give final expression to the author's habitual philosophy and dramatic system. According to these, man is a plaything of destiny, and in fate's unconscious cruelty lie the dramas of life.

The outstanding features of Hervieu's plays, viewed all together, are their many points of resemblance with French Classic drama, and the supremely national character of the author's dramatic qualities. In no respects are such characteristics more marked than in his plots. These have a brevity, simplicity and concentration equally removed from the too theatrical system of the well-made play and from the rudimentary and incomplete conception of the slice of life exemplified by the Naturalists. It is interesting especially to note the brevity of his pieces. Of the nine serious plays considered here as characteristic of the author, one, *Le Dédale,* is in five acts, and another, *La Course du Flambeau,* in four. Two of the others have only two acts and the rest have three, which may be taken as the norm of his dramatic construction in this respect.

Not infrequently the concentration of action and plot is carried to the point of conforming in part, or in whole, to the unities of time and place, and this is evidently not due to the author's feeling under any obligation to follow these former rules of drama. He attained this unity, as did the Classicists, by his tendency to choose a moral crisis for his subject, and especially by the unswerving logic and mathematical precision of his plot development. As already indicated, he sometimes carried this dramatic virtue to the point where it became a fault, and his dramas may seem bare and harsh on that account. This judgment is somewhat confirmed by the fact that *Le Dédale,* his only five-act play, has largely avoided this criticism. In any case, Hervieu's tendency toward the Classic practice in plot and construction is clear, and it is just as evident that this is the working out of the native and racial qualities of his genius and not an attempt to revive an obsolete genre.

Hervieu's style is no less notable for its Classic qualities. It is marked especially by correctness, elegance and precision, but falls short of the best Classic traditions in its lack of the shades and flexibility of a Racine, and by its deficiency in the wit and humor of a Molière. The uniformity, for which Hervieu may be reproached, is partly because he dealt only with the educated and cultured classes, but it is also certain that he lacked the power to project himself into the different characters and give them individuality. It has often been said that they all talk alike, and like Hervieu himself.

His style is clearly the expression of himself, of precise and methodical thinking, without imagination, or spontaneity. It is exact and well-balanced, but rarely with the flashes of inspiration that make the *coups de théâtre* of so many French dramatists. The deficiency in wit and humor is particularly striking in a French author, and its almost complete absence is apparently due both to natural qualities of the dramatist's genius, and to an intentional elimination of all comic touches from the thoroughly serious plays he has written.

Quite naturally Hervieu's characters show the same lack of color and of marked individuality that were noted in his style. They have usually been identified with the universal and even abstract types of Classic drama. However, the differences are considerable, and probably are due to a different conception. It is doubtful whether Hervieu's figures have been created by a personification of abstract qualities; they are rather the products of observation, with the elimination of most of the minor qualities or details which would give them color and individuality.

The dramatist has often been accused of making his characters too completely the instruments of his deductions and plot developments. Nevertheless they are not weak puppets; on the contrary, they are for the most part notable for will and determination. Their failure to control their own destiny is inherent in the author's philosophy or dramatic conception, which is to bring this will and determination to a struggle — usually ending in defeat — with the great primary and controlling instincts of life. In any case, the characters of Hervieu present certain merits not always found in the dramas of his day. They are not false to life and they are not monsters; still more, they are regularly respectable, often representative, and consequently much above those of Becque and the *comédie rosse,* although their conception has occasionally been slightly affected by the Naturalistic practice.

Hervieu's philosophy has been mentioned more than

once in connection with his plays. It looks on life as controlled by a few primary instincts, such as egoism and the preservation of the species. Compared with these, all the acquirements of civilization form but a thin veneer covering the primitive man beneath. In the great crises of life, this veneer is broken through and the original savage in man appears.

The author's most frequent conception of the drama is to show civilized man in these moments of crisis, in the grip of these instincts, which are quite as inexorable as the hand of fate. This emergence of the primitive and savage in man is necessarily a grievous or tragic spectacle, and the doctrine of its supremacy is a pessimistic one.

No doubt, there is much ground for this conception, and even its truth, in a very remote and general sense, might be admitted, but it is questionable whether Hervieu is warranted in carrying it as far as he sometimes does in practice. One might admit that such civilized virtues as honesty, filial respect and conjugal duty are the painted card-board of life's stage rather than actual stone walls, and still find them sufficient to turn back the human animal that has always respected them.

Because of the Classic qualities already mentioned, and particularly on account of this basic conception of drama found in the philosophy just described, where the instincts of life play a rôle similar to that of fate in the drama of the ancients, Hervieu has often been given credit for the reëstablishment of a genuine French *tragédie*, comparable to that of Classic drama. With due allowances for important differences, the comparison is admissible. But it must be noted that this is, at most, a bourgeois tragedy, which lacks the poetry and the heroic tone and proportions of the Classic. However, it is in accord with its age, and, for that reason perhaps, is the only genuine tragedy possible today.

The themes to which Hervieu has confined his drama are decidedly of narrow range. Except for a play or two, and in these to a secondary extent, he has scarcely touched the large rôle of money in modern society. Also, of the two great fields of the passions, ambition and love, he has confined himself to the second, and has cultivated this in part only. But at least he has limited himself to that with which he was in personal contact, to the class he knew at first hand.

In a final analysis, he would seem to be best described as a Classic realist. The numerous Classic qualities of his drama have been fully brought out. But it must not be overlooked, also, that he is a genuine realist, who came on the stage following Becque and in the time of the Théâtre Libre. He undoubtedly represents, to an extent, the reaction against these extreme Naturalistic influences, but he was none the less affected by them. He has turned from the sordid life depicted by Becque and the *comédie rosse,* but his realism has the same hard, scientific and impersonal character as that of the author of *Les Corbeaux.*

It is strictly French realism, without any of the mystic faith and religion of the Russian, or of the feeling of sympathy and comradeship of the English. Here is probably the chief difficulty his drama encounters in making a wide or popular appeal, especially outside of France. In this country particularly, we have failed to find in his plays, despite the high intellectual qualities shown, the warm humanity and interest that we see, for example, in the social pity of Brieux's pieces.

It is of interest to note further that the character of Hervieu's thought, his intellectual qualities, are as thoroughly French as is his realism. Certainly he stands high in these respects. He is a psychologist and a philosopher, and, throughout the development and arguments of his plays, strictly intellectual. But he is not interested in the curious or exceptional psychological problems and characters which are so often treated by Curel, nor is his thought of the speculative sort of his contemporary. His is the orthodox and mass psychology, and his philosophy is supremely that of his age, the positivism of Compte, which holds itself rigidly within the realm of fact. He represents perfectly the French rationalism of the first years of the twentieth century.

CHAPTER XIV

OTHER RECENT PLAYWRIGHTS AND TENDENCIES

LAVEDAN, DONNAY, LEMAITRE, PORTO-RICHE, BATAILLE, BERNSTEIN

In order to follow main currents and emphasize important tendencies in the modern French theatre, it has been necessary not only to pass over the playwrights who seem less significant but to select among those who are outstanding. In connection with Rostand, Brieux, Curel and Hervieu, an attempt has been made to treat the forms and phases of recent drama that are most characteristic of the French and that promise most for the future. These forms do not represent all the aspects of the present French stage, nor do the names mentioned include all those who stand high in popular favor.

Every year there appear in the Paris theatres more native plays than in any city of the world. Quite naturally most of these are not masterpieces, and the great mass of them fall into a very simple category. Many are written in conformity with successful formulae, for an audience whose preferences are known, and to be given by actors of certain capabilities. Such plays may be called the " *théâtre à succès.*" This may or may not mean that the authors have subserviently catered to the appetites of the crowd; often no doubt such pieces are genuine products of the playwright's own tastes and ideas.

Since the days of the two Dumas, at least, the greater number of these pieces are dramas of guilty love and passion and are most frequently known as triangle plays. The astonishing vogue of such pieces is perhaps after all entirely explicable. Love and passion have always been the greatest resource of the theatre, both in France and elsewhere; the pattern and technique of this genre were demonstrated and taught by one of the greatest masters of the modern realistic stage; and the frankness of French manners and speech allow unusual freedom for the discussion of immoral love and sex problems. The taste of audiences was formed for such dramas, and playwrights knew exactly how to write them.

But these plays do not represent the best theatre of the French, nor their creative dramatic art, any more than a ready-to-wear establishment would offer the best products of the original or artistic efforts of French designers. Mere vogue or popularity means little. Assuredly we should hardly wish the serious promise of our own stage to be judged by the millions who have flocked to see *The Bat* or *The Thirteenth Chair,* or by the prevalency in general of the mystery play and the bedroom farce. Such plays please the crowd and can be manufactured cheaply.

It is obviously difficult to select the most worthy French dramatists whose work happens to fall mainly in the above category of the *théâtre à succès,* even in the cases where such drama may be the sincere and original product of the author's talent and philosophy, so closely will it resemble the many imitative examples of the commercial theatre. It seems necessary, however, to give a summary treatment to a few names, at the risk of inviting the inclusion of a number of others who must be omitted for the sake of brevity. The following recent or present-day dramatists are all widely known in France, and in some cases have been exceedingly popular. The permanency of their fame can, no doubt, be questioned, but the final judgment of posterity has not yet been passed, and at least they have in nearly every case written some plays of sufficient literary merit to warrant discussion in a history of French literature.

HENRI LAVEDAN (1859–   )

Henri Lavedan is perhaps the most eminent, and is certainly the most versatile, of those contemporary dramatists who have made a specialty of psychological love drama and character analysis. He was born at Orleans in 1859 but was mostly educated at Paris, where, like so many young Frenchmen, he was prepared for law. His career as a writer began rather in journalism, and his earliest pieces in dramatic form are mere dialogues, not intended to be played. In fact, a considerable part of his work is on the borderline between the real play and the literary dialogue.

Several of his pieces, while enjoying considerable popularity in Paris, will hardly be of interest elsewhere or bear the light of serious study. *Une Famille* is scarcely more than his early dialogues strung together; *Viveurs* and *Le nouveau Jeu,* although often amusing, are exaggerated pictures of a class already extreme; the subject of *Le vieux Marcheur* is not worth the effort; *Sire* and *Servir* border on melodrama; and about the most one can say for *Catherine* is that there is no harm in it. His best, or most notable, plays are *Le Prince d'Aurec* in 1892, *Le Marquis de Priola* in 1902, and *Le Duel* in 1904.

Le Prince d'Aurec often recalls *Le Gendre de M. Poirier* of Augier, and the imitation is even conscious at times. The Prince is a Gaston, without either the charm or the possibilities of reform of the latter, and his mother is a paler and less inspired Poirier. The chief difference between the two pieces — and this difference is enormous from the dramatic standpoint — is that *Le Gendre de M. Poirier* is a real play, while *Le Prince d'Aurec* is only three scenes of character analysis, which are not welded into an inseparable whole nor made vitally effective as a play.

Le Marquis de Priola is a Don Juan play. Priola is portrayed as a dilletante or connoisseur in the art of seduction. This drama is a striking study of character, cleverly and often keenly done, but it is rather difficult to justify such a Don Juan portrait as a finished piece of art, and its moral lesson is obviously of limited application. Priola is not any too convincing, and his speeches and actions border on pose. Much of his perversity is recounted by himself and is without sufficient motive. There would seem to be three possible ways of treating this famous subject: one making Don Juan ordinary and comic, another by making him Satanic and tragic, and a third, halfway between, in which he is only disagreeable or obnoxious. Lavedan's portrait falls too largely in the last category.

Le Duel is the play which does Lavedan the greatest honor and which has the widest and most enduring interest. It is one of the very early dramatic themes, a debate betweeen the soul and the body, or, in action, a struggle between the flesh and the spirit. It is a play of penetrating psychological insight and of considerable dramatic interest, but is far from perfect as a whole. Its characters are incomplete or inconsistent and fail to carry entire conviction, and, when all is said, we are not sure of the author's purpose. Despite this criticism, Lavedan has, on the whole, ably treated a most difficult subject without resorting to any cheap appeals.

What is best in Lavedan is keen psychological analysis; what he lacks is a corresponding power of synthesis and composition. He is most clever in laying bare the vices or qualities of his persons, without seeming to be able to combine these into a convincing, autonomous character, who can be used effectively in a drama.

As a moralist his effect is similar. He is keen in showing the weaknesses and crimes of life without passing any very certain judgment on them. The criticism is not that he fails to point an obvious moral — this might well be a virtue — but that he does not always leave us on ground firm enough for us to find our own way out. He seems, on the whole, too versatile in his sympathies, and without the strong conviction or high earnestness necessary to strike fire in his characters and move deeply an audience.

MAURICE DONNAY (1860–   )

Maurice Donnay is probably the most artistic of the contemporary realistic dramatists who furnish the Parisians their daily — or rather nightly — bread, the love play. No doubt his real talent and exceptional qualities are less recognized than they should be, owing to his cultivation of a form of which every variety and color have been discovered and developed to the point of standardization.

The most characteristic plays of Donnay are *Amants, La Douleureuse, L'Affranchie,* and *L'Autre Danger;* and of these, the most perfect example is *Amants,* which appeared in 1895. It is a play of free love, but without vulgarity and without any tragedy, at least of the ordinary, physical sort. The usual moral questions, such as the sanctity of marriage and marital fidelity, are practically absent from this play, as are all the other serious interests of life except those of love and sentiment, and these latter are sufficiently refined so that they are hardly colored by the sensual. This is a condition perfect for the genius of Donnay, who is an unusual combination of poet and realist, a sort of Musset whose more highly colored Romanticism has been evaporated by the distilling irony of a Henri Becque.

The popularity of Donnay with the Parisians is legitimate. His work offers an almost perfect blend — not a mixture like Sardou's — of the qualities they most appreciate in literature and in life: wit, satire, sentiment and good sense, made with admirable taste and presented in a style of almost Grecian purity and beauty. It should be noted that the *esprit* is in its latest dress, that the satire is not ill-humored, that the sentiment never overflows into sentimentality, and that the good sense is manifested largely as measure and restraint. The word his drama most suggests is exquisite. Certainly it does not offer a very hearty drink. It is rather one of those rare old *liqueurs*, distilled to a quintessence and served in a glass so small that only a born Parisian can sip from it a whole hour of aroma.

Donnay's philosophy is the right to love. He deifies love almost as much as the Romanticists did, and is hardly more concerned than they were with its strictly moral problems. But his love is not, on the whole, a terrible and tragic god. It does not usually kill, as Antony's did, and one can even jest a little with it, or at least one can smile at it a bit through one's tears. Donnay's characters suffer, and no one can find better the simple, tender words that move to tears, longing or regret, but his men are not violent — they remain seated — and his women pull down the blinds to hide their swollen eyes. They are sincere but they remain civilized. The brute of the Naturalists is rarely seen.

Most of the characters of Donnay are little concerned with the positive and practical interests of life, such as work or money. They have nothing to do but sip this exquisite dessert of life. This is the greatest restriction to the value and appeal of his theatre. The most of the world has no dessert, and the greater number of those who have can give only a limited amount of time to it.

No doubt some exception can be taken to this restriction of the field and importance of Donnay's theatre. In *Georgette Lemeunier* he has stressed moral love and duty, in *Paraître* he has treated love and money, and in various plays he has shown himself in touch with all the questions of his day. But in none of these where he departs from his usual theme of love is he at his best, or even better than numerous other playwrights who need not be mentioned here.

His characters are thoroughly well drawn, entirely human and natural, but they do not stand out as striking. This lack of relief is partly due to his usual practice of dividing the interest among several characters in each play rather than of concentrating it in only one or two, and partly due to the fact that love — at least as he conceives it, without its manifestations of all-consuming passion or devastating jealousy — does not form a sufficient basis on which to build outstanding characters.

Jules Lemaître (1853–1914)

Jules Lemaître was one of the best known and most versatile of recent men of letters in France. His greatest success has undoubtedly been in the field of criticism, for which he was endowed with an exceptional talent, but he has also won distinction as a dramatist and has written more than a dozen plays.

It is not easy to choose as outstanding any one of these pieces, since all have merit and qualities of certain interest, just as they all lack the striking relief, character or purpose which marks a work of the highest dramatic effect. Perhaps the most representative and the best of these dramas are *Le Député Leveau* (1890), *Le Mariage blanc* (1891), *Le Pardon* (1895), *L'Ainée* (1898), and *La Massière* (1905).

The good qualities of Lemaître's plays are certain and numerous. His characters are natural, typical, and predominantly respectable; his action is not forced; his scenes are in good taste and true to life; his psychological insight is keen and sure; and in general the literary merits are what we should expect from one of the most cultured of French critics. Also there is nothing in his work of the pedant or literary snob that might be assumed to exist because of his service as a professor and his position as a literary critic. The life he portrays is, on the contrary, much more likely to be of the natural and average sort than that found in the plays of many of his fellow dramatists.

But, despite the eminently respectable character of Lemaître's plays, they do not seem to bear a sufficiently strong dramatic impress to place him among the most significant of recent French dramatists. They lack a strong individual note, but particularly they appear to be deficient in dramatic distinction, in marked purpose and conviction. Undoubtedly one of the most charming and valuable qualities of Lemaître as a critic was his broad sympathy, his taste and versatility, which, without impairing his independence of judgment, enabled him to fall in step with, to appreciate and to interpret the most widely separated of authors and literary productions, from the ancient and severely classic to the ultra modern. It is probably this same broad catholicity of taste and sympathy, which was so precious to him as a critic, that has impaired his effectiveness and force in the narrower limits to which the dramatist is confined.

What we fail most often to find in Lemaître's plays is theatrical interest and power in his plots and situations, and genuine originality in his characters. Perhaps we foresee too clearly the final outcome of his dramatic intrigues and are too sure of his characters. The latter, especially, are in general too well balanced to figure in any very exciting dramatic escapades. They may depart from the normal paths of virtue, good sense or fixed principles — they would hardly be human otherwise, — but we feel sure of their quick return to their orbit, which is plainly marked. In reality most of his characters are too much like the great mass of humanity to figure in highly interesting dramas.

When *Le Député Leveau*, one of the author's best plays, first appeared, Sarcey wrote, " ce n'est pas du théâtre," and Lemaître replied, " Je m'en moque si c'est de la vie." Both were justified in their analysis of the play, and their judgments would hold good for Lemaître's work as a whole. It is a picture of life, and even a most representative one, but Sarcey was right in not finding it really dramatic, and it is Sarcey's criticism that is especially pertinent. Certainly drama must keep its feet firmly planted on life, but not all life is dramatic, and in a sense the best, the most natural, or in any case the most nearly average life is the least strikingly dramatic. To be able to make it dramatic on the stage is a rare gift.

In Lemaître, then, we can find most of the literary virtues, and particularly the racial ones of the French, such as clarity, measure, good sense, taste, keen psy-

chology, and purity of art; his dramas are equally removed from the *comédie rosse* of the Naturalists and the
artificial and empty technique of Scribe and Sardou, and
are good portraits, realistically and spiritually, of life
and character; but he really lacks the dramatic gift.
In fact his case is perhaps one of the clearest proofs
that there is such a gift.

GEORGES DE PORTO-RICHE (1849–)

Porto-Riche is not absolutely the most popular recent
dramatist in France, nor has he escaped wholly un-
scathed from some of the serious French critics, but the
popular favor shown him is great enough, and the place
often assigned him by criticism is sufficiently important,
to call for some consideration. Like Donnay, he is a
specialist in love, but much narrower and much more a
dilletante.

His first play to attract any attention was the one-
act *Chance de Françoise,* played by Antoine in 1889, but
his earliest real success was *Amoureuse,* in 1891. This
has been often revived since and is unquestionably his
best play. The superior merit of *Amoureuse* is that it
is natural and not over-emphasized; its action is not
forced and above all is not too elaborated and long drawn
out.

There are only two characters in any of Porto-Riche's
plays — in fact it is not certain that there are more
than one — whatever the number of rôles may be. One
of these characters is a woman who lives on love and
finds her joy in the torments of jealousy. The other is

probably a woman also but plays the rôle of a man. The most important difference between the two is that the first is a monogamist and the second a polygamist. The play is their conversation. As a picture of character, the first type is more pleasing. It is perhaps rather an accepted idea that women may make love the sole business of life. But the men are sad heroes. If they were ruthless Don Juans they would seem less contemptible, but their only weapons are deceit and lying.

The later plays of Porto-Riche that are most important are *Le Passé*, in 1898, *Le Vieil Homme*, in 1911, and *Le Marchand d'Estampes*, in 1918. They present the same characters, the same situations and the same themes of conversation that are found in *Amoureuse*. About all they add to his first play is length. They are among the longest pieces of the contemporary stage — *Le Vieil Homme*, for example, is of some four hundred pages — and what is more, all of these dramas seem even longer than they are. This is doubtless owing to the time spent by the author in writing and elaborating them. He is supposed to have devoted a dozen or more years to *Le Vieil Homme*, and one can believe this when he reads it.

This feeling of length is not due alone to the excessive elaboration of these plays, it is partly caused by their lack of progressive action. The situations are incredibly prolonged. The characters seem to do nothing but hesitate — and talk. They are like guests who get up to leave at eleven, and at twelve are still standing and talking. Exasperated, you turn twenty or forty pages and find them at the same spot, holding the door open.

There is also a peculiarity in style which the author has developed to a striking degree in his later plays. This is his tendency to short speeches. Possibly we should commend his avoidance of the tirade — at least such abstinence is unusual with the French — but there is much more than this. The number and brevity of the speeches are probably unparalleled in drama. On twenty consecutive pages in *Le Passé,* one character has eighty speeches with an average of six words per speech. Perhaps some day an obliging Ph.D. candidate will count the infinite number of these speeches, with their average number of words, and tell us what all this means. Until that time, we shall have to rely on impressionistic criticism, and the impression is sometimes that of a mannerism carried to insufferable lengths.

The particular effect of these long series of short speeches is to give a sort of rhythmic swing to the dialogue. In brief passages this might be rather agreeable, but played all evening, this swinging barcarolle affects the nerves like some refrain that runs endlessly through the head of a fever patient.

With all this, there is no denying the keenness of the author's analysis of his characters in their passion of love. The subject, as he restricts it, is very narrow, but it is thoroughly probed by a skillful hand. Also the dramatist knows how to translate every tremor to the spectator. A more persistent and effective prodder of the sensitory (and sensual) nerves it would be difficult to find.

Porto-Riche's philosophy of love is not notably different from Donnay's. If he does not proclaim the inalienable right to love, as the latter does, he, at least, asserts its fatal necessity — which is much the same. But the effect obtained from this philosophy is very different in the two dramatists. With Donnay it is often agreeable, a thing of tender feeling and memory. It has much of sentiment. With Porto-Riche it is an incurable passion, sensual and tormenting.

No doubt this brief analysis of Porto-Riche hardly explains the popularity of some of his plays with the Parisians, and, except for *Amoureuse,* it appears difficult to find a sufficient explanation to give. Even the vogue of plays of passion and the French appreciation of clever and delicate character analysis hardly seem adequate reasons. It is true that the endless dialogues found in these plays will be appreciated somewhat differently in France, where an audience in one night will endure, and even enjoy, an amount of conversation — provided it be clever — that would last an Anglo-Saxon public for an entire season.

It would be misleading to give the impression that all Parisians unqualifiedly approve these plays. The later ones have certainly not had the success of *Amoureuse.* However, the popularity of *Amoureuse* is at least understandable, and, despite the unnecessary suggestiveness found in this piece, the favor shown it is on the whole legitimate. In any case, it is a real stage play. But if *Amoureuse* proves that Porto-Riche was able to write a good stage play under ordinary conditions, *Le Vieil Homme,* taken with other, similar examples, should show that it was impossible for the author to do so by spending a dozen years elaborating the same work.

HENRI BATAILLE (1872–1922)

Henri Bataille was one of the well-known recent dramatists who have specialized in the field of love and guilty passion, and in certain respects he was one of the most representative. His field is admittedly narrow, and some of the influences he reflected are not of the best, but at least he combined an unusual number of qualities. His basic character and temperament seem to have been largely poetic and idealistic, with leanings, even, toward symbolism and mysticism. But on this native stock was grafted a realism in some respects as rank as that of Zola. The fruit of this combination has quite naturally been mixed.

In the more than a score of plays which he produced during some thirty years of dramatic activity, there have been a number of popular successes, some mainly won through their sensational appeals and others achieved somewhat more legitimately. *Maman Colibri* (1904) was his first piece to win striking favor. It is the love adventure of a middle-aged woman, of which the chief novelty lies in treating the heroine primarily as a mother. If it is a real success it is assuredly one of bad taste.

La Femme nue (1908) is one of his best plays — one in which the purely sensual is least marked. In situation and sentiment it resembles often Donnay's *Amants*, but it is much inferior in tone, style and artistry.

Les Flambeaux (1912), placed in a scientific *milieu*, is one of the author's most ambitious plays. In this piece he attempts philosophic and symbolical flights, but does not entirely neglect the usual appeal of sensual love.

L'Amazone, in 1916, proves that even the exaltation of war and the mask of symbolism could not change or destroy the author's tendency toward a materialistic and physical love appeal. In the absence of a real guilty passion, the author builds his most tensely dramatic scenes on the assumption of guilty love.

Bataille disclaims a Theatre of Ideas, and at least his pieces are not Thesis Plays in the regular sense of this term. None the less, he frequently introduces themes of elevated or philosophic thought, although it is difficult to say that his dramas are consistently constructed with such thought as a basis, and at times one is almost tempted to look on his practice in this respect as a sort of cloak or pretension, in order to give more dignity or respectability to less worthy appeals.

In any case, much of the dramatic effect is sensual, and if it can not be called immoral, it is doubtful if it is wholesome. He is very often highly dramatic — in some plays almost frantically so — but it is not usually in the more elevated realm of ideas that this is true. He does not so much present a moral or mental crisis as he does an attack of the nerves.

In dramatic power he is the superior of Porto-Riche, but he is less a real psychologist, and is certainly less clear. In short, he is a very good example of the conflicting tendencies and cross-currents to be found in French drama in this first quarter of the twentieth century, when it has been freed from the strictly theatrical control of the *pièce bien faite* and has recovered from the Naturalistic orgy. This has left it in a state of freedom which certainly favors new creative efforts, but which may quite as well invite confusion.

HENRI BERNSTEIN (1876–   )

Henri Bernstein has had so much theatrical success in France, and even in other countries, that it seems imperative to take some account of him, little justified as his claims may be to a place in a book where the drama is considered as a branch of literature. It is perhaps briefer to treat him than to give the reasons for not doing so.

His first play was *Le Marché*, given at the Théâtre Antoine in 1900. It was very successful, as in fact have been practically all of his pieces. The most perfect types of the Bernstein play are *La Rafale*, *Le Voleur*, *Samson* and *Israël*, which appeared from 1905 to 1908. Each of these is a breathless drama filled with tense situations and violent action. So intense and concentrated are they that they approximate the observance of the Classic unities, but, instead of being mental and moral crises, they are only nervous and emotional fits.

Perhaps the most widely known of these is *Le Voleur*, which under the title of *The Thief* has been played in the United States. It is the story of a woman who steals from her hosts — or, more exactly, uses the son of her host to steal for her — and is discovered and forced to confess, by her husband. Most of Bernstein's subjects might be taken from the criminal court records of the newspaper.

The scene of this discovery and confession is characteristic of Bernstein's methods. It progresses with increasing suspense, with agonizing torture at each turn of the screw, to a dénouement of panting exhaustion. The emotion and distress it causes are largely physical, and it is based on physiology rather than psychology; more than once it is quite unnecessarily, if not shamelessly, suggestive. Its sheer theatrical force is undeniable and irresistible. It is as difficult to believe that any one could sit through it unaffected, as it is to imagine that any one would not be a little disgusted and ashamed afterward for allowing himself to be moved by it.

La Rafale and *Samson* are almost as exciting as *Le Voleur,* and their tone and characters are less respectable. However, there is somewhat more dignity and less violence in *Israël.* None the less, this play lacks anything worthy or notable in ideas or appeal. It is also less continuously interesting — almost the entire effect being placed in one tense scene and the rest being dull by comparison.

In later plays, such as *L'Assaut, L'Élévation* and *Judith,* which appeared from 1912 to 1922, Bernstein has obviously intended to include more than the purely theatrical qualities of his earlier pieces. *L'Assaut,* for example, attempts to appeal both through its ideas and its sentiment or tenderness, but in neither respect is it very convincing. *Judith* is doubtless his most nearly successful effort to find a new manner.

Bernstein possesses an unusual talent as a playwright, but his appeals are theatrical rather than properly dramatic. Often they border on melodrama. In any case, he offers little food for serious thought or reflection. He constructs his plays about, and for the sake of a few strong situations. His characters, which are speed models, seem built for the sole purpose of carrying the action, as swiftly as possible, over the thin places in his drama into these gripping scenes, and they are convincing only in action. Considering them at leisure, we find a lack of keen psychology in their conception, and they appear without true feeling or sentiment. They are not human beings; they are only actors. No doubt they act better than human beings, but we are not deceived.

Bernstein, then, has obviously continued the tradition of Scribe and Sardou. He has adopted their point of view — which is to look at the theatre rather than life. Only his method is different from theirs. He does not rely, as Scribe did, on suggestion to motivate his plot, nor so often renew his intrigue, and he is still further removed from the eclecticism and multifarious appeals of Sardou. But just as little as they does he seem to have observed and pondered life and to have reflected it in his dramas. We find in them no adequate philosophy.

It is regrettable that Bernstein, like Scribe and Sardou, has been played in countries outside of France more frequently than certain other recent French dramatists whose work is more serious or significant. No doubt it is largely because his qualities are so readily exportable, and also because his popular successes have tempted the commercial manager. Neither French drama nor French life is likely to have gained much in foreign esteem through this preference, and it would be unfair to both to accept Bernstein's plays as thoroughly representative. It is true that he shows the usual French aptitude for dramatic technique, but he lacks the higher artistry of style and form, which is not less characteristic of French dramatists. We fail to find in him the usual observer and moralist of the French theatre, and he is still more exceptional in his lack of concern for ideas.

The present state of the French theatre is one of unusual freedom. The rigid technique and the too exclusively theatrical aim were destroyed by the Naturalistic movement near the end of the nineteenth century. This movement was followed by the reaction against the Naturalistic régime itself. Today no special form or kind of drama is obligatory. With this freedom have developed naturally multifarious tendencies, of which many are experimental and uncertain. This development has been aided by foreign influence, which, beginning with the Théâtre Libre, and reinforced by the Great War, has been the most considerable to be found in any period of the modern French drama since the Romantic school. However, the influence of foreign plays is still comparatively small and does not promise to affect profoundly French drama. In the same way the revolts against rigid technique and stage conventions have in no permanent manner brought disorder or anarchy in form and composition. The French national genius for logic, clarity and ordered purpose has quickly reasserted itself, and badly or loosely composed plays are still the exception.

Some of the tendencies of contemporary drama are only continuations of earlier movements, and others perhaps are promises of future development. In the idealistic theatre, the brightest recent light has been Rostand, who inherited directly from the Romantic school, and although verse drama is a smaller stream, there is no indication that it will ever run dry in France. The French love of form, rhetoric and style is almost universal, and this is a powerful aid to the verse play. It is surprising to note the number of playwrights who have at least one or two verse plays to their credit, even if these are often nothing more than youthful indiscretions.

For good examples of the Symbolistic theatre — since the symbolism of both Rostand and Curel is restricted and very special — we have to go outside of France to the Belgian Maeterlinck, and Maeterlinck's fame in other countries, compared with his influence in France, shows clearly how little French national genius is inclined to this kind of literature.

Brieux is obviously a continuer of the Social drama initiated by Dumas and Augier, and his appeal proves the vitality of this form. In fact, when one considers the importance of social problems in present day society, and the popularizing tendency in all forms of art caused by the conditions of modern democracy, it would be rash to say that he represents a belated form. In some respects the tendencies he shows are likely to persist or to go still further.

However, one is tempted to find the purest French tradition in Curel and Hervieu. The markedly intellectual character of French literature is exemplified by both. In Curel we have some of the finest examples of psychological drama, and in Hervieu French rationalism and logic are again in complete control. There is no better recent example in France of the Theatre of Ideas than *La Nouvelle Idole*, and *La Course du Flambeau* is — if we ignore dates — a Classic drama, even in its purity of form.

In nearly all the recent French dramatists there is a

marked tendency to turn from purely external realism and facts to analysis of character and mental states. Until some master work appears to inaugurate a new school, it would be vain to predict what form the French drama may take in the future, but it seems fairly safe to suppose that it will again be in the nature of the mental and moral crisis, which, with only brief variations, has marked the centre of the French stage for the past three hundred years.

CHAPTER XV

MAURICE MAETERLINCK, SYMBOLISM, AND STATIC DRAMA

MAURICE MAETERLINCK (1862–   )

IT would no doubt be quite as easy to explain the omission of Maeterlinck from a book on the French theatre as it is to justify his inclusion. Belgian literature is nationally distinct from the French, and is in racial qualities sufficiently autonomous to be quite different. None the less, Maeterlinck is the best representative, writing in French, of certain forms of recent drama which have received some attention in France. Particularly he has developed symbolism further than any native French dramatist of importance, and he is responsible for introducing on the stage elements of mystic philosophy. Finally he may be called the creator of Static Drama.

An even greater interest offered by Maeterlinck's plays is the chance they give for contrast with the more strictly native works of the French theatre. Indeed this comparison may be of still broader extent and value. Maeterlinck is quite as much an international figure as he is a Belgian, or a representative of French literature, and this wide popularity affords an excellent opportunity to note dramatic tastes and to study the trends of certain forms of the theatre outside of France, and particularly in England and America.

Finally, without questioning the autonomy of Belgian literature, one should not forget that it is, at least, in large part a French literature and that Maeterlinck's first distinctively literary influence comes from his early sojourn at Paris. Later he definitely adopted France as his place of residence, and he has not only done most of his mature work since he came to live in that country but the influence of his French environment, and particularly of his French marriage, is clearly evident in his plays, and highly important in the evolution of his ideas and philosophy.

Maurice Maeterlinck was born in Ghent, in 1862, and passed his early life in that old Flemish city. Its shadow seems to have hung heavily over him, and, although this has gradually been lightened by the bright sun and Latin clarity of his long residence in France, it gave a somber background to all his early plays. These are set in old ruined castles, by broad, sleepy canals, under skies which rarely open to the sun and in a vague and often gloomy atmosphere.

He was several years in a Jesuit school and studied law in the University of Ghent. He even appeared at the bar but his legal career was of the briefest. In 1886 he went to Paris, ostensibly for further study, but actually his time there was given to art and literature. Particularly he fell under the influence of the French symbolists, who, headed by Verlaine and Mallarmé, were active just then, and this influence, according doubtless with his own temperament, was decisive. He turned definitely against realism, which was so widely prevalent at this time and which one might have expected his materialistic Belgian environment to encourage.

The next ten years, which are marked by the appearance of two collections of poetry and a few of his earlier plays, are very important in Maeterlinck's literary formation. The greater part of this time was spent in Ghent, where he was being drawn still deeper into symbolism and mysticism by a study of literature of this character. The writers who have contributed to this formative period of his life are very numerous and include, besides some of the great mystics and philosophers, many who are more properly moralists and idealists. A few whose influence was paramount are Plato, Marcus Aurelius, Behmen, Ruysbroeck, Spinoza, Schopenhauer, Shakespeare, Carlyle, Novalis and Emerson.

In 1896 Maeterlinck definitively took up his residence in France, at first in Paris, but in later years, after he became famous, in the provinces. His winter home is in a beautiful villa in the south near Grasse, and in summer he occupies the famous old Norman abbey of Saint Wandrille, which he bought and restored after it was left by the Benedictine monks. Beginning with the period of his French residence one notes especially the influence of his first wife, who was formerly the actress Madame Georgette Leblanc. No one could be more modest in his attitude toward, and appraisal of his own literary works, nor more unassuming and retiring in his private life and tastes.

Maeterlinck's first play was *La Princesse Maleine*, of which thirty copies were printed on a hand press by the author himself in 1889. It brought him extravagant, and, on the whole, unfortunate praise. Octave Mirbeau, in the *Figaro*, claimed to discover in it an absolute masterpiece, the equal or superior in beauty to any of the works of Shakespeare; but this assertion is more eloquent of Mirbeau's incomprehension of Shakespeare than it is of his real acuity in seeing unusual merit in Maeterlinck.

The play is an obvious imitation of Shakespeare in some of its leading characters, in certain striking scenes and in numerous minor devices and details. Doumic was able to reply effectively to Mirbeau by asserting that it was made up from Shakespeare's rags.

But whatever merit there is in this drama is not in its pale copies of Hamlet, Lady Macbeth and King Lear and even less in Shakespearian portents and scenes of violence and madness. It is a merit not easy to isolate and more difficult still to describe, especially where it is so obscured by a borrowed and foreign emphasis. In spite of that, we can discern here at times what is so much clearer in his later plays that are unencumbered by Shakespearian trappings, namely, the power to suggest or evoke an interior drama, a travail of the spirit that is quite apart from the many second-hand and second-rate elements of the piece. It is a drama of poetry and mystery, or rather it becomes one later, for it is only foreshadowed in this apprenticeship play.

It should be said, to Maeterlinck's credit, that he disavowed most sincerely this attempt to make him a Belgian Shakespeare. Moreover, he took the lesson to heart in a practical way — which seems to be his usual reaction toward criticism. He is certainly a genuine admirer of Shakespeare. One could hardly be more so. Shakespeare's masterpieces are constantly the touchstones of his dramatic judgments. But he never again entered the shining, tumultuous lists of Shakespearian drama; he remained in his own garden and cultivated the flowers and fruits of his native genius.

In sketching the important evolution that characterizes Maeterlinck's dramatic career, it is impossible to ignore his volumes of essays, and especially *Le Trésor des Humbles,* collected and published in 1896, *La Sagesse et la Destinée* in 1898, *Le Temple Enseveli* in 1902, and *Le Double Jardin* in 1904. Whether most of his ideas and philosophy were first conceived in connection with the composition of his plays or formulated in his mind in the more complete systems of his essays is a question beyond this sketch. What must be noted is that these essays furnish the only solid basis for grouping and judging his plays, since they not only avow the philosophy and ideas on which his theatre is built but often contain definite explanations of his dramatic intentions and systems.

The particular system in which are to be placed most of his early plays, after *La Princesse Maleine,* is explained in his essay on *Le Tragique Quotidien,* found in *Le Trésor des Humbles,* which begins:

" There is an every-day tragedy which is more real, deeper and more in keeping with our true existence than the tragedy of great adventures. . .

Is it while I am fleeing before a naked sword that my existence attains its most interesting point? . . .

I admire Othello but he does not seem to me to live the

august life of a Hamlet, who has the time to live because he does not act. Othello is admirably jealous. But is it not perhaps an ancient error to believe that the moments when such a passion, and others of equal violence, rule us are those in which we most truly live? I have come to think that an old man, seated in his armchair, simply waiting beside the lamp, listening, without knowing it, to all the eternal laws that reign about him, interpreting, without understanding it, what there is in the silence of the doors and windows and in the small voice of the light, undergoing the presence of his soul and of his destiny, leaning a little his head, without suspecting that all the powers of this world are intervening and watching in his room like attentive servants, not knowing that the sun itself sustains the little table on which he rests his elbows and that there is not a planet in heaven nor a power of the soul which is indifferent to the dropping of an eyelid or the disclosure of a thought — I have come to think that this motionless old man was living in reality a deeper, more human and more general life than the lover who strangles his mistress, the captain who wins a victory or the ' husband who avenges his honor.'

It will be said perhaps that a motionless life would hardly be visible, that life must needs be animated by certain movements and that these various movements which are acceptable are to be found only in the small number of passions that have been utilized up to the present. I do not know if it is true that a Static theatre is impossible. It seems to me even that it exists."

And Maeterlinck is inclined to find the nearest approximation of this static quality in the brief action of the Greek theatre, and the most promising attempt to suggest or evoke symbolically a deeper and more mysterious tragedy, or a dramatic dialogue, without actually putting it in words, in some of Ibsen's plays.

The system described above, of which Maeterlinck is the chief creator, is the one best known by the expressive and yet somewhat inadequate term, Static Drama. It might be noted that the dramatist's choice of common, every-day life is in complete accord with the theory and practice of the Naturalistic theatre then in vogue, but that his ability to see real tragedy in such life was quite different from the prevalent realistic conception of a drama or comedy that was often trivial and uninspiring. However, a fundamental difference is that Maeterlinck concerns himself exclusively with the interior drama, and would merely evoke this, often by the vaguest symbols, while the Naturalists occupied themselves mostly with the drama of fact, with external and physical details plainly and often baldly expressed.

The fatalistic and pessimistic philosophy which is the basis of Maeterlinck's early tragic system is fully expounded in his essays, but its most concise expression is in the preface to his plays, which, written later, is somewhat of a confession and criticism.

" In these plays," he says, " one believes in tremendous powers, invisible and fatalistic, of which no one knows the intentions, but which this conception of drama supposes to be malevolent, attentive to all our actions and inimical to joy, life, peace and happiness. Innocent, but involuntarily hostile lives are there united and divided to the ruin of all, beneath the grieved eyes of those who are wisest and who foresee the future, but who can in no way alter the cruel and inexorable tragedy that Love and Death play with human beings. And Love and Death, and the other powers, display here a kind of malicious injustice, whose penalties — for this injustice does not reward — are perhaps only the whims of Destiny."

The plays that illustrate more or less perfectly this system and this philosophy are: *L'Intruse, Les Aveugles, Les Sept Princesses, Pelléas et Mélisande, Alladine et Palomides, Intérieur* and *La Mort de Tintagiles,* appearing in the order named, from 1890 to 1894. The first of these, *L'Intruse,* is one of his good examples of Static Drama, as well as one of his effective plays; the one where his peculiar method of evoking thoughts and drama which lie behind the words uttered seems most natural.

A family at night are sitting around a table next to the room where the sick mother is lying. The Grandfather is blind, and is anxious and troubled despite the assurance that his daughter is better. Gradually his uneasy inquiries communicate his unformulated fears to the others. A sister is momentarily expected, and the surmises with regard to her coming are skillfully used to suggest the approach of the Intruder, Death.

" THE DAUGHTER. I am sure that some one has entered the garden. You will see.

THE UNCLE. But she would answer me.

THE GRANDFATHER. Are not the nightingales beginning to sing again, Ursula?

THE DAUGHTER. I no longer hear one in all the fields.

THE GRANDFATHER. And yet there is no noise.

THE FATHER. There is a silence of death.

. . . .

THE GRANDFATHER. Are the windows open, Ursula?

THE DAUGHTER. The glass door is open, grandfather.

THE GRANDFATHER. It seems to me the cold is entering the room.

THE DAUGHTER. There is a little wind in the garden, grandfather, and the rose leaves are falling.

THE FATHER. Well, shut the door, Ursula. It is late.

THE DAUGHTER. Yes, father. I can not shut the door, father.

THE TWO OTHER DAUGHTERS. We can not shut the door."

In this manner, with sentences of primer-like simplicity, the dramatist continues to develop the growing uneasiness and fear of the group, through their comments on incidents, natural in cause but portentous in their suggestions, such as the silence of the nightingales, the fear of the swans, the sound of the gardener's scythe, noises on the stairway and the flickering of the dying lamp, until there are hurrying footsteps in the adjoining room and the attendant nun opens the door and makes the sign of the cross to indicate the mother's death. Action, in any proper sense, is practically absent, but there is a dramatic progression which is based on keen psychologic insight. Also the main drama is not in the actual dialogue spoken but in the train of thought that it constantly suggests.

Intérieur is a play of very similar method and effect. In this piece a young girl has been drowned and the whole drama is expressed in the dialogue of the persons who have to inform her family of the tragic event, and who stand looking in at the window, lacking the immediate courage to destroy the scene of contentment and happiness they see there.

It will be seen that the characters of this play in

whose tragedy the audience is interested are neither seen nor heard on the stage — only their shadows appear through the window — and the sorrow and anguish which are closing in on them are merely evoked in the minds of the spectators and not acted. In this manner the author eliminates the actual appearance and personality of the actor, against whose deformation of the masterpieces of poetic drama he has more than once protested. Also there is no action whatsoever on the real stage.

Intérieur, then, is the one play where the conditions of Static Drama are perfectly realized. It is, moreover, both in style and in the character of its thought, less childlike than *L'Intruse,* and for these reasons it has sometimes been considered the author's finest example of this form of drama. However, its dramatic effect is not as intense as that of certain other of his pieces.

Les Aveugles is also characteristic of the same system. It is the conversation of a group of blind patients, who have been taken into the forest by an old priest. While seated in the woods their guide has fallen dead, without their being aware of it, and they are left groping helplessly before an approaching storm and death.

This play has been given an allegorical explanation by making it symbolize Humanity wandering in the dark after the death of its guide, the Church, and similar allegorical interpretations have been made for the other dramas of the author, whether they were all so intended by him or not.

This collaboration of Maeterlinck's admirers has been a craze, especially in countries outside of France, and has doubtless prejudiced against him a number of serious lovers of literature. It has become difficult to imagine any play that he might sign whose source would not be found by some erudite German in a solar myth, or for which some American or English professor of hermeneutical psychology would not discover a symbolical system of Swedenborgian correspondences.

Les Sept Princesses is a mere dream, a pale wavering picture seen through a glass darkly, and is undoubtedly the slightest thing Maeterlinck has done. Various meanings have been put into it, the more easily apparently since the author himself seems to have put none.

Alladine et Palomides is a piece with highly romantic and even mystical scenes and settings, which, like its figures, might have been taken directly from the Arthurian romances, only they have "suffered a sea-change" in their transportation, through being drenched in the strange, unearthly atmosphere so characteristic of Maeterlinck's early plays. Like these others its ending is entirely fatalistic.

If *Les Sept Princesses* can be called a pale dream, *La Mort de Tintagiles* should be thought of as a horrible nightmare. The sole tragic effect is concentrated in a final scene, where a helpless child cries in terror behind an iron door, and pleads for aid while being gripped and choked to death by a monster — whether human or not we never see — and while his sister tears her nails on the steel walls, and begs and curses alternately this murderous Fate. Even if this piece is intended to symbolize the merciless crushing of Humanity by inexorable Death, it seems difficult to justify such unmotivated, tragic horror, and still more difficult to understand Maeterlinck's alleged preference for this drama. It is true that the rebellion here of the sister against fate is strikingly symptomatic of an important evolution that was soon to take place in his philosophy. His victims are no longer entirely passive and resigned, but are beginning to struggle, still in vain, in the grip of the fatalistic powers in which he places them. Later this beginning develops into a very different dramatic conception.

Pelléas et Mélisande is the most beautiful play of Maeterlinck, the one nearest a real masterpiece, and which does most toward justifying his conception of a symbolic, spiritual drama. It is the old story of Paolo and Francesca, similarly infused with poetry and treated without any moralistic preoccupation that might hinder its pure artistry. This last point is important, and we shall see that Maeterlinck was entirely sincere in this doctrine of the moral unconsciousness of the soul; it was a part of his philosophy.

In his essay on *La Morale Mystique* he asks what would happen if our soul should suddenly become visible, disclosing all of our thoughts and wearing the most secret acts of our life.

" For what would it blush? What would it wish to conceal? Would it go, like a modest woman, throwing the long mantle of its hair over the numberless sins of the flesh? It has not known them, and these sins have never touched it. They have been committed a thousand leagues from its throne; and the soul even of the Sodomite would pass through the midst of the crowd, without suspecting anything, and carrying in its eyes the transparent smile of the child."

From Jane Cowl's production of *Pelléas and Mélisande*—1923

We are concerned, for the moment, only with the importance of this philosophy in our play, and recalling that Maeterlinck's particular dramatic conception was to express by symbolic methods a spiritual drama, a pure drama of the soul, we can see that it is fundamental. Furthermore, it is perhaps the only basis, in a love story such as this, from which the author could raise with genuine conviction a work of chaste and sincere spiritual beauty. In his eyes at least he was working with pure marble, there was none of the clay of material life.

In this case also the spiritual value and beauty of the play is enhanced, or better, it is made more mysteriously poetic by the Maeterlinckian atmosphere and setting: the old castle, the gloomy gardens and forests, and the mysterious fountains and grottoes.

The author's early conception of fatality is still maintained, only here the chief compelling force is Love, and not Death as it is in most of the other early plays. In fact, Death would have been here almost a haven to be sought rather than a terror to be faced, if the dramatist had ended his play with the fourth act, an abbreviation that would have left a more harmonious work of art.

However, there are in *Pelléas et Mélisande* decided superiorities over his other early plays. Its figures — one hesitates to call any of them characters in the flesh and blood sense — are more life-like, and its story is more dramatic. Moreover, it has a number of truly theatrical scenes and dialogues, not only in the drama evoked but in that which is actually expressed, and it is, no doubt, in the beauty and power of these scenes, harmonious in their ensemble but without dramatic progression, that one finds the secret of the play's wide appeal. The hauntingly mysterious meeting at the beginning between Golaud and Mélisande in the forest; the beauty and symbolism where Mélisande plays with her ring and loses it in the fountain; the supremely lyrical appeal where she leans from the castle window and her hair falls around Pelléas standing below; the daringly theatrical effect when Golaud holds Yniold up to the window to report on the actions of Pelléas and Mélisande; and finally the last scene of the fourth act, reminiscent of Tristan and Isolt, where the lovers meet in the garden, watch their shadows enlaced in the moonlight, see Golaud spying on them, and exchange their first, and last, kiss of passion before they are killed; these alone are sufficient to explain the popular appeal of this romantic and poetical drama.

Maeterlinck's other early plays illustrate his dramatic philosophy, and show his power to suggest an interior drama, but *Pelléas et Mélisande* is the one in which this inner spiritual drama is most perfectly transmuted into the pure gold of idealism and poetry. Later plays show an evolution of his philosophy that results in decided dramatic improvements over his early work, but it is doubtful if any one of these is better representative of the native genius of the author, and certainly none is so much a work of pure beauty.

Aglavaine et Sélysette, in 1896, marks the beginning of an important evolution in Maeterlinck's philosophy and a turning point in his dramatic system. It is the date when he went to France to live, and we should see here some

French influence and particularly that of Georgette Leblanc. He has fully recorded these developments in his
essays. Speaking of his early philosophy and dramatic
conception whereby human beings are merely the resigned
puppets of Fate, he says: " Such a conception of life
is not healthy, whatever show of reason it may seem to
possess." " Hamlet thinks a great deal but he is hardly
wise." " Hamlet is unhappy because he walks in gloomy
darkness and it is his ignorance that completes his misfortune. There is nothing in the world that is obedient
longer than Fate to those who dare to give it orders."
" Intelligence and will, like victorious soldiers, should
accustom themselves to live at the expense of all that wars
against them."

His departure from his former views is not a break,
it is an evolution. He still believes that we can have
little influence over exterior events, the decisions of fate,
but that we can do everything in transforming these
events — our sorrows and our misfortunes — into elements of strength and beauty in our character; and it is
these elements that determine our happiness. We see
then that he is far from the helpless resignation and despair of his former philosophy, and well on the road
toward a doctrine of moral strength and happiness. In
drama this is translated into terms of greater force of
character and will-power; man is not master of Fate but
he is master of his own moral fate.

Aglavaine et Sélysette is an attempt, only partially successful, to realize this philosophy. It is one of the most
modern of his dramatic situations, a triangle play of
which two of the corners are feminine. Its characters

are clearer and can live in the sunlight. They have individuality, and strength at least to struggle with destiny. However he is not yet free from his former system, and Death still wins a victim, but, on the whole, one who comes willingly, impelled by Love, and who dies almost happy.

It is an interesting play but far from perfect. Méléandre is a weak character. Sélysette, representing simple, unconscious goodness, is its most appealing figure but she is much like Maeterlinck's earlier heroines. Aglavaine, who stands for most of the author's new philosophy, is intended to be conscious goodness, and she is — too conscious — and unless you happen to be in the mood for her, an insufferable bore and blue-stocking. We grow tired of her talk about beautifying souls and wish she had a little common sense.

Ariane et Barbe-bleu, in 1901, completely realizes the author's new philosophy. It is based on the well-known Bluebeard legend. Ariane, in the rôle of triumphant intelligence and will, comes to Bluebeard's Castle and releases his former wives, who are only intimidated and imprisoned and not decapitated. These wives, quite aptly, are named Sélysette, Mélisande, Ygraine, Bellangère and Alladine, Maeterlinck's former weak-willed heroines. They have lacked the strength to escape from their prison. Ariane breaks the windows, lets in the light, frees them and departs, leaving Bluebeard (Fate) defeated and humble. But his other wives choose to remain with him. They prefer submission and perhaps are unable to bear the light. This piece offers a beautiful picture but has very little dramatic value.

The same might be said of *Soeur Béatrice* which appeared in the same year. It is the well-known legend of the nun who flees from her convent, leads a worldly life, and, on returning broken to die, finds the Virgin had taken her place and that she had become a saint. As a stage piece its dramatic value is hardly the equal of the Old French miracle play of the fourteenth century from which most of the modern adaptations are derived, and Maeterlinck himself denied that it was intended to have any particular significance — which has not, however, discouraged his various interpreters.

What these three plays above have in common is their trend away from the philosophy of inertia and despair toward light, strength and optimism. The ruling force now is Love; Death has been dethroned or at least robbed of his terror. The evolution of this philosophy is completed and its fruits are seen in a riper form in three later pieces: *Monna Vanna*, in 1902, *Joyzelle*, in 1903, and *Marie Magdeleine*, in 1913.

Monna Vanna is historic drama of an orthodox sort, without allegory or mystery and practically without symbolic suggestion. Its style even approaches the argumentative, rhetorical character of the traditional French drama. It has had considerable stage success, and contains strong theatrical scenes with fully drawn, independent characters, particularly that of Monna Vanna. The theme is the ennobling power and victory of love, represented as sincere and self-sufficient, without weakness or renunciation. Maeterlinck's philosophy of love, and life, is distinctly against renunciation and sacrifice, in which he differs fundamentally from Rostand.

The rank of *Monna Vanna* in the work of Maeterlinck is still, perhaps, debatable. It is clearly not an insignificant play, but in testing his dramatic genius on the traditional ground of French drama, it is doubtful if he has gained enough in the orthodox virtues to compensate for those of his former manner which he has been forced to give up, and which are probably more deeply rooted in his temperament and character. Also the play is at times tiresome.

Joyzelle is a return toward mysticism although not to pessimistic philosophy nor to the omnipotence of Fate. It is based both on Shakespeare's *Tempest* and on the Arthurian romances. Like the preceding play its theme is love, all powerful, all-wise and triumphant. In style also it is nearer his later manner.

Marie Magdeleine is the last of this trilogy where love is apotheosized — not the irregular love of the Romanticists, despite the title of this play, but a love that is ennobling and beneficent, and in this case mystically divine. This can hardly be considered one of the author's best dramas. Like Rostand in *La Samaritaine*, he seems to have wandered too far afield, and his treatment will hardly satisfy either the devout or the profane.

Maeterlinck's most popular stage piece is *L'Oiseau bleu*, a fairy play that first appeared in 1908. Written to the level of children and almost equally interesting to adults, it has been one of the great popular, theatrical successes of the times. This is the more interesting in the case of an author whose book popularity has usually been much greater than that of the acted play.

The *Blue Bird* is an allegory from beginning to end,

but a child can understand some of this allegory, and what he cannot comprehend affects little his enjoyment of the play, and affords the adult a good excuse for the childish pleasure he takes in it. Its saving grace is its humor; and it is moreover really a stage play, within the limits of its particular genre.

The piece is too well known to require comment of any kind, but it might be noted that its symbolism, or rather allegory, which is here quite obvious, conforms entirely to the later philosophy of the author. The quest is for the Blue Bird " which symbolizes the great secret of things and of happiness." For Maeterlinck had come to consider wisdom or knowledge, both objective, as in the natural sciences, and introspective, the knowing of one-self, as necessary to self mastery and to happiness. In fact in this later period of his career, wisdom, love and happiness have come to mean much the same thing in Maeterlinck's philosophy, and it is a philosophy of opti-mism. This delightful and genial play is one of its clearest reflections.

A sequel to the *Blue Bird* is *Les Fiançailles* which ap-peared in 1918. It is in the same vein and manner but less entertaining. Tyltyl, the hero of the *Blue Bird*, is to choose a wife, and much of the play turns on the strength and importance of heredity, on the rôle of the ancestors in making this choice. However, in the end, it is not the ancestors who decide but the children-to-be: the last word would seem still to be that of the mystic. The treatment of Fate is particularly interesting as show-ing the complete transformation of the author's early conception. In the begining of this quest Destiny is a stern giant who grips Tyltyl and drags him along, but Fate shrinks with each new revelation until in the end he is a babe who has to be carried.

Two plays of Maeterlinck lie quite outside of the accepted categories, *Le Miracle de Saint Antoine* and *Le Bourgmestre de Stilemonde*. The first of these, written before the war and published in German and English translations, is the author's only outright comedy. It is difficult to see any of Maeterlinck's usual manner in this play and it would be much easier to ascribe it to Shaw. It is highly ironical from the first word to the last.

Le Bourgmestre de Stilemonde, in 1918, is a war play, and for that reason, doubtless, is also not in Maeterlinck's usual style. So far as internal evidence goes it might have been written by one of a number of recent French dramatists.

Maeterlinck's style has been variously appreciated. In his early plays, such as *L'Intruse,* its primer-like simplicity and astonishing repetitions have been mentioned. It is undoubtedly effective there in evoking an interior dialogue, but it would be tiresome in longer plays, and in fact its repetitions often approach the ridiculous. In his more poetic dramas there is sometimes a sort of cadenced prose that approaches verse. In his later works, however, such as *Monna Vanna,* there is a marked progression, especially in the long philosophical speeches. Still it rarely attains the smooth-flowing rhetoric of many French writers. Its strongest quality is its symbolic power.

Maeterlinck's drama is above all subjective and not

the product of observation. However, it is not primarily an expression of the personal feelings and emotions, as in the case of Musset and other Romanticists, but is a consistent reflection of his thoughts, ideas and philosophy, perhaps at times of his somewhat mystic visions. We could hardly think of an incident in life, a fact, or a story, as the exciting cause for any of his plays: the facts, plots and figures of his dramas are the indispensable but subordinate media for the expression of his ideas and philosophy.

To understand his plays, then, we must understand his philosophy and follow the development of his thought. This evolution has been indicated in the treatment of his dramatic career. The starting point is in his early conception of an inexorable and hostile Fate in whose hands human beings are helpless puppets. Since there could be no valid action by these helpless figures the sole interest is in their interior life, their thoughts and emotions, their visions and fears. These, following his mystical inclinations, he seeks only to suggest or evoke, in a symbolic manner, and not to formulate completely in precise dialogue. This is his early system of Static Drama.

The evolution of this philosophy, which was gradual but in the end sufficiently great to approach repudiation, is marked both by a weakening of the tyranny of Fate and by a strengthening of its former helpless victims. Fate is no longer considered as necessarily hostile, it does not always destroy, and it may even allow sufficient autonomy for complete self development and happiness. The wisdom of human beings then is not to remain helpless in the hands of Fate, nor even to fight against its decrees and its punishments, but to seek to coöperate with these, and especially to transform them into strength of character and self mastery. This alone can bring happiness.

These different stages of Maeterlinck's thought and the logic of its evolution are clearly recorded in his plays, and a history of the basic ideas of these dramas is only the reasoned philosophy of the author from the time of its first expression down to the present day. This philosophy from its earliest phase to its final form, teaches that true wisdom is not to be afraid of Fate (*Maleine, L'Intruse, Les Aveugles*), not to fight against or curse it (*Mort de Tintagiles*) nor to be broken by it (*Pelléas, Aglavaine*), but, since one cannot master Fate, to be master of one's own life (*Ariane, Monna Vanna, Joyzelle*) and to seek to know the secrets of Fate — which is to know nature and oneself — and to coöperate with it (*Oiseau bleu, Fiançailles*).

A comparison suggests itself at this point. Maeterlinck's idea of the rôle of the fatalistic powers is strikingly like Hervieu's control of life by the primitive instincts. However, the difference between their dramas is absolute, and this is not solely because one is a realist and rationalist and the other an idealist and mystic. Hervieu's characters are from the beginning endowed with will and determination, and the drama is their struggle and the tragedy their defeat. When Maeterlinck's evolution allowed him to create characters of comparable strength, they are made to coöperate with Fate and seek happiness, and there is no tragedy. Maeterlinck's philosophy develops from a pessimistic to an optimistic one, while Hervieu's remains unchanged.

It is difficult to evaluate finally Maeterlinck's drama to-day, when its merit is still being denied through incomprehension or obscured through over-praise and superinterpretation, and the attempt may even seem rash, since the author is in the maturity of his powers and still writing. But there is ample room for true criticism between the two extremes mentioned, and neither the character of the author's recent plays nor his trend toward the essay gives great promise of further original drama.

The merits and faults of his early system of Static Drama have already been fairly well seen. It gave needed emphasis to interior, spiritual drama, and its method of symbolistic evocation has many possibilities. It may even have given a new dramatic shudder, but, if so, it is a very brief and limited one. It lacks action, which is the real substance of drama. Moreover, its philosophy is not only undramatic but it is demoralizing. The victims of this dramatic conception are like the occupants of a small boat, lost in the fog and suddenly surprised by the liner's siren without knowing the direction from which it is approaching. No doubt they shudder but they can only sit with folded arms and wait. This is an unhealthy conception of life and Maeterlinck himself has recognized it.

As to the value of his allegory, symbolism and mysticism, which are the really constant features of his work, opinions will differ greatly, according to whether one looks on his dramas as stage plays or as pieces of idealistic literature. From the point of view of the theatre there is much to criticize, and this criticism has been frequently voiced, especially in France, where the dramatic sense and stage technique are so highly developed. Most of these pieces lose in representation and some are hardly suitable for it. The vague, mysterious atmosphere in which a number of them were conceived, and with which their spirit accords, can hardly be maintained on the stage. Too often he takes us:

> " hard by the dim lake of Auber,
> In the misty mid region of Weir "

and wanders with Psyche, his soul. And the dim, mysterious atmosphere of poetry is dissipated by the glare of the footlights, and the ethereal pallor of Psyche is destroyed by the stage make-up.

However, Maeterlinck's dramas are more widely known through reading than through their performance, and they are entitled to be judged as works of literature, whatever may be their value or influence on the stage. Besides it is not entirely true that they always show life " through a glass darkly," even those most romantic. Should we not see rather in *Pelléas et Mélisande,* a beautiful series of pictures, like those from *Tristan and Isolt,* done in the marvelous stained-glass windows of some ancient cathedral, whose art and color we lack today the mystic medieval faith to restore! The most enduring element of Maeterlinck's dramatic work should be this beautiful poetry, which is probably created by his character as a mystic and which is certainly heightened by its symbolistic quality. The purely dramatic merit of

Maeterlinck may be doubted without questioning his position as an original, creative artist.

As we have seen in the case of Curel, other French dramatists have employed symbolism. But the symbolism of Curel is entirely realistic and intellectual, and, compared with the mystical quality of Maeterlinck's, is almost algebraic in purpose and effect. A case more in point would be that of Rostand, who is also an idealistic dramatist and who has made use of symbols. But again the symbolistic plays of Maeterlinck and Rostand are as widely separated as were their birthplaces, and it is much farther from Ghent to Marseilles in terms of race and temperament than it is measured in miles. It is like the difference between moonlight and sunlight. The symbolism of Rostand is burned in and exaggerated by the Provençal sun on the firm lines of Parisian art; it is intense and brilliant in color and effect, but it is far removed from the vague, mysterious character, hauntingly suggestive of immaterial worlds, which gives much of the charm and poetry to Maeterlinck's work.

In Maeterlinck's most original contributions to the drama he is very little characteristic of the French theatre, and the main French influence by which he was affected would seem to be that of the Symbolistic school of Verlaine and Mallarmé, which was primarily a movement of lyric poetry. He is a romantic dramatist, on the whole, but with a small " r "; he has little affiliation with the school of Hugo and Rostand.

BIBLIOGRAPHY

THE following Bibliography is very brief, intended for the students who may wish some further reliable information and criticism in the field of the modern French drama; in some cases the choice of reference texts is dictated by their possible availability in small libraries.

The lists of plays for the greater number of dramatists include all their important pieces, but in a few instances, such as those of Scribe and Ponsard, where the number of plays is very great or some are of no present-day interest, only the most representative dramas are given. The dates are usually those of the first performance but there are many exceptions, due to the fact that numerous pieces were published before they were played or were not played at all.

The best or most significant dramas of each author appear in capitals.

GENERAL

BACOURT AND CUNLIFFE, *French Literature During the Last Half-century*, 1923.

BENOIST, ANTOINE, *Le Théâtre d'Aujourd'hui*, 1911–1912.

BORDEAUX, HENRY, *La Vie au Théâtre*, 1907–1919.

BRISSON, A., *Le Théâtre*, 1913.

CHANDLER, FRANK W., *The Contemporary Drama of France*, 1920.

CLARK, BARRETT H., *The Continental Drama of To-day*, 1914; *Contemporary French Dramatists*, 1915.

DOUMIC, RENÉ, *De Scribe à Ibsen*, 1893; *Les Jeunes*, 1895; *Essais sur le Théâtre Contemporain*, 1905; *Le Théâtre Nouveau*, 1908.

FAGUET, ÉMILE, *Propos de Théâtre*, 1903–1907.

FLAT, PAUL, *Figures du Théâtre Contemporain*, 1912–1913.

GAUTIER, THÉOPHILE, *Histoire de l'Art dramatique en France depuis vingt-cinq ans*, 1858–1859.

HALE, EDWARD EVERETT, *Dramatists of To-day*, 1911.

HENDERSON, ARCHIBALD, *European Dramatists*, 1913.

KAHN, ARMAND, *Le Théâtre Social en France*, 1907.

LEMAÎTRE, JULES, *Les Contemporains*, 1885–1899; *Impressions de Théâtre*, 1888–1898.

LENIENT, CH., *La Comédie en France au XIXe Siècle*, 1898.

MATTHEWS, BRANDER, *French Dramatists*, 1914.

PARIGOT, H., *Le Théâtre d'Hier*, 1893.

PETIT DE JULLEVILLE, L., *Le Théâtre en France*, 1889; *Histoire de la Langue et de la Littérature Française*, 1895–1899.

SAINT-AUBAN, E., *L'Idée Sociale au Théâtre*, 1901.

SARCEY, F., *Quarante Ans de Théâtre*, 1900–1902.

SOREL, A. E., *Essais de Psychologie dramatique*, 1911.

THALASSO, A., *Le Théâtre Libre*, 1909.

WEISS, J. J., *Le Théâtre et les Mœurs*, 1889; *À Propos de Théâtre*, 1893.

ZOLA, E., *Nos Auteurs dramatiques*, 1881; *Le Naturalisme au Théâtre*, 1881.

DRAMATISTS AND PLAYS

ÉMILE AUGIER (1820–1889). *La Ciguë*, 1844; *Un Homme de Bien*, 1845; L'AVENTURIÈRE, 1848; *L'Habit vert*, with Musset, 1849; GABRIELLE, 1849; *Joueur de Flûte*, 1850; *Diane*, 1852; *Philiberte*, 1853; *La Pierre de Touche*, 1853; Le GENDRE DE M. POIRIER, with Sandeau, 1854; *La Ceinture dorée*, 1855; *Le Mariage d'Olympe*, 1855; LA JEUNESSE, 1858; *Les Lionnes pauvres*, with Foussier, 1858; *Un beau Mariage*, with Foussier, 1859; *Les Effrontés*, 1861; LE FILS DE GIBOYER, 1862; MAÎTRE GUÉRIN, 1864; *La Contagion*, 1866; *Paul Forestier*, 1868; *Le Post-scriptum*, 1869; *Lions et Renards*, 1869; *Jean de Thommeray*, with Sandeau, 1873; *Le Prix Martin*, with Labiche, 1876; *Mme Caverlet*, 1876; *Les Fourchambault*, 1878.

Special references: Morillot, Paul, *Émile Augier*, 1901; Parigot, H., *Émile Augier*, 1890.

BATAILLE, HENRI (1872–1922). *La Belle au Bois dormant*, with d'Humières, 1894; *La Lépreuse*, 1897; *Ton Sang*, 1897; *L'Enchantement*, 1900; *Le Masque*, 1902; MAMAN COLIBRI, 1904; *La Marche nuptiale*, 1905; *Poliche*, 1906; LA FEMME NUE, 1908; *Le Scandale*, 1909; LA VIERGE FOLLE, 1910; *Le Songe d'un Soir d'Amour*, 1910; *L'Enfant de l'Amour*, 1911; LES FLAMBEAUX, 1912; *Le Phalène*, 1913; *L'Amazone*, 1916; *Les Sœurs d'Amour*, 1919; *L'Animateur*, 1920; *L'Homme à la Rose*, 1920; *La Possession*, 1921; *La Tendresse*, 1921; *La Chair humaine*, 1922.

Special reference: Amiel, Denys, *Henri Bataille*, 1909.

BECQUE, HENRI (1837–1899). *Sardanapale*, 1867; *L'Enfant prodigue*, 1868; *Michel Pauper*, 1870; *L'Enlèvement*, 1871; *La Navette*, 1878; *Les honnêtes Femmes*, 1880; LES CORBEAUX, 1882; *Le Frisson*, 1884; LA PARISIENNE, 1885; *Madeleine*, 1896; *Une Exécution*, 1897; *Le Domino à quart*, 1897; *Veuve*, 1897; *Le Départ*, 1897; *Les Polichinelles* (unfinished), 1910.

Special references: Dawson, Eric, *Henri Becque, Sa Vie et son Théâtre*, 1923; Got, Ambroise, *Henri Becque, Sa Vie et Son Œuvre*, 1920.

BERNSTEIN, HENRI (1876–   ). *Le Marché*, 1900; *Joujou*, 1901; *Le Détour*, 1902; *Le Bercail*, 1904; *La Rafale*, 1905; *La Griffe*, 1906; LE VOLEUR, 1906; SAMSON, 1907; ISRAËL, 1908; *Après Moi*, 1911; *L'Assaut*, 1912; *Le Secret*, 1913; *L'Élévation*, 1917; JUDITH, 1922.

Special reference: Benoist, A., *Le Théâtre d'Aujourd'hui*, vol. 2, pp. 223–249.

BORNIER, HENRI DE (1825–1901). *Le Mariage de Luther*, 1845; *Dante et Béatrix*, 1853; *Le 15 Janvier*, 1860; *La Cage du Lion*, 1862; *Agamemnon*, 1868; LA FILLE DE ROLAND, 1875; *Dimitri*, with Silvestre, 1876; *Les Noces d'Attila*, 1880; *L'Apôtre*, 1881; *Mahomet*, 1890; *Le Fils de l'Arétin*, 1895; *France — d'abord*, 1900.

Special reference: Sarcey, *Quarante ans de Théâtre*.

BRIEUX, EUGÈNE (1858–   ). *Bernard Palissy*, with Salandri, 1879; *Bureau des Divorces*, 1880; *Ménages d'Artistes*, 1890; *Fille de Duramé*, 1890; BLANCHETTE, 1892; *M. de Réboval*, 1892; *La Couvée*, 1893; *L'Engrenage*, 1894; *La Rose bleue*, 1895; *Les Bienfaiteurs*, 1896; *L'Évasion*, 1896; LES TROIS FILLES DE M. DUPONT, 1897; *Resultat des Courses*, 1898; *L'École des Belles-mères*, 1898; *Le Berceau*, 1898; LA ROBE ROUGE, 1900; LES REMPLAÇANTES, 1901; LES AVARIÉS, 1901; *La petite Amie*, 1902; *Maternité*, 1903; *La Déserteuse*, with Sigaux, 1904; *L'Armature*, with Hervieu, 1905; *Les Hannetons*, 1906; *La Française*, 1907; *Simone*, 1908; *La Foi*, 1909; *Suzette*, 1909; *La Femme seule*, 1913; *Le Bourgeois aux Champs*, 1914; LES AMÉRICAINS CHEZ NOUS, 1920; *L'Avocat*, 1922; *L'Enfant*, 1923.

Special references: Thomas, P. V., *The Plays of Eugène Brieux*, 1913; Scheifley, W. H., *Brieux and Contemporary French Society*, 1917.

COPPÉE, FRANÇOIS (1842–1908). LE PASSANT, 1869; *Deux Douleurs*, 1870; *Fais ce que dois*, 1871; *L'Abandonnée*, 1871;

Le Rendez-vous, 1872; LE LUTHIER DE CRÉMONE, 1876; *La Guerre de Cent Ans,* with Artois, 1878; LE TRÉSOR, 1879; *Mme de Maintenon,* 1881; *Severo Torelli,* 1883; *Les Jacobites,* 1885; LE PATER, 1889; *L'Homme et la Fortune,* 1889; POUR LA COURONNE, 1895.

Special reference: Gauthier-Ferrières, *François Coppée et son Œuvre,* 1908.

CUREL, FRANÇOIS DE (1854–   ). L'ENVERS D'UNE SAINTE, 1892; LES FOSSILES, 1892; *L'Amour brode,* 1893; *L'Invitée,* 1893; *La Figurante,* 1896; LE REPAS DU LION, 1897; LA NOUVELLE IDOLE (pub. 1895), 1899; LA FILLE SAUVAGE, 1902; *Le Coup d'Aile,* 1906; *La Danse devant le Miroir,* 1914; *L'Âme en Folie,* 1919; *L'Ivresse du Sage,* 1922; *La Terre inhumaine,* 1922.

Special reference: Le Brun, Roger, *François de Curel,* 1905.

DELAVIGNE, CASIMIR (1794–1843). *Les Vêpres Siciliennes,* 1819; *Les Comédiens,* 1820; *Le Paria,* 1821; *L'École des Vieillards,* 1823; *La Princesse Aurélie,* 1828; *Marino Faliero,* 1829; LOUIS XI, 1832; *Les Enfants d'Édouard,* 1833; *Don Juan d'Autriche,* 1835; *Une Famille au Temps de Luther,* 1836; *La Popularité,* 1838; *La Fille du Cid,* 1839; *Le Conseiller rapporteur,* 1841; *Charles VI,* with G. Delavigne, 1842.

Special reference: Sambuc, ed., *Casimir Delavigne,* 1893.

DONNAY, MAURICE (1860–   ). *Lysistrata* (new version, 1919), 1892; *Pension de Famille,* 1894; AMANTS, 1895; *La Douloureuse,* 1897; L'AFFRANCHIE, 1898; *Georgette Lemeunier,* 1898; *Le Torrent,* 1899; *La Clairière,* 1900; *Éducation de Prince,* 1900; *La Bascule,* 1901; *La Vrille,* 1902; L'AUTRE DANGER, 1902; *Le Retour de Jérusalem,* 1903; *Oiseaux de Passage,* with Descaves, 1904; *L'Escalade,* 1904; PARAÎTRE, 1906; *La Patronne,* 1908; *Le Mariage de Télémaque,* with Lemaître, 1910; *Le Ménage de Molière,* 1912; *Les Éclaireuses,* 1913; *L'Impromptu du Paquetage,* 1914; *Le Théâtre aux Armées,* 1917; *La Chasse à l'Homme,* 1919; *La belle Angevine,* with Rivoire, 1922.

Special reference: Le Brun, Roger, *Maurice Donnay,* 1903.

Dumas, Alexandre (1803–1870). HENRI III ET SA COUR,
1829; *Christine*, 1830; ANTONY, 1831; *Charles VII chez ses
grands Vassaux*, 1831; *Napoléon Bonaparte*, 1831; LA TOUR
DE NESLE, 1832; *Angèle*, 1833; *Don Juan de Maraña*, 1836;
Kean, 1836; *Paul Jones*, 1838; *Mlle de Belle-Isle*, 1839;
L'Alchimiste, 1839; *Les Demoiselles de Saint-Cyr*, 1843.

Special reference: Parigot, H., *Le Drame d'Alexandre Dumas*, 1899.

Dumas fils (1824–1895). LA DAME AUX CAMÉLIAS, 1852;
Diane de Lys, 1853; LE DEMI-MONDE, 1855; *La Question
d'Argent*, 1857; LE FILS NATUREL, 1858; *Un Père prodigue*,
1859; *L'Ami des Femmes*, 1864; LES IDÉES DE Mme
AUBRAY, 1867; *Une Visite de Noces*, 1871; *La Princesse
Georges*, 1871; LA FEMME DE CLAUDE, 1873; M. AL-
PHONSE, 1873; *L'Étrangère*, 1876; *La Princesse de Bagdad*,
1881; *Denise*, 1885; *Francillon*, 1887.

Special references: *Entr'Actes* by A. Dumas fils, 1804;
Noël, C. M., *Les Idées Sociales dans le Théâtre de A. Dumas
fils*.

Hervieu, Paul (1857–1915). *Point de Lendemain*, 1890; *Les
Paroles restent*, 1892; LES TENAILLES, 1895; *La Loi de
L'Homme*, 1897; L'ÉNIGME, 1901; LA COURSE DU FLAM-
BEAU, 1901; *Théroigne de Méricourt*, 1902; LE DÉDALE,
1903; *L'Armature*, with Brieux, 1905; *Le Réveil*, 1905; *Modestie*, 1908; *Connais-toi*, 1909; *Bagatelle*, 1912; *Le Destin
est Maître*, 1914.

Special reference: Estève, Éd., *Paul Hervieu, Conteur,
Moraliste et Dramaturge*, 1917.

Hugo, Victor (1802–1885). *Cromwell*, 1827; MARION DE-
LORME, 1829; HERNANI, 1830; *Le Roi s'amuse*, 1832;
Lucrèce Borgia, 1833; *Marie Tudor*, 1833; *Angelo*, 1835; RUY
BLAS, 1838; *Les Burgraves*, 1843.

Special references: Cappon, J., *Victor Hugo*, 1885; Gautier,
Th., *Victor Hugo*, 1902; Glachant, P. et V., *Essai sur le Théâtre de Victor Hugo*, 1902–3.

LABICHE, EUGÈNE (1815–1880). *Embrassons-nous Folleville,*
1850; LE CHAPEAU DE PAILLE D'ITALIE, 1851; LE
MISANTHROPE ET L'AUVERGNAT, 1852; *Les deux
Timides,* 1860; LE VOYAGE DE M. PERRICHON, 1860;
LA POUDRE AUX YEUX, 1861; *Célimare le Bien-aimé,*
1863; LA CAGNOTTE, 1864; *Moi,* 1864; LA GRAMMAIRE,
1867; *Le plus Heureux des Trois,* 1870; *La Cigale chez les
Fourmis,* 1876.

Special references: Doumic, *De Scribe à Ibsen,* pp. 143–
153; *Lacour,* in *Nouvelle Revue,* VI, pp. 593–628.

LAVEDAN, HENRI (1869–   ). *Une Famille,* 1891; LE PRINCE
D'AUREC, 1892; *Les deux Noblesses,* 1894; *Viveurs,* 1895;
Catherine, 1898; *Le nouveau Jeu,* 1898; *Le vieux Marcheur,*
1899; *Les Médicis,* 1901; LE MARQUIS DE PRIOLA, 1902;
Varennes, with Lenôtre, 1904; LE DUEL, 1905; *Sire,* 1909;
Le Goût du Vice, 1911; *Servir,* 1913; *La Chienne du Roi,*
1913; *Pétard,* 1914; *Dialogues de Guerre,* 1916; *Les Sacrifices,*
with Zamaçoïs, 1917; *Portraits enchantés,* 1918; *La belle Histoire de Geneviève,* 1920.

Special reference: Benoist, *Le Théâtre d'Aujourd'hui,* vol.
I, pp. 157–208.

LEMAÎTRE, JULES (1853–1914). *Révoltée,* 1889; LE DÉPUTÉ
LEVEAU, 1890; MARIAGE BLANC, 1891; *Flipote,* 1893; *Les
Rois,* 1893; *L'Age difficile,* 1895; LE PARDON, 1895; *La
bonne Hélène,* 1896; L'AINÉE, 1898; *Bertrade,* 1905; *La
Massière,* 1905; *La Princesse de Clèves,* 1908; *Le Mariage de
Télémaque,* with Donnay, 1910; *Un Aventurier,* 1920.

Special reference: Sansot-Orland, *Jules Lemaître,* (in Célé-
brités d'Aujourd'hui) 1903.

MAETERLINCK, MAURICE (1862–   ). *La Princesse Maleine,*
1889; L'INTRUSE, 1890; *Les Aveugles,* 1890; *Les sept Princesses,* 1891; PELLÉAS ET MÉLISANDE, 1892; *Alladine
et Palomides,* 1894; INTÉRIEUR, 1894; *La Mort de Tintagiles,* 1894; AGLAVAINE ET SÉLYSETTE, 1896; *Ariane et
Barbe-bleue,* 1901; *Sœur Béatrice,* 1901; MONNA VANNA,
1902; *Joyzelle,* 1903; L'OISEAU BLEU, 1908; *Marie Magde-*

leine, 1913; *Les Fiançailles*, 1918; *Le Bourgmestre de Stile-monde*, 1918; *The Miracle of Saint Anthony*, 1918 (French original earlier).

Special references: Bever, A. Van, *Maurice Maeterlinck*, 1904; Bithell, J., *Life and Writings of Maurice Maeterlinck*, 1913.

MUSSET, ALFRED DE (1810–1857). *La Nuit Vénitienne*, 1830; A QUOI RÊVENT LES JEUNES FILLES, 1832; *André del Sarto*, 1833; LES CAPRICES DE MARIANNE, 1833; FANTASIO, 1833; LORENZACCIO, 1834; ON NE BADINE PAS AVEC L'AMOUR, 1834; *La Quenouille de Barberine* (revised as *Barberine* in 1853), 1835; *Le Chandelier*, 1835; *Il ne faut jurer de rien*, 1836; *Un Caprice*, 1837; IL FAUT QU'UNE PORTE SOIT OUVERTE OU FERMÉE, 1845; *Louison*, 1849; *On ne saurait penser à tout*, 1849; *Carmosine*, 1850; *Bettine*, 1851.

Special references: Lafoscade, L., *Le Théâtre d'Alfred de Musset*, 1901; Donnay, M., *Alfred de Musset*, 1914.

PAILLERON, ÉDOUARD (1834–1899). *La Parasite*, 1860; *Le Mur mitoyen*, 1861; *Le dernier Quartier*, 1864; *Le second Mouvement*, 1865; *Le Monde où l'on s'amuse*, 1868; *Amours et Haines*, 1869; *Les faux Ménages*, 1869; *L'autre Motif*, 1872; *Hélène*, 1872; *Petite Pluie*, 1875; *L'Age ingrat*, 1878; L'ÉTINCELLE, 1879; *Le Chevalier Trumeau*, 1880; LE MONDE OÙ L'ON S'ENNUIE, 1881; *Pendant le Bal*, 1881; *Le Théâtre chez Madame*, 1881; *Le Narcotique*, 1882; *La Souris*, 1887; *Cabotins*, 1894.

Special reference: Weiss, *Le Théâtre et les Mœurs*, pp. 215–236.

PONSARD, FRANÇOIS (1814–1867). LUCRÈCE, 1843; CHARLOTTE CORDAY, 1850; L'Honneur et l'Argent, 1853; *Le Lion amoureux*, 1866.

Special reference: Latreille, C., *La Fin du Théâtre romantique et François Ponsard*, 1899.

PORTO-RICHE, GEORGES DE (1849–   ). *Le Vertige*, 1873; *Un Drame sous Philippe II*, 1875; *Les deux Fautes*, 1879; LA

CHANCE DE FRANÇOISE, 1888; *L'Infidèle*, 1890; AMOUREUSE, 1891; *Le Passé*, 1897; *Les Malefilâtre*, 1904; LE VIEIL HOMME, 1911; *Zubiri*, 1912; *Le Marchand d'Estampes*, 1918.

Special reference: Marx, Claude, *Georges de Porto-Riche*, 1912.

RICHEPIN, JEAN (1849-   ). *L'Étoile*, with Gill, 1873; *La Glu*, 1883; *Nana Sahib*, 1883; *M. Scapin*, 1886; *Par le Glaive*, 1892; LE FLIBUSTIER, 1894; *Vers la Joie*, 1894; LE CHEMINEAU, 1897; *Les Truands*, 1899; *Don Quichotte*, 1905; *Le Carillonneur*, 1913.

Special reference: Doumic, *Théâtre Nouveau*, pp. 341-353.

ROSTAND, EDMOND (1868-1918). LES ROMANESQUES, 1894; *La Princesse lointaine*, 1895; *La Samaritaine*, 1897; CYRANO DE BERGERAC, 1897; L'AIGLON, 1900; CHANTECLER, 1910; *La dernière Nuit de Don Juan*, 1921.

Special references: Haraszti, J., *Edmond Rostand*, 1913; Suberville, J., *Le Théâtre d'Edmond Rostand*, 1919.

SARDOU, VICTORIEN (1831-1908). *La Taverne des Étudiants*, 1854; *Les Pattes de Mouche*, 1860; *La Famille Benoîton*, 1865; LA PATRIE, 1869; RABAGAS, 1872; LA HAINE, 1874; *L'Oncle Sam*, 1875; *Dora*, 1877; *Daniel Rochat*, 1880; DIVORÇONS, 1880; *Fédora*, 1882; *Théodora*, 1884; *La Tosca*, 1887; *Thermidor*, 1891; MADAME SANS-GÊNE, with Moreau, 1893; *Robespierre*, 1899; *La Sorcière*, 1903; *L'Affaire des Poisons*, 1907.

Special reference: Hart, J. A., *Sardou and the Sardou Plays*, 1913.

SCRIBE, EUGÈNE (1791-1861). *Une Nuit de la Garde nationale*, 1815; *La Somnambule*, 1819; *Le Mariage enfantin*, 1821; *Le Mariage de Raison*, 1826; *Le Diplomate*, 1827; *Le Mariage d'Argent*, 1827; BERTRAND ET RATON, 1833; *La Camaraderie*, 1837; LE VERRE D'EAU, 1840; *Une Chaine*, 1841; *Oscar ou le Mari qui trompe sa Femme*, 1842; ADRIENNE

LECOUVREUR, 1849; LA BATAILLE DE DAMES, 1851; *Mon Étoile*, 1854; *Les Doigts de Fée*, 1858.

Special reference: Arvin, N. C., *Eugène Scribe and the French Theatre*, 1924.

VIGNY, ALFRED DE (1797–1863). *Le More de Venise* (Othello), 1830; *La Maréchale d'Ancre*, 1831; CHATTERTON, 1835.

Special reference: Sakellaridès, E., *Alfred de Vigny, Auteur dramatique*, 1902.

INDEX OF NAMES